COMING TO COLORADO

Coming to
COLORADO

A Young Immigrant's Journey to Become an American Flyer

Wolfgang W. E. Samuel

UNIVERSITY PRESS OF MISSISSIPPI / JACKSON

www.upress.state.ms.us

The University Press of Mississippi is a member of the
Association of American University Presses.

Photographs courtesy of Wolfgang W. E. Samuel

First edition 2006

∞

Library of Congress Cataloging-in-Publication Data

Samuel, Wolfgang W. E.

Coming to Colorado: a young immigrant's journey to become an American flyer /
Wolfgang W. E. Samuel. — 1st ed.

p. cm.

Continues: German boy.

ISBN–13: 978–1–57806–902–6 (cloth: alk. paper)

ISBN–10: 1–57806–902–5 (cloth: alk. paper) 1. Samuel, Wolfgang W. E. 2. Colorado—
Biography. 3. World War, 1939–1945—Refugees—Biography. 4. Air pilots, Military—United
States—Biography. 5. United States. Air Force—Biography. I. Samuel, Wolfgang W. E.
German boy. II. Title.

CT275.S3175A3 2006

940.54'4943092—dc22   2006001990

British Library Cataloging-in-Publication Data available

TO MY SON CHARLES

IN MEMORY OF MY SON TOMMY

TO ALL YOUNG PEOPLE WHO NURTURE A DREAM

Contents

Illustrations

Preface

On the morning of January 24, 1945, I had no idea of the length and nature of the journey upon which I was about to embark that evening; had no inkling that after sunset I would never again play the games of childhood. Nor could I have imagined the sorrow I was to witness and experience along the way. Like a wisp of windblown straw on the waters of a raging river I floated along for six long years with no ability to influence the direction or nature of my journey. In my struggle for survival I seldom gave the world I lived in a second thought; just to survive demanded all I had to give to get me from one day to the next, from one week to another, from one season to the one that followed, winter always being the worst, until it all added up to six years to the day, when that raging river of life spit me out upon a ship sailing for the United States of America. I don't recall precisely how I survived, nor what it was I did that was so different from others who perished. I was just a child and did not understand the world I was born into. *German Boy*, my first book, recounts the story of that part of my life.

Like that earlier January day in 1945, January 24, 1951, was equally cold and gray. Like then, I was leaving my home for an uncertain future. Unlike then, there were no tanks, warplanes, or hate-filled soldiers threatening my life. This gray and windy January day I stood at the railing of the USNS *George W. Goethals*, a World War II Liberty Ship converted to the mundane task of hauling passengers across the North Atlantic between the ports of New York, Southampton, and Bremerhaven. As the *Goethals* exited the Weser River estuary and entered the windswept waters of the North Sea, I stood alone on deck, my overcoat tightly wrapped about me, watching intently the receding shoreline of the land I called home for the past fifteen years. As I stood watching, the shoreline suddenly disappeared like something dropping off the edge of a table. One moment I saw the distant shore, the next it was gone. All that remained were the ever present gulls and masts of ships sunk long ago sticking out of watery graves like bony fingers of a fallen giant.

As the cold wind tousled my hair and the vibrations from the ship's engines reverberated through the wooden deck planks into my body, tears sprang to my eyes. Would I ever see Germany again? I was only fifteen and never really had the chance to get to know the land of my ancestors. Only six years earlier I was a happy boy of nine living in a small, unimportant town in the east of Germany. Then war suddenly was upon me and I lost my home, my friends, and everything else that until then anchored my life. I became a refugee, unwanted in my own land. As the light of day faded and darkness hid the bow of the ship from view, I understood that I had to focus on the future, leave the past behind.

Our crossing was stormy, as it was apt to be in January on the North Atlantic. As we traveled by Greyhound bus from New York City to Denver, Colorado, I was overwhelmed by the vastness of this land called America, by the distances covered, and by the distances remaining to reach the other shore. In Colorado my romantic notions of America gained from reading the books of James Fenimore Cooper and Karl May merged with reality. Whatever that reality, for the first time in years I felt safe from bullets and bombs, felt free to be a boy again. Maybe I could just be another American boy, that was my dream.

Coming to Colorado, the sequel to my first memoir, *German Boy*, is the story of my struggle to become a part of a new and wondrous world, leaving behind all that was familiar—country, customs, language, friends, and family. I soon learned how difficult it was to exchange the familiar, no matter how awful, for something utterly different and new. My first lesson in America: it is not easy to be an immigrant. A violent past made it difficult for me as a teenager to deal with my incipient manhood. Depression dogged me while I struggled to learn a new language and gain an education at the same time. To fly, a dream since early childhood, gave my life focus, and in time healed my invisible wounds. *Coming to Colorado* is my story of failure and ultimate success in the land of my childhood dreams, a story of kind and generous people who were there when I needed a helping hand, a story of opportunity offered and taken.

While *German Boy* was written from the perspective of a child recounting experiences as they occurred, in *Coming to Colorado* I chose to look back on life as I lived it. This approach allowed me the literary freedom to present a fuller perspective and include details which would not have been possible otherwise. My thanks go to Craig W. Gill, editor in chief at the University Press of Mississippi, for his incisive advice and gentle nudges every writer needs now and then to excel. I wish every writer to be so fortunate as to have a Craig Gill as an editor. I thank my wife Joan for her incisive review of the manuscript—and my country for having me and giving me so many opportunities.

—WOLFGANG W. E. SAMUEL

Colonel, U.S. Air Force (Retired)
Fairfax Station, Virginia

COMING TO COLORADO

CHAPTER 1

The Way Things Were

When the mailman came, it was high noon. Always a busy time in the Rheinische Bäckerei Krampe at Detmold Strasse 1, near the center of the bomb-scarred city of Hannover. The *Postbote* carried his scuffed leather pouch before him like a mother might carry her baby, providing him ready access to the mail, I presumed, as he walked door to door sticking letters and postcards into the narrow slits of row upon row of apartment house mailboxes. To me it seemed a backbreaking way to carry a heavy load. In time, I thought, he would injure his back. Carrying the mail was a steady job that paid well, with the promise of a life-time pension in future years when he would no longer be able to work. Jobs like the mailman's were hard to find in the Germany of 1950, and if it meant injuring your back, then that was the way it had to be.

Every day, precisely at noon, the mailman entered the little pastry shop adjacent to the bakery where I worked, doffed his cap respectfully to the woman working behind the counter, either Frau Krampe or her sister Emma, reached into his vast pouch to extract a carefully bundled packet of letters and postcards, and handed them across the counter with a grimace charading as a smile. Then he politely touched the bill of his ski cap with two fingers of his right hand, as if giving a military salute, turned around with some difficulty, and hobbled up the concrete stairs to the cobblestone courtyard above. The mailman's routine was so familiar to me, I actually believed I knew him, yet he and I never exchanged a word. For me, he became a marker in time, because of his unfailing punctuality, and a caricature, with his predictable delivery ritual: doff cap, grimace, hand over mail, salute, turn around slowly, then hobble up the stairs. His routine never varied.

What might he have been in another life? I wondered. To me he appeared neither young nor old, his age masked by his past, a haggard face, eyes reflecting pain and suffering, a slight limp in his left leg. Yet there was something disciplined and upright about the man that caught my eye. He had the look of a soldier, used to keeping his shoulders straight and his head held high. Whatever he might have been in years past, whatever his eyes may have seen, he now was simply a mailman making his daily rounds as precisely as he undoubtedly once executed his military duties. He reminded me of my grandfather Samuel who served in the kaiser's army in the Great War. No matter how Opa dressed, or what he did, his posture betrayed the soldier he once was.

For some unexplained reason I felt compassion for the mailman, noting his coming and going as I noted everything else going on about me at work, at home, or out in the open—everything. It was an ability I acquired five years earlier in January 1945 after leaving behind my childhood when advancing Russian tanks abruptly forced my family to flee from our comfortable home in the small town of Sagan, Lower Silesia, into the bitter cold of a wintry night. At not quite ten, I quickly learned that danger could come from anywhere, at anytime, from anyone. Sensing danger became second nature to me, rather like someone noting the smell of freshly baked bread when approaching a bakery, or the fleeting scent of roadside flowers. Of course the mailman represented no danger, nor did my place of work—unless I was careless with the dough knife and cut my finger, which I had done twice already. By 1950 times had changed. I hadn't. In my mind and heart I was still a refugee, a *Flüchtling*; still running, looking over my shoulders, always fearing what my next step might lead to. The next step for me out of school in 1950 had been an apprenticeship in Krampe's Rheinische Bäckerei, not something I had ever imagined doing.

It was mostly the way Herr Krampe treated me which made me resent the place, brought me at times close to despair. Nearly three years of my apprenticeship still lay ahead—three years of running errands, delivering bread to favored customers, scrubbing concrete steps, floors, and tiled walls, day in and day out. On the side, or so it seemed, I was to learn how to make and bake bread. In return for a fourteen-hour work day, six days a week, Herr Krampe provided me the opportunity to learn to be a baker; not a baker of fancy pastries, just a baker of bread and *Brötchen*. Each morning I was provided breakfast, and at the end of the day, a large plate of sandwiches accompanied by a bottle of *Seltzer Wasser*. As monetary compensation for my labor I received a meager salary of four marks at the end of each month, less than a dollar. A sparsely furnished, damp room with cold running water in a burned-out house ruin next to the bakery was where I slept.

After three years I would be able to take a *Gesellenprüfung*, a comprehensive examination of my acquired baking skills, before a group of master bakers to whom I had to prove that I was worthy of elevation to journeyman, *Bäckergeselle*. Once a *Bäckergeselle*, I would still be far from becoming a *Bäckermeister*, a master baker. Many more years of low pay would follow before I would be allowed to take my *Meisterprüfung*. It was clearly a medieval system designed to exploit the young, at least that's how I viewed my situation. I didn't particularly like the way my future was evolving, but I knew if I wanted to earn an honest living I had to learn a trade. Any skill, even that of a baker, was better than being a *Stundenarbeiter*, a lowly paid and looked-down-upon day laborer.

In April 1950, five years after war's end, I finished the eighth grade in Fassberg. Less than one hundred kilometers northeast of Hannover, Fassberg sat in the middle of the Lüneburger Heide, surrounded by dense pine forests, proliferating junipers, and a profusion of heather blooming each August in purple splendor. Beyond Fassberg squatted small, medieval villages, connected by narrow, winding, cobblestone-paved roads lined with weathered oak, horsechestnut, or weepy birch trees. The often huge, half-timbered farm houses, some dating back to the fourteenth century, were built with sturdy timber cut from ancient oak trees, locally burned red brick, and stones ground smooth and round by the retreating ice age glaciers—the same stones used to pave roads since Roman times. Reeds from nearby marshes were used to thatch roofs which could last for well over a hundred years. Half of each farm house was built for human occupation, the other half for the farmer's animals—horses and cows, which provided the energy to till the fields and the milk and cheese so essential to the diets of their owners. Living together under one roof was a practical arrangement. The animals helped keep the building warm for man and beast. The steep, reed-covered roofs were adorned on each gable with wooden, oftentimes elaborately carved, crossed horses heads which according to legend kept away evil spirits. Superstition did not die easily in the Lüneburg Heath, a world touched by few outsiders. When winter storms raged it was said to be Wotan, the Germanic god of war and his horde of fire-spewing horsemen who stampeded across the skies and threw bolts of thundering lightning at the mere mortals below. At least those were the stories told to children huddling near kitchen fires on long winter evenings, their eyes rolling around in their heads in fear of the night and the strange beings in the sky. The sandy black soil of the heath was perfect for raising potatoes, beets, and rye. The wind and rain, which defined the heath, did little damage to such hardy crops, but after years of unrelenting punishment most roadside trees leaned in an easterly direction, their west-facing sides covered with a thin layer of moss. The predominant color of this region was green—green grass, green leaves, green moss. While other colors came and went, green endured year-round, along with the gray of the often angry skies.

As a youth I endured many a fierce winter storm that savaged the Lüneburg Heath, not huddled in one of the sturdy stone and timber farm houses, but in a flimsy, aging former Wehrmacht barracks near the northwest end of the Fassberg airbase runway referred to as the Trauen *Flüchtlingslager*, refugee camp. A rotting barracks with a leaky tar paper roof and dangerous aluminum electrical wiring, in a camp of like barracks, all with leaky roofs and fire prone wiring, I called home beginning in December 1946 when my mother and I first arrived, after fleeing the Russian zone of occupation. The Trauen refugee camp was a world of want and depravity. I found myself in a constant struggle between the despair caused by the apparent hopelessness of my situation, and my equally strong belief that there had to be a better world out there, somewhere, a world where I wouldn't be labeled a *Flüchtling*, where I wouldn't have to live in a stinking camp filled with the human debris of an evil war. It was that near irrational belief in a better world that kept me going from one dreary gray winter day to the next.

Most of my Fassberg classmates found a *Lehrstelle* to their liking, at least the boys did. Most of the girls stayed at home, expecting to meet a boy who would marry them in exchange for steady sex, bearing their children, housekeeping, a hot meal at noon, and *Abendbrot* in the evening. A few *Mädchen* apprenticed as salesgirls in local stores, or went to work in low paying positions as kitchen help or cleaning women at the Fassberg Royal Air Force station. But most stayed at home helping their mothers keep house, primping, and heading for the dance hall on Saturday evenings, or to one of the many fairs, such as the *Schützenfest*, the *Maifest*, or *Erntedankfest*, all good opportunities for a girl to meet her man.

My best friend Arnim, the only refugee boy from the east in my eighth grade class besides myself, found a *Lehrstelle* with our local butcher. I found it hard to believe that Arnim wanted to be a butcher, but he assured me he did. "Somebody has to make the *Wurst* and the *Kassler Rippchen* you like so much, Wolfgang, *Ja?*" Arnim said jokingly when I questioned him about his choice of occupation. Then he added emphatically, "I'll never go hungry. You've never seen a starving butcher have you?" Arnim pushed out his belly, patted it vigorously with his left hand, then laughed loudly. I always liked Arnim's confident, in-your-face laugh. I knew Arnim would do all right. He had the build to be a butcher, the muscles needed to lift heavy animal carcasses. Arnim's father kept two pigs behind their barracks and had established a working relationship with the Fassberg butcher who slaughtered and processed the pigs each year in return for half the meat. Arnim helped out with the butchering and the meat processing, and when the time came for him to choose a trade, butchering was what he knew. I knew what really drove Arnim to that decision was the memory of hunger, the deep kind of hunger, that makes you pull your belt tight around your middle to lessen the pain. Arnim, like me, knew hunger all too well, and he never again wanted to experience it.

Other classmates of mine found apprenticeships as plumbers and electricians, something I had aimed for but was unable to get. There were just too few positions like that to go around. Most of the coveted apprenticeships were filled "under the table," never listed with the *Arbeitsamt* in Celle, the labor exchange at the county seat. Getting a desirable apprenticeship was all about having connections, the only thing that counted in hard times. Being a local boy helped as well. I was neither a local boy nor did my family have connections. I was simply a *Flüchtling*, a refugee from the east. So I became a *Bäckerlehrling*, a baker's apprentice.

Not all of my classmates apprenticed in the coveted trades promising steady employment, a bit of status, and good pay—job features also noted by girls looking for husbands. My friend Karl accepted a position as streetcar driver in a large industrial city. At the time I thought that a rather strange choice even considering the difficult times we lived in. I think Karl just wanted to get out of Fassberg, get to a city where there were more opportunities, then change to something else. Wolfgang went to work for the post office, a position which I thought had a good future. Gerd, of all things, chose to become a shepherd. Sheep played an important role in the Lüneburg Heath for as long as people could remember, providing not only meat, wool, and shaggy gray and black skins, but also efficient foraging skills which kept the ever expanding pine forests at bay. The sheep ate pine seedlings down to the ground, making it impossible for the forest to establish itself and destroy the heath. The heath depended on the sheep for its health and survival. The hardy breed of *Heideschnucken* in turn depended on the heath for their survival. The result of this mutually supportive relationship was that in late summer the usually green-brown heath turned into a showy carpet of purple for as far as the eye could see. The heath in full bloom was an unforgettable sight, in good times drawing nature lovers from near and far. But few had time for such pastimes in the postwar years when every moment available to man, woman, and child was devoted to securing the basics of life—food, shelter, clothing, and fuel to cook and stay warm in the long winter months. Yet the heath bloomed whether it was appreciated or not, and aside from providing a splendid panorama, its bloom served as the basis for an important economic sideline—honey. Every farmer, and many ordinary citizens, kept one or more beehives in their backyards. It didn't take much skill and space to keep a few swarms of honey bees, and it was an easy way to supplement meager rations. Standing in the heath in mid-August, as I often did on my way home from school, I felt the air reverberating from the wing beats of millions of hard-working insects. I loved the heath. It was the one place in my desperate world of want that provided peace and tranquility.

None of us continued school beyond the eighth grade. No one went to the Gymnasium, high school, or *Mittelschule*. Eight years of education was all the state was prepared to offer the children of war. For those of us born in 1935 a ninth year of education had been added by the state of Niedersachsen, to make up for all the school days lost in 1945 by nearly every German child. Nothing new was added to the curriculum though to increase our knowledge. Who made the decisions about who went to school where and for how long? I didn't know. No one ever asked me if I wanted to continue my schooling. Someone, somewhere must have determined that my education would end in 1950 at age fifteen. I had missed two full years of school since fleeing Sagan in January 1945 and probably wouldn't have passed a high school admission's test, but I thought at least I could have been asked. Maybe I just missed my turn. We fled the Russian zone of occupation in December 1946. I didn't start school again in Fassberg, in the English zone, until January. In the postwar Germany I lived in, there were no second chances given for missed opportunities, least of all to refugees. I was one of millions of refugees whose numbers inundated what was left of a truncated Germany. We were blamed for much of what was wrong with life. Every imaginable calamity quickly became the fault of the refugees from the east. I didn't like being a *Flüchtling*, unwanted even by my own countrymen, but that's what I was. I couldn't help what war had done to me and my family—it was the way things were.

Fassberg was not a town in the traditional sense, but rather a large housing development built to accommodate the families of construction workers, Luftwaffe personnel, and civil servants who began to arrive in 1933, at the beginning of the Nazi era. The White housing area was constructed first in 1936 for the families of laborers who built and maintained the airfield. The Red housing area came next in 1937 and was reserved for families of Luftwaffe officers and higher ranking civil servants. Finally, in 1938, the Gray housing area, similar to the White, was built for sergeants and lower level civil servants. The houses in the prestigious *Rote Siedlung* were mostly two-story duplexes built of red brick; some single family homes were built as well, for the highest ranking officers and their families. The *Rote Siedlung* houses, substantially larger than those in the *Weisse* or *Graue Siedlung*, had full basements, in contrast to root cellars, and central heating, full bathrooms, and separate toilets. Some even had balconies, patios, and verandas. Such luxuries were not wasted on the simple one-story houses in the White or Gray subdivisions.

As a community Fassberg offered little—a butcher shop, a grocery store, a dry goods store, a bookstore, and a pharmacy. No hotel, no movie theater, not even a *Gasthaus* where an ordinary citizen could drink a beer or order a modest meal. Clearly, the town planners were interested only in getting ready for war. An elaborate officers club was built on the airfield, but that facility was not accessible to ordinary citizens. Fassberg was a town built in a hurry to support the adjacent airfield without any thought given to anything but the absolute necessities of ordinary life. In 1945, the British occupation forces took over many of the best houses in the *Rote Siedlung*.

On my way to school I walked through the *Rote Siedlung*. Whenever I entered the tree-shaded Red housing area with its paved streets, clean sidewalks, and pretty fences, I felt a load lifting off my shoulders, a distinctly physical feeling of relief. Here life appeared to be lived the way I once lived years ago as a young child: in a real house with a bathroom, a kitchen, a living room, and bedrooms. I looked with envy at the houses and the people privileged to live in them, whether German or English. In contrast to my world of rotting barracks, cold, filth, and deprivation, the *Rote Siedlung* seemed a world of peace and tranquility, a place of solace and healing, offering a hint of that better future I so tenaciously continued to believe in. Maybe someday I would live like that again. Maybe. Someday.

On my way home in the afternoon I walked more slowly than in the morning. I felt the burden of my own circumstances settling again on my shoulders as I left the *Rote Siedlung* behind and entered the sandy path through the pine forest which led to my world of rot and foul smells. The squalid refugee camp had no paved streets, no sidewalks, no indoor toilets, no running water, no central heat. It was a place of utter misery defined by the color gray—gray barracks, gray skies, gray soil, and most of all the gray and sallow faces of its occupants. A single pump provided water for nearly two hundred of us, people of different nationalities from all parts of the former German Reich. Mud, dust, swarms of flies, and the stench from the outdoor latrine defined the world I lived, slept, and breathed in. I never missed a day of school, the opportunity to get away from it all. Only once did I stay away—when I came down with pneumonia and nearly died.

At noon the mailman left a packet of letters with Frau Krampe's sister Emma who was serving customers in the small pastry shop next to the bakery. A narrow entry was all that separated the bakery from the shop. I could easily look into the shop from where I worked. By the time the mailman dropped off the mail we were at our busiest, getting the day's product out of the ovens and to the downtown store. Herr Krampe made certain everyone worked as hard as they could. He was not inclined to tolerate idleness, not even a smile on a face which might betray thoughts other than of baking bread and *Brötchen*. If I went to the lavatory, Herr Krampe timed me, and I'd better be out in minutes or an avalanche of verbal abuse would descend upon me when I emerged. He was forever intent on getting the most out of everyone, be it master baker or lowly apprentice. His demeanor toward the cake and pastry baker, however, was decidedly different, almost deferential. Baking pastries and cakes was a rare skill, more art than function, much in demand, and this baker was paid substantially more than the rest of us.

I, as an apprentice, received next to nothing, other than my room and board. My *Lehrvertrag*, the training contract I signed with Herr Krampe, called for me to receive four marks pocket money each month in my first year, which would increase to eight marks in the third year. Such a pittance wasn't enough to buy a third-class train ticket home on occasional weekends, unless Herr Krampe provided a little more now and then. While it seemed totally out of character for him to do anything of a generous nature, he would in fact do so on occasion. One day we were driving in his three-wheeled delivery van from the downtown store back to the bakery when he suddenly stopped in front of a bicycle shop, pressed two hundred marks into my hand and said, "Go in and buy yourself a bicycle." I sat there astonished, stared at the money, not comprehending what he had just told me to do, until he asked in an annoyed tone of voice, "Don't you want a bicycle?" Having that bike allowed me to get out and ride around the *Maschsee*, Hannover's city park and lake, on Sunday afternoons. It was a generous gesture, with strings attached. Herr Krampe insisted I take his dog, a German shepherd, along whenever I went on one of my Sunday rides. The bicycle also freed him from having to drive me every other week to my mandatory trade school classes. Strings or no strings, the bike provided a measure of freedom. I was grateful for it.

The small shop next to the bakery was staffed by whoever happened to be available, either Frau Krampe or her younger sister Emma. Krampe's main store was located downtown on one of Hannover's most prominent streets, Georgstrasse, across from the opera house and near the famous Café Kröpke. With a crew of seven, counting Herr Krampe and me, we could barely keep up with demand for the several varieties of bread, *Brötchen*, cookies, cakes, and *Torten* that we turned out six days a week. Around Christmas and during the Lenten season Herr Krampe added marzipan to his traditional holiday offerings, and the pastry baker was busy from morning to late at night turning out marzipan piglets, lady bugs, butterflies, sausages, and varied other forms of the almond and sugar concoction.

My day, which started at two o'clock in the morning, usually ended around four in the afternoon. My last task of the day was to clean the bakery, a chore assigned to the most junior member of the crew. I mopped the concrete floor, washed off tables and bread boards, washed and dried all cutting and mixing tools, bowls, and variously shaped forms and pans. On Fridays I mopped the stairs leading up to the courtyard, still surrounded by ruins of houses burned in a devastating British night raid late in 1944. On Saturdays, when everyone else left by two o'clock in the afternoon, I washed the floor-to-ceiling tile walls. I never finished my chores before four o'clock, and at times it took a little longer. The fourteen-hour work days, six days a week, kept me in a near permanent state of exhaustion. All I seemed to be able to do was work, eat, and sleep, and not enough of the latter.

Once I finished my chores I went next door into the pastry shop to eat. The shop closed at two o'clock in the afternoon. Without fail, on a little table where customers could be seen earlier in the day enjoying a piece of exquisite *Torte*, Emma would have a plate of liverwurst and salami sandwiches waiting for me—my dinner. Emma was a full-breasted woman in her early twenties, not unpleasant to look at, always courteous, even kind to me, in contrast to her sister, Frau Krampe, who openly displayed her disdain toward anyone she deemed below her own station in life. As a lowly *Lehrling* I was never deserving of more than a dismissive comment from her. Frau Krampe had an overbite which made it seem as if she was perpetually smiling. Far from it. I found her to be a bitter, bossy, and cold-hearted woman, who used the often uncovered stump of her right arm, lost in that 1944 bombing raid, as a ghastly pointer to emphasize her orders. Emma, in contrast to her sister, would seek me out and try to console me on occasions when Herr Krampe had been especially abusive toward me.

This afternoon, as I was hungrily working my way through a huge pile of sandwiches, Emma came over and handed me a letter that had arrived with the noon mail. The letter was from Hedy, my mother. I carefully put the letter in the breast pocket of my flour and dough smudged white jacket, intending to read it in the quiet of my room. Emma busied herself behind the counter where she stayed until I finished eating. I bade Emma a good afternoon when I finished, and she responded cheerfully, "*Schlaf gut* Wolfgang," giving me a long, lingering look as I left, a look I didn't know how to interpret. I was certain though that the way she looked at me on occasion had nothing to do with baking bread and making sandwiches. At times, when she brought me another bottle of water, or as a special treat an Afri Kola, Emma leaned over me, her ample bosom pressing against me, making my young heart pound.

The ruin where I lived had that peculiar smell of rot and death, like all house ruins I'd ever been in. Every time I entered I automatically recalled the terrible air raid of February 3, 1945, on Berlin, when a thousand American B-17 bombers dropped twelve thousand five-hundred-pound bombs in a massive attack against the city. I remember sitting in the cellar of our apartment house on Schönhauserallee, choking on dust shaken off whitewashed cellar walls by the bomb explosions. The dust filled the cellar like a dense fog. I felt the explosions coming closer and closer. The flyspecked light bulbs on the ceiling flickered on and off, yet the electricity remained on. I wanted to scream and run out of the cellar, run away from all the madness, but I sat there quietly like all the other children, waiting to be buried alive. But God was with us that day, and we survived to live yet another day. Every time I stepped into that burned-out apartment house, its smell took me back to that day in Berlin when the bombers came and I thought I was going to die. I hated living in that building. Hated its smell of death. Hated the memory.

There were no steps leading to my room. I had to jump up to the door from the rubble-strewn hallway. My room had one bare light bulb hanging from a gray ceiling, an ordinary cast-iron sink with cold running water, a table, a small dresser, bed, and one chair. The room was damp, cold, and dark like a prison cell. Herr Krampe had not yet installed a stove for the winter. Maybe he never would. At times I even wished I was back in the run-down barracks in Trauen. I washed up, sat down on my bed, and carefully opened my mother's letter. Her news was electrifying. I forgot all about being tired, about my depressing room and the smell of death. She wrote that their papers were finally in order. She and Leo had received permission to marry. "We have set the date for October 14. If you come for the wedding it would make us both very happy."

Hedy met Technical Sergeant Leo B. Ferguson while working at the Fassberg Base Exchange, the BX, during the Berlin airlift, which began in late spring 1948. A year later Leo asked Hedy to marry him. She accompanied him in October 1949, when the airlift ended, and Leo was transferred to Fürstenfeldbruck air base. I reread my mother's letter several times. Its message was like a ray of sunshine suddenly entering my gloomy room through the curtainless window. If everything turned out alright, maybe I wouldn't be here much longer. Maybe I could go back to school again, someday, somewhere—in America.

Whatever excitement I felt the next morning was tempered by the fact that I feared Herr Krampe's verbal response to my request for time off to attend the wedding. I had returned only recently from a brief visit to Fürstenfeldbruck, a picturesque Bavarian town west of Munich. I knew Herr Krampe wouldn't be happy about my wanting time off so soon again. Mustering all my courage, I stood up straight and approached him just before he left for the downtown store. He didn't like my request, as I had expected, but neither did he yell at me. I didn't say anything to my co-workers as we stood around the large table cutting and kneading dough balls, but if they looked closely they surely must have read excitement in my eyes.

Whenever Herr Krampe was gone we relaxed. Talk and laughter made the day seem to go by faster. At times like that it was even fun to work here. One of the master bakers was married to a nice looking woman and lived in an apartment above the bakery. He didn't have to show up until six in the morning, a privilege that came with his position, and he left again by two in the afternoon. He liked talking about his bachelor days, including dating Emma. "I took Emma out a few times," he said, boasting. "She wasn't bad in bed. But then she wanted to get married, and naturally I couldn't do that. Just imagine me being in the Krampe family?" He looked around the table and laughed so hard tears came to his eyes. He told that story more than once, each time adding little details about him and Emma in bed. When he washed his hands to leave, he would wink at us and say, "You know what I'll be doing when I get upstairs, don't you?" I laughed along with the others, but I didn't know what he meant.

The war in Korea was an ongoing topic of discussion. The Americans had just chased the North Koreans back across the thirty-eighth parallel, and the pastry baker who seemed so gleeful over the Americans' misfortunes earlier in the year now kept to himself and didn't get involved in our discussions anymore. He had a work area separate from ours. Occasionally I stuck my head into his room to give him a status report on the progress of *my American army*. All he ever said was, "Just wait and see." I decided he was probably the sort of person who was happy when bad things happened to others, *Schadenfreude*. It was a trait I was taught by my mother Hedy not to admire nor indulge in.

On Thursday, October 12, I took a fast *D-Zug* from Hannover to Munich, then the slow *Personenzug* from Munich to Fürstenfeldbruck. The *Personenzug* stopped in every tiny village along its route and sat in every station seemingly forever, its engine belching clouds of white steam and black soot, accompanied by loud belching noises. When I finally arrived in "Fürsty," as Americans referred to Fürstenfeldbruck, only Leo awaited me at the station. Mutti was probably busy, I thought, preparing for the wedding reception they intended to have at the NCO Club, a requisitioned villa near the center of town. As I got off the train and approached Leo, I felt something wasn't right. He was smoking in quick, short puffs, uncharacteristic for a man who usually enjoyed smoking his cigarettes slowly and deliberately. Leo also had a frown on a face that nearly always wore a smile. When he saw me coming, his expression lightened. Discarding his half-smoked cigarette, he shook my hand vigorously. "Wolfgang, dear Wolfgang," he said, "it's wonderful to see you again." With that he grabbed my suitcase, and I followed him out of the station. His new, blue air force uniform was impeccably tailored and freshly pressed. I thought it made him look taller than the brown army uniform he used to wear when I first met him in 1948.

"Your mother couldn't come," he said in a strained tone of voice as we walked down the familiar, tree-lined lane toward town. "Soon after she wrote you, she had to go into the hospital. She was carrying our baby and something went wrong. She started bleeding and had a fever and they were forced to operate."

"Is Mutti all right?" I asked. Leo spoke little other than *Gasthaus* German, and I spoke nearly no English. Yet somehow, with all our linguistic impediments, Leo and I managed to communicate.

"Yes, she is doing well," he said, or I assumed that's what he said, "and the doctors think we can get married on Saturday after all. But it will have to be in the hospital." He smiled when he said that. Leo obviously loved my mother. He had always loved Hedy; I knew it the first time we met. I remembered that day clearly. Mutti came home from work, accompanied by this American sergeant. Leo wore the usual brown uniform, an Ike jacket with large sergeant stripes on his sleeves. I was immediately attracted to him, a feeling I never had about any of my mother's other friends. After lighting a Camel cigarette and taking a long first drag, he said to me in twangy, slow American English, "My name is

Leo Ferguson. Call me Leo," and stretched out his hand to shake mine. As I took his hand, I noticed his long slender fingers and the clean, manicured nails. I didn't understand all he said. He could tell. "Leo," he said again. "I am Leo."

"Ich bin Wolfgang," I replied, grasping that he had told me his name and wanted to know mine. He smiled, his teeth regular and white, his brilliant blue eyes laughing at me. "W-o-l-f-g-a-n-g," he repeated slowly, "that's a fine name. I like it." We laughed together and I knew in that instant that he liked me as much as I liked him. I felt certain he didn't see any of the things others had seen in me, in my family, in the place where we lived—my worn-out clothes, the sandals I wore made from German airplane tires, the mud, the flies, the smell of the camp latrine, the snot-nosed kids walking around half naked. After he left, my mother asked me, "*Wie magst du den Amerikaner?*"

"I like him very much," I told her. "His eyes are gentle and warm. They have no hate in them."

I thought my mother loved Leo as well, but in a different way. Of course, I didn't really know what adult love was. I loved Hedy, loved my little sister Ingrid, loved my grandparents Wilhelm and Anna Samuel. That was a different kind of love, I presumed, from the love between Leo and Hedy. I wasn't sure I ever wanted to experience their kind of love. It seemed to include so much pain, at least what I had seen of it, filled with more sorrow than happiness. My mother and father Willie must have loved each other at one time, but they divorced. Over the years I experienced men forcing women to their wills; my own mother selling her body to a Russian officer for a can of soup in the dark days of 1945 so my sister Ingrid and I could live another day. Was that adult love? Love was confusing for me, and the changes I began to feel in my own body didn't make finding an answer any easier. Whatever kind of love there was between Hedy and Leo, at least at the moment, seemed to make both of them happy.

Frau Buck, Leo and Hedy's landlady, greeted me at the front door of her house, set in a neatly kept garden of flowers, rose bushes, and fruit trees. Herr Buck sat at the kitchen table wearing his usual well-worn, shiny knee-length *Lederhosen*. He gave me a hearty "*Grüss Gott*," the Bavarian greeting, as I passed by the kitchen.

"*Grüss Gott*, Herr Buck," I replied. When I opened the door to Hedy and Leo's room, I discovered a surprise—Ingrid. At last Leo was smiling again, the open, uncomplicated smile of a compassionate man. Leo had kept that little secret from me, and when he saw how delighted I was to see my sister, he freely shared in our joy. Leo had become more like a father to me than my own father. Ingrid, who had arrived earlier in the day, had already visited Mutti at the hospital. "Mutti looks just fine," Ingrid said. I was pleased to hear the news.

On Saturday, Mutti's hospital room was decorated with flowers sent by friends. The German marriage ceremony was performed first in the presence of her attending doctors and nurses. In addition to Ingrid and me, only one other couple was allowed to be present, friends of Hedy's and Leo's who served as witnesses. Then an American air force chaplain performed another brief ceremony. Hedy and Leo were married at last under German and American law. After cake and coffee, none for Hedy, the nurses ushered us out of the room saying, "She needs her rest." Their voices were gentle, but their hands were firm. "You may return tomorrow," they assured us. Leo went back to work, even though it was his wedding day.

On Monday evening Ingrid and I took a train back to Hannover, she continuing on to Hamburg and Bad Oldesloe where she lived with our father and his new wife Erika—a war widow with two children, a boy and a girl, Friedhelm and Karin, about Ingrid's and my age. Ingrid and I sat across from each other. The clickety-clack of the wheels, the whistle of the wind pushing against speeding cars, and the occasional hoot from the locomotive provided a near musical background of sleep-inducing sounds. Ingrid promptly fell asleep. My mind wandered. I thought of all the effort it took Hedy and Leo to get married. In addition to the many forms and letters they had to submit to this and that authority, there were mandatory interviews and counseling sessions. One form I remembered well. It stipulated that when they were married the German wife would not be permitted any privileges: commissary, post exchange, government quarters, medical or dental care. Hedy and Leo still got married.

Herr Krampe was pleased to see me return so soon, and within a day it seemed as if I had never left. In my absence he had a cast-iron stove installed in my damp room in the house ruin, which meant he intended for me to live there for the winter. When the union representative came to approve my apprenticeship and evaluate my working and living conditions, Herr Krampe coached me not to say anything about my room in the ruin. "It's only temporary," he said. "I'll show him a bedroom in my apartment, the one you slept in when you first arrived."

Pyongyang, the capital city of North Korea, was captured by the Americans on Thursday, October 19, 1950. I couldn't help myself and rushed into the cake baker's workroom as soon as I heard the news. In a solemn voice I made the announcement to him. I felt vindicated by *my American army*. I knew it was the best army in the world after all. The cake baker made his usual comment, "Just wait and see."

As part of my apprenticeship I attended mandatory trade school classes, which turned out to be exceedingly dull and uninformative. I thought I would learn the theory of my craft, but the first year proved to be merely a generalized curriculum for all apprentices, regardless of speciality. In our biweekly afternoon sessions we covered basic arithmetic, social issues, and German—many students couldn't read or write well. The teacher preferred talking about his wartime experiences instead. I didn't really care what my instructor said, did, or thought. I had half a day off, and that's what mattered to me. One afternoon our discussion turned to America. One of the apprentices said, "In America," and he insisted that he had heard this from reliable sources, "everyone has a helicopter. You know, those airplanes without wings." No one challenged him. I was speechless when I heard such ignorance expressed in a classroom. I kept quiet as one apprentice after another chimed in about how easy life was in America. I knew Leo and his soldier friends lived a good life in Germany, but they too worked for a living. Leo's family didn't have a helicopter. In a picture my mother showed me of Leo's brother Raymond and his family, standing in front of a simple basement house, Raymond looked like someone who worked hard with his hands, not like a helicopter pilot.

When class let out that day, I rode my bike back to the bakery, lost in deep thought about what I might find on the other side of the Atlantic should I accompany Hedy and Leo to America. I realized that most of what I knew were old, romantic descriptions of a land and people changed long ago. I knew Leo came from a state called Colorado. I thought that was where we were going. In my mind a picture emerged of a majestic mountain chain rising from a grassy plain, snowy alpine peaks glistening in the sun, and forest-covered ledges dropping off steeply into deep, dark canyons. In my imagination I visualized herds of elk grazing on verdant mountain meadows, giant bears strolling through immense forests, and mountain lions prowling unseen, looking for prey. Overhead, sustained by invisible updrafts, I visualized eagles and vultures drawing lazy circles in an azure blue sky. Blue sky and sunshine were central to my vision—freedom and open spaces. Down below the snow-covered mountains I imagined a city rising from a grassy plain stretching to the far horizon, its skyscraper windows sparkling in the morning sun. I visualized trout-filled streams and rivers rushing from steep mountain slopes to spend themselves on the plain below. My mind conjured up a land of bliss and wonderment, a reflection of my deepest wishes—a place without war. My vision of Colorado didn't include helicopters, nor did Raymond's basement house fit into it. A small, gray cloud of uncertainty drifted through my otherwise blue sky of high expectations. But whatever America was like, I thought, it had to be a better place than where I lived.

My life quickly fell back into its familiar routines of work and sleep, work and sleep, day in and day out, interrupted only briefly by my trade school classes and a brief few hours off on late Saturday afternoons and Sundays. If the weather was nice on Saturday or Sunday, I rode my bike around the *Maschsee*. Or I went to the Amerika Haus near Krampe's downtown store and tried to learn more about America, though I didn't find much useful information. The spacious rooms of the Amerika Haus were filled with huge pictures of workers in large automobile factories, and of landscapes of blooming deserts and ripening fields of grain. The few books I found were mostly picture books, and I had the uneasy feeling that they were propaganda, rather than books telling the truth about a land that was such an enigma to me.

As the month of November 1950 came to an end, stories of Korea appeared again in the papers. The talk was about the Chinese coming into the Korean War. Our pastry baker joined our speculative discussions again. "Just wait," he said, shaking his finger at us, and particularly at me. "You just wait. The time will come." And then the time he was apparently talking about came. The Chinese attacked across the Yalu River and the American army was again on the run. I chose to ignore the pastry baker's prophesies of doom. I admitted I didn't understand what was happening in Korea. I hardly knew where the place was, much less its climate and topography. Still, I decided that *my American army* would somehow do the right thing and prevail.

CHAPTER 2

A Child Once More

On Monday, November 27, 1950, I received another letter from my mother, this one telling me to come to Fürstenfeldbruck. "We have an appointment at the American Consulate in Munich on Tuesday morning, the sixth of December," she wrote. This time I knew I would not have to return to Hannover. While I was sorry to leave my friends, my fellow workers who had always been helpful and supportive, Herr and Frau Krampe I wouldn't miss. That night I went to sleep with my blanket pulled over my head and visions of Colorado coloring my dreams.

I rose as usual at fifteen minutes before two, washed up, and got dressed in my baker's uniform—white jacket, black and white checkered pants, white hat. I had a smile on my face that just wouldn't go away. I decided to tell Herr Krampe that I was leaving at ten o'clock that morning, the time when he always left the bakery for the downtown store. When the time came, I was suddenly afraid; my heart pounded furiously, and I didn't think I could speak. I watched Herr Krampe take off his white apron, wash his hands under the cold-water tap across from the ovens, wipe his hands on the smudged towel hanging next to the sink, then proceed to exit the bakery. "Herr Krampe, please," I said a bit too loudly, scrambling toward him from behind the cutting table. I was surprised at how firm and strong my voice sounded, as if it came from someone else. "Could I have a minute of your time, please?" He stopped at the door, apparently surprised at being addressed by me in such a direct manner.

"Be quick about it," he replied. He never addressed me by my name. I followed him out the door.

"*Ja?*" he inquired impatiently as we faced each other.

"I received a letter from my mother," I looked him straight in the eyes. "She wants me to be in Munich by the sixth of December. We need to be at the American Consulate that morning to get our visas to go to America."

Herr Krampe looked at me calmly, then said, "I am not surprised. I expected something like that. Not quite so soon though. So, you will leave here on the fifth of December, *Ja?*"

"*Ja*, Herr Krampe." I was relieved that the feared verbal outburst didn't materialize.

"Then let's get back to work," he said almost gently, as he turned to go.

On the second of December, a Saturday, after finishing my chores, I took a train from Hannover to Celle where I transferred to the narrow gauge which took me to Trauen. The standard and narrow gauge stations in Celle were adjacent to one another, making it easy to transfer from one train to another. I wanted to say *auf Wiedersehen* to my grandparents Samuel. I needed their blessings for the long, uncertain journey that lay ahead. I couldn't leave for America without seeing them one last time. When I arrived at the Trauen station, a ramp with a siding and a locked and untended station house, I jumped off the two-car train before it came to a full stop and ran all the way up to the barracks nestled in their grayness against the edge of a brooding pine forest. It looked all so familiar, yet different. The barracks had finally lost their hold over me. I knew that I would never have to live here again.

My grandparents lived in the same two-room apartment which at one time in early 1947 housed seven of us—Oma and Opa Samuel, my parents Hedy and Willie, my sister Ingrid, my cousin Vera, and me. That was after my mother and Opa Samuel returned to the Russian zone of occupation at considerable risk to themselves and brought out Vera and Ingrid. Ingrid had been left behind with my grandmother Grapentin when my father, mother, and I fled Strasburg in December 1946, eluding the communist police and arrest by a scant hour. My father had come to Strasburg searching for us after being released from an American prisoner-of-war camp. A communist spy reported his presence, forcing us to flee on a moment's notice, leaving Ingrid behind with my grandmother. Hedy was obsessed with retrieving her daughter, and within days of our arrival in the English zone, she turned around to rescue Ingrid. Bringing Vera along was a spur of the moment decision. Vera was my mother's niece, her deceased sister Marie's oldest daughter. I believe my mother saw a little of herself in Vera, wanted to do the right thing by her sister, and hoped to give Vera a chance at a better life than what she was facing in the Russian zone. Vera, at age fifteen, had been raped daily by Russian soldiers for several weeks in April and May 1945, until my grandfather Grapentin found a secure hiding place for her in an abandoned well in a remote apple orchard. Vera came close to committing suicide after losing her mother to the same cruel and degrading ordeal. In the end, Vera chose life.

When I walked in the front door of Oma and Opa Samuel's small apartment, Oma was puttering around the stove, as I expected she would be. Oma was never far from her stove or her garden. Opa, on his knees, was stacking firewood by the stove. Still out of breath, I kissed Oma on the cheek and hugged her, knowing that she would give me a scolding for ruffling her apron and dress. Opa wore his old, black sweat-stained ski cap. His blue eyes smiled when he saw me, his cold pipe clenched between his teeth. I hugged him, kissed his stubbled cheek. "My dear boy," was all he said, never taking the pipe out of his mouth. His love for me was cradled in those three words, "*Mein lieber Junge.*" I would miss him saying that to me. He wore a blue, long-sleeved shirt, buttoned all the way to the top. He probably learned to do it that way in the kaiser's army and never buttoned his shirts any other way since. He wore an old, worn gray tweed jacket with all three buttons buttoned as well. I smiled at the brave, kind, and generous old man, my dearest grandfather. I loved him beyond saying. Never an unkind word toward me passed his lips; all he ever gave me was love and wise counsel. He once told me as I rambled on about things long gone, "Never look back my boy. You cannot change the past. Put your efforts toward the future." He never looked back on his own life, although he achieved much and lost it all—not once, but twice. The first time, when raging inflation after the Great War robbed him of his savings and possessions; the second time, in 1945, when he and Oma were evicted by Russian forces from their beautiful house near the Baltic Sea and put on a cattle car to a refugee camp in the English zone of occupation. I once asked Opa to tell me what happened when the Russians came. "Some other time," he said. I knew the subject was closed; he would never speak of it. His gray pants, worn like his tweed jacket, gave no evidence of ever having had a crease; bulging at the knees from frequent kneeling when fetching wood from the barn and stacking the firewood next to Oma's stove. I had to turn away from these two wonderful, precious people to keep them from seeing the emotion welling up in my eyes. My grandfather noticed anyway.

"Tell me, my dear boy, what brings you here today?" he said gently, pushing a chair in my direction. I sat down as he wanted me to. My grandmother stood watching from near the stove. "We are happy to see you," Opa continued, "but we are surprised at the suddenness of your visit. Is it something good that brings you to us?"

"Yes, Opa," I replied softly, trying hard to keep my voice from breaking, "I am going to America."

"Oh, my dear God," Oma said loudly, folding her swollen, rheumatoid hands in a praying gesture, lifting them up high, tears running down her hollow cheeks. "I will never see my dear Wolfgang again. First his father wanted to go to America. Now his son is leaving." She bravely tried to wipe her tears away. I leapt off my chair and put my arms around her. This time she didn't protest when I pulled her close to me.

"No, Oma, I will be back to see both of you again many times. You are my dearest grandparents and I can't imagine not seeing you again. Don't worry. I'll be back. At least I don't have to be a baker anymore," I said, trying to make light of the situation. Oma smiled at me through her tears. Opa motioned for me to follow him. We left the kitchen and walked to the barn in the pine forest where we looked after his chickens.

"Oma needs a little time to herself, Wolfgang," my grandfather said softly, looking for eggs the hens may have laid since he checked last evening. "They don't lay much this time of year." A pig grunted in its sty. I boxed the pig in the head and scratched its back with a brush. The pig stood still, enjoying the attention. Opa filled his basket with wood from logs he had sawed to the right length in late summer and then split into pieces small enough to fit into Oma's stove. At age seventy-two he did nearly everything himself. He allowed me to carry the basket as we slowly walked back toward the barracks. The basket was heavier than I expected. Opa wove the basket himself from pliable willow boughs which he cut down by the Örtze River, a small stream which ran through the nearby village of Trauen, down the road from the barracks.

As we walked side by side, I couldn't take my eyes off my grandfather's beard-stubbled face. Throughout my childhood he was the one who had always been there when I needed someone. He was the one who listened to me, talked to me like I was a real person, came to Sagan by train every time I had a school vacation. Every spring and fall I went with him to Schlawe, where he and Oma lived in a big house with an even bigger garden filled with flowers, cherry, apple, and pear trees, gooseberry and currant bushes. Then he wore a suit to work with creases in his pants. I remembered how I loved to hold his hand as we walked to the train station, wondering, as little boys are apt to do, all the things his hands must have done—from holding a rifle when he was a soldier, to harnessing horses on his father's farm, to laying bricks when he learned to be a bricklayer. I always held onto his hand real tight, feeling totally safe in his presence—like nothing could harm me when I was with my grandfather.

Later in the summer of 1947, when I was twelve, I drove a team of horses and a wagon with my grandfather to a nearby artillery range to get our wood for the winter. Opa worked on a potato farm in Trauen to help make ends meet. The farmer lent him the horses and wagon. On the way back Opa taught me how to drive the team. Giving me the reins he said, "Hold them loosely," a lesson in leadership I would recall in later years. "Apply just enough pressure for them to know you are there. They'll do a few quirky things to test you. Remain steady, and they'll settle right in and accept you." The horses did what Opa said they would. As we rode along that day, with only the sounds of creaking leather, wagon wheels crunching against cobblestones, and the clip-clop of laboring hooves to break the stillness of the afternoon, he said something I never forgot. His pipe had gone cold. He took it out of his mouth, then said to me, "You can never stand still, my son. The world keeps changing and you must change with it. Those who don't, are left behind. Don't you ever be left behind, my dear boy. Keep your eyes on the future. Have faith in yourself. Your time will come. You will know when it does." He stroked my hair back slowly, lovingly, with the hand once hit clean through by a Rumanian rifle bullet in the Great War.

After dinner that evening, we three sat together in the kitchen. Opa lit his pipe as Oma pulled her chair between the two of us. She sat there listening to Opa and I talk about days long gone, days in Schlawe, days that seemed to have been only yesterday for her, or at best the day before.

She leaned forward on her cane, its handle encircled by her swollen, arthritic fingers. Around her head a simple black cotton scarf failed to contain a few strands of her salt and pepper hair hanging loosely over her cheeks. She listened to us talk, and I could see in her watery eyes that she was back in Schlawe, up near the Baltic Sea, in her beloved house and garden, remembering a little boy who once came to visit, who was leaving her now forever for a strange land called America.

I was as fond of my grandmother as I was of Opa Samuel, but in a different way. She too was raised on a farm. Her father Martin Blume, my great-grandfather, farmed a large estate in the east, near the town of Gnesen. When he found clay on his property, Oma told me, he opened a brick works. He opened a butcher shop as well and became a successful veterinarian, and not surprisingly, the village doctor by default. From the stories Oma told of her childhood it seemed there was nothing her father was unwilling or unable to do, and he succeeded in everything he tried, including raising a family of twelve children. Opa Samuel was in the cavalry when he and Oma met at a dance in Gnesen. Oma's place was in the kitchen of her father's farm, and she learned all there was to learn about cooking and baking, from making and baking bread to process-ing a pig into tasty sausages, hams, and bacon. She did "women's" work around the house and farm, but at harvest time, like the men, she spent much of her time in the fields. Only on Sundays was there a moment of rest for her, and the only book she read was the Bible. Oma Samuel was a devout Lutheran, the Bible never far from her side, and the word God never passed her lips lightly for fear of committing blasphemy. According to her, God was always near us in good times and in bad, heard and saw everything we said and did—at least His emissaries were always near us, his angels. According to Oma, God had legions of angels at his dis-posal. She told me more than once that "Everyone had an angel. You, too, Wolfgang." One day when we were laughing about something, she pointed a finger at me and said, "Yours is a girl angel for sure." Oma had a lovely laugh, clear as a silver bell, yet warm and inclusive. I loved my grandmother for all her quirky little ways. Since our escape from Russian tanks in late April 1945, when our wagon broke down by the side of the road in a hail of rocket and artillery fire, since that time I truly believed in God. Not in a church-going way—that was not my family's tradition; after all we were Protestants—but in my heart. I believed all Oma Samuel told me about angels and God. How else could I explain the many occasions when my family and I were saved from almost certain death?

It was late when I turned in that night, sleeping in the old hospital bed I had purloined years earlier from the abandoned Trauen V-2 rocket research center just up the road from the barracks and adjacent to the Fassberg airfield. I could still hear Oma puttering around, doing something near the stove in the adjacent room, trying to grasp what was happening to her only grandson, when I fell asleep. The wall separating the two barracks rooms was constructed from thin pine boards, one reason why there were never any secrets in this refugee compound. The next-door neighbors were privy to every conversation above a whisper and any other sound that was made, including sex. I remember our barracks Communist—there was always at least one Communist in every refugee camp I had ever been in—speaking to me about the workers' paradise across the border to the east and how wonderful life was in a place where everybody was equal. He never went to check things out for himself though. He liked sex, and perhaps he was even a little bit of an exhibitionist as well. His apartment was directly behind ours when Mutti, Ingrid, and I still lived in a barracks across from Oma and Opa Samuel's. On purpose or by accident his bed sat right next to the wall separating his apartment from our living room—the room with the stove where we did our cooking and where I slept. All winter long I had to listen to him groan on the other side of the thin wall as he mated with his wife. The woman never made a sound, but he became louder and louder as he approached his climax. If it happened in the afternoon, there was no pretending that we didn't hear. My cousin Vera, who lived with us at the time, would point at the wall and say, "There he goes again." Mutti, if she was present, acted as if she didn't hear. I felt ashamed listening to something I thought should be private, something I didn't really understand. But of course there was nothing private in the barracks, and no one explained anything to me about sex.

I awoke during the night and heard my grandfather's regular breathing. After all he had seen and experienced in life, he was a man at peace with himself. He blamed no one for anything that had happened to him and never complained about his lot in life. Last evening before we went to bed he mentioned to me that he would build another house. He didn't know where and when, but he would build one just the same, and I knew my grandfather made no idle promises. I looked up into the darkness of the room, remembering the debilitating years of life in this camp. My mind traveled back to the winter of 1947, a winter so cold that many of us thought dying would be preferable to going on with life. Many people, including my mother, had lost their jobs at the airfield. Cold winds blew off the storm-whipped North Sea and rattled the windows of our aging barracks. Hopelessness raised its dispiriting head, the hopelessness that came with the certainty that our lives would never change for the better. If it didn't rain, then a fine, cold mist persisted in the air, chilling our ill-clad bodies as well as what was left of our spirits. I remembered how the first snows came gently at first, then more persistently. Finally winter arrived with bitter vengeance, as if it had a score to settle with us, the most vulnerable and destitute of people. The mud around the barracks, churned up by many feet and the huge tires of British army trucks, froze into steel-hard ridges, making it difficult to walk to the one pump that provided our small community with water. The danger of fire was ever present as I pushed wood into our stove by the basketful. That cast-iron stove provided the only heat for our apartment and had just enough space on top for one pot to prepare our meals. I kept a wary eye on the ceiling, hoping to catch a fire before it became uncontrollable. I slept in the room with the stove and never went to sleep until the fire was out; then our apartment turned bitter cold. When the wind howled outside and drove the snow before it, I could feel the frigid air come through the cracks in the walls, from between the floor boards, and under the door, and around the window frames. The wind drove snow as fine as powdered sugar into the room and onto my bed. Mutti, Ingrid, and I slept with our clothes on, with every blanket and coat we possessed spread over us, yet we were cold. By morning the water in the water bucket was covered with a thin layer of ice.

I remembered turning thirteen in February 1948, nearly three years after the war ended. There was no thought of a birthday celebration. Slowly people were coming to see themselves as being at the end of their wits. Men and women, mothers and fathers, were beginning to doubt their ability to sustain their families, to keep their young children alive one more day. No amount of ingenuity could hold the old uniforms and ancient pieces of clothing together much longer. Everything was worn through and out. Clothes were permanently stained with rings of sweat and the dirt of years, dirt impervious to hard water and the bars of clay we used in place of soap. For a time back in November it never stopped raining, and our compound swam in a sea of mud. The roofs of the barracks leaked, and we had nothing with which to stop the leaks. I tried to keep our beds dry with the few pans and bowls at my disposal. The smell of dirt and decay wrapped itself around us, smothering the little spirit we had left. I felt like I was drowning, slowly sinking into the ooze around me. At night, when I went to bed, the thought of maybe not waking up the next morning provided a macabre option, a welcome sense of possible relief. Why not? There was nothing to live for anyway.

I struggled to find something to hold on to, to give me hope to hang on until tomorrow. One night, when it was so cold my bones hurt, I remembered the brave German soldier who stopped for us in Strasburg in April 1945 amidst the chaos of a fleeing army. He rescued us from the Russians, saved our lives. That memory made me forget my pain, and I went to sleep thinking of him. On subsequent nights, I tried to recall other people who gave us a helping hand. And as the nights passed I began to see things differently, discerning a glimmer of light on my dark horizon of life. I quit feeling sorry for myself. In the long nights of that cold winter of 1947 the memory of what others had done for us gave me comfort and hope.

When I awoke the next morning, Opa and Oma were already up doing their chores. After breakfast my grandfather slipped me some money. "Go buy yourself something, dear boy," he said with a cracking voice, patting me on the back. Then he went out to the barn. Oma prepared two salami sandwiches for my trip back to Hannover. "Will you say *auf Wiedersehen* to my father for me?" I asked Oma as she was busy fixing my sandwiches.

"Yes, I will," she replied. "He doesn't come home regularly anymore from Munster-Lager now that he remarried. When I see him I will tell him that you came to say *auf Wiedersehen*." She handed me my sandwiches, carefully wrapped in wax paper. Then she said in a surprisingly firm voice, "Go now, my dear boy. May God bless you on your long journey. Write soon. Don't forget your Oma and Opa." How could I?

Oma walked out front with me, stopping at the corner of the barracks to watch me walk down the familiar path to the train station. The potato fields to my left lay fallow this time of year; the forest to my right stood as it had when I first arrived in the winter of 1946—a silent witness to our misery. Oma held her cane in her left hand and leaned slightly forward as she waved *auf Wiedersehen* to me with her right. She continued to wave until I reached the station. As the two-car train pulled away from the platform I saw her lonely figure still standing next to the barracks, resting on her walking stick and occasionally raising her arm for a final wave. By early afternoon I was back in Hannover.

On Monday, December 4, 1950, I said goodbye to my friends in the bakery. They revealed to me that as soon as they learned my mother had married an American they knew I wouldn't be staying around much longer. I listened to what they had to say and smiled at them. To my surprise, the cake baker came out of his room, ceremoniously wiped his hands on his white apron smudged with flour and remnants of pastry dough, and took my hand. He shook it vigorously. "I wish you much luck, my young friend," he said, looking me in the eye. "And I hope that you will remember us now and then. Write us a letter and tell us about what you find in that America you love so much. We would like to know what it is really like over there. Have a good trip. And don't worry," he said as he turned away from me to return to his world of cakes, *Torte* and marzipan, "*your* American army in Korea will do just fine." I was surprised and taken aback by the sincerity of his comments. As I watched him walk back to his room I knew I had probably misjudged him. Maybe he knew more about armies and war than I thought. Maybe he had not always been a cake and pastry baker.

"*Auf Wiedersehen*," I called after him as he passed through the door, but I don't believe he heard me. My few possessions fit into my old cardboard suitcase which had been with me since we fled Sagan in January 1945. I packed on Monday evening after work and the next morning, December 5, Herr Krampe drove me to the train station in his odd-looking, three-wheeled delivery truck. He shook my hand and wished me a good trip. He looked like he meant it. Before I left that morning Emma fed me an extra large plate of sandwiches. For a moment her eyes seemed watery. Then she grabbed my hand and said, "*Auf Wiedersehen*, Wolfgang, *und eine gute Reise nach Amerika*." She then ran off to ready her wares to take to the downtown store. Frau Krampe was her usual self, shaking my left hand with her left hand, the stump of her right forearm covered with a knitted sock-like garment, smiling her perpetual cold smile. She wished me well without meaning it.

Herr Krampe dropped me off at the *Hauptbahnhof*. Not until his truck sputtered from view did I grasp the handle of my suitcase, straighten up and resolutely walk toward the station, toward my new future. "I am free," I said out loud to myself over and over again, not caring if anyone heard, "I am free." And for the first time in nearly six years I really did feel free and unfettered—felt like a child once more.

CHAPTER 3

Leaving for America

The ticket window at the Hannover railroad station looked just like the window I remembered from Sagan in January 1945, when my mother, Ingrid, and I got on the last train to Berlin, fleeing the terror of the Red Army. As I stood in line to buy my ticket to Fürstenfeldbruck, a vision from my past popped into my head. My mother and Ingrid had somehow managed to get on the crowded train. As much as I tried, I couldn't find a way, surrounded as I was by hundreds of screaming, pushing, clawing, desperate people wanting to do the same. Then the train began to move, slowly at first, then faster and faster, with me running alongside. When I realized that I wouldn't be able to get on, that the train was leaving without me, taking my mother and sister with it, when I understood that terrifying truth—I wanted to die. I was only nine years old then, cold, hungry, tired, filled with fear. As I approached the end of the platform, resigned to my fate, strangers reached out of a passing train window and grabbed me by my uplifted hands, my hair, my coat, wherever they could find a grip, and as the train thundered across switches into the darkness of night the strangers struggled with their burden until they pulled me to safety onto the speeding train. But this was 1950. I was on a train platform in Hannover, waiting for a train that would take me to my mother, not away from her. I shook my head vigorously, as if by doing so I could shake off the past like sweat pearling on my brow. The war was long over, yet it lived on in my head. I seldom thought of the past consciously, but it intruded all too often in my sleep, when I couldn't keep it out, and at times of its own choosing. There was no total escape.

The blue-jacketed attendant took my money, stamped my apprentice pass which gave me a special fare, handed me the one-way ticket to Fürstenfeldbruck, and never once looked up. I walked over to the platform where my *D-Zug* was scheduled to arrive. I was early. The station smelled of the many thousands of people who had passed through it before me; it smelled of urine, coal, steam, and cheap tobacco. I saw daylight at the far end of the platform. Once out in the open I felt better, freer. I sat down on a bench, alone with myself and my thoughts. I began to understand that I was about to start a new life, have a new beginning, like being born for a second time. The thought was thrilling, also intimidating: To have another chance at life. How many people got such a break? Would I be able to take advantage of this opportunity?

When the train arrived, I hardly felt the weight of the suitcase in my hand as I walked down the line of green cars looking for an empty compartment. I wanted to be alone with my thoughts, savor every second, every minute of this precious day. I found a compartment in a car to the rear of the train and made myself comfortable in a window seat, looking aft, to have a lingering view of the countryside. Maybe it would be the last time to see the land of my birth. I didn't know if I would ever be able to return. It was a beautiful December day filled with sunshine, mellow and diffuse, gently warming. There was no wind, or very little of it. A touch of coolness in the air presaged the chill of winter days to come. As the train carried me south I was captured by its rhythm, just as I had always been as a child, captured by the rush of air pushed aside by speeding cars, by the clickety-clack of cast-iron wheels racing across shiny rails, and by the occasional hoot of the engine at the head of a long string of cars obediently following behind like little chicks following a hen. At times, when negotiating a long curve, I could see the train to its full length: an enchanting sight of fluid motion, nearly a living thing it seemed to me.

The haze of late autumn lay draped across the land providing a sense of tranquility that came with the stable air of the season when nature was at peace with itself. I felt at peace with myself and watched Germany glide by my window. First we crossed the Lüneburger Heide with its expanses of heather and thickly bunched junipers, dark pine forests abruptly giving way to fields and meadows, alternating in regular, predetermined patterns. Nothing wild here, everything had been assigned its role and place a long time ago. Then the train passed through the *Mittelgebirge* of central Germany, a more rugged, heavily forested region, filled with legendary castle ruins and the imaginary denizens of the tales of the brothers Grimm. There was little color remaining, only shades of gray and the occasional evergreen. The forests were largely denuded of their leaves, allowing at times a spectacular view into deep valleys and black chasms nurturing rapidly flowing streams spanned by high-flying bridges miraculously saved from war or quickly repaired after the shooting stopped. The train entered narrow tunnels as black as night to again emerge suddenly into near blinding sunshine.

What captured my greatest attention though was not the beauty of the land, nor the castle ruins of lives lived long ago, nor the occasional palaces, which spoke of opulence amongst poverty with their hundreds of glistening windows looking down from some lofty mountain, but the seemingly endless sea of ruins as we passed through Germany's cities. It didn't matter which—Hannover, Kassel, Würzburg, Nürnberg, Munich—they all had that same devastated look of street after street of houses with hollow eyes, one-time doors and windows now leading nowhere. Ruins empty of life, hiding the human agony of their destruction. I was again overcome by the magnitude of the disaster that had befallen my country. Seeing Germany's savaged cities and towns gliding by was unnerving, and it brought back the horrors of many days and nights in wartime Berlin when we children huddled with our mothers in a basement cellar built to store coal and personal belongings, not to withstand the brutal explosive power of massed five-hundred pound bombs released in profusion from up high by American or British bombers. The aircrews only saw smoke and flashes of light below, not the agony of life lived and life taken by their exploding freight.

My tenth birthday was on February 2, 1945, the day before the Berlin inferno. It was cloudy that day. Herr Schmitt, our kind Berlin host with whom we were staying said, "The Americans won't come today. They prefer sunny, cloud-free days for their air raids." The next day, February 3, 1945, was one of those sunny, cloud-free days. Mutti kept Ingrid and me close to her, knowing that soon an ominous warning would come over the radio: "*Achtung. Achtung,*" the radio announcer commanded, "*Feindliche bomber Formationen im Anflug auf Berlin. Sofort in Deckung gehen. Ich wiederhole . . . .* Enemy bomber formations are approaching Berlin. Take shelter immediately." Then the sirens wailed and we took a few things and slowly walked down the stairs from our fifth-floor apartment to the cellar below. Everyone walked slowly, no one ever ran. Everyone knew that our turn to die would come. As I heard and felt the bombs exploding nearby in chaotic rhythm, I shut it all out of my ten-year-old mind, and instead thought of the Americans flying those airplanes high above as people.

I wondered if they really hated me? How could they. They didn't even know me. I had done nothing to them. I thought of the American flyers as men who came from the land of the Mohicans. What were they really like, I wondered. What did their faces look like? Did they have children like Ingrid and me? Were their children being bombed by someone else? From that day on I played mind-games to distract myself from reality the instant we stepped into the basement. We left Berlin in late March 1945, to stay with my mother's parents in Strasburg, a small, bucolic country town less than a hundred miles north of Berlin. There, war seemed as remote as the moon. That soon changed as well.

I pressed my forehead against the window pane as the train passed through the cities, passed by row upon row of burned-out buildings, street after street without a man, woman, or child in sight. Remnants of walls stared back at me with their hollow eyes. I knew that at one time these ruins were blazing infernos, and children like Ingrid and me and mothers like Hedy suffered horrible deaths within. Many were buried in the cellars below the rubble, slowly dying as their life-giving oxygen was depleted and fumes from bombs and burning buildings seeped into their sanctuary turned mausoleum. How could all this have happened? Whenever I asked anyone, even my grandfather Samuel whom I trusted to tell the truth, I received no explanation that I, as a teenager, could understand. It was no use looking back, that's what my grandfather said. Look to the future, he told me. I was trying hard to look to the future.

Since I had no chance to write my mother I wasn't surprised to find no one waiting for me at the train station in Fürstenfeldbruck. It was cold, with some snow on the ground. I wore my new brown overcoat, which I bought in Hannover with the money my grandfather Samuel had given me. The coat was a size too large, but it was all I could find. It was warm, and that was all that really mattered. I could feel the spring in my steps as I took the familiar path to Frau Buck's house. When I knocked on the door, Frau Buck opened and greeted me in her usual friendly manner. I shook her hand and followed her inside. I knocked on Mutti's door. Leo opened and let me in. Their faces lit up when they saw me. I was welcome. I was home. Hedy, Leo, and I were a family.

Very early the next morning, December 6, the three of us walked to the station to catch the first train to Munich. That day we spent most of our time in the American consulate sitting on old, hard, discolored wooden benches in poorly lit rooms—waiting and waiting. Then someone called our names and we filled out papers and had our pictures taken. I was ushered into a doctor's office—alone, without my mother. I felt intimidated, never having been to a doctor before in my life. I sat for a while on a chair by a desk until the doctor entered the room. He looked at the floor as he entered and said nothing. Then, in fluent German, still not looking at me, he said, "Please drop your pants and let me look at you." His German was perfect, without a trace of accent, yet I didn't believe he was German. He moved differently than Germans did, had different mannerisms. His request shocked me into inaction. Perhaps I hadn't understood him correctly. I remained seated without moving a muscle or saying anything.

"Please get up," he repeated matter-of-factly, without any expression showing in his face or in his voice, "and drop your pants, including your underpants." This time I rose slowly, undid my belt and unbuttoned my fly. Looking at him for encouragement, but receiving none, I first pulled down my pants and dropped them on the floor, then pulled down my underpants, olive green American army issue underpants Leo gave me when he was still stationed in Fassberg. I stood exposed, feeling like the only thing I thought I still possessed and could call my own, my dignity, had just been taken from me. For me, the war was still going on, just by different means. The doctor approached and examined my genitals with some care. Then he said, "I am finished. You may put your pants back on." I did as I was told. He washed his hands, went to his office door, opened the door, and indicated with his hand for me to leave. I don't believe he ever looked me in the eye while I was in his office. I stepped outside. Wounded. Hurt. Hedy went in next. I sat quietly next to Leo on the hard bench in the waiting room. My English wasn't good enough to ask him about what had just happened to me. When my mother emerged from her examination, we walked downstairs to a cafeteria for soup and sandwiches. I found a moment during lunch to tell her about my experience in the doctor's office.

"Oh," she said lightly with a laugh, putting an arm around my shoulders and pulling me close, "that can be embarrassing for a young boy. I should have talked to you. The doctor was only checking to see if you had venereal disease. He checked me too. We are both fine." I didn't know what venereal disease was; I hadn't heard those words before. I let it go at that. I still felt violated.

We were issued a passport that afternoon with visas for my mother and me to enter the United States of America. I couldn't believe it was really happening. It had taken nearly a year for Mutti and Leo to obtain this coveted document, a small, ugly frog-green booklet. On its front, in gold capital letters in English, French, and German, it read TEMPORARY TRAVEL DOCUMENT IN LIEU OF PASSPORT FOR GERMAN NATIONALS. It was issued by the Combined Travel Board of the Allied High Commission for Germany. In it, the bearer was described as Hedwig Ferguson, accompanied by one child, me, "under 16 years." On page four was a picture of my mother, along with her signature. What I was looking for I found on page eight—our visas. I ran my fingers over the eagle and the words "Consulate General of the United States of America, Munich, Germany," impressed with a metal stamp upon the page. My mother's visa number was 794, a very low number I thought. Written next to it was the word "nonquota." My number was 20,488 and it was annotated "quota." Both of our visas were certified by the American consulate general at Munich, George I. Churchill. I didn't know what quota and nonquota meant, and I didn't care. What mattered was that with this document in hand I could travel to America, to the land of the Mohicans, to Colorado, the land of my dreams.

While I thought we would leave within days after our consulate visit, that didn't happen. The month of December passed slowly. I had become used to fourteen-hour work-days. Suddenly I had nothing to do. I got restless. On Christmas Eve it began to snow, lightly at first, then quite heavily. There was no wind, and the flakes tumbled out of a gray sky as if shaken loose by some mysterious source. I went outside into the garden and looked up at the leaden sky, at the swirling snowflakes taking shape at the last moment as they approached my face, making me dizzy as I tried to focus my eyes on them. I opened my mouth and let flakes fall in as I had done when I was a little boy in Sagan. The next morning, when I got up and pushed the curtains aside, I was greeted by a fairytale landscape. Field and forest were covered with a foot thick blanket of fluffy snow. The bulbous cupola of a Catholic church was visible in the distance, its gold dome contrasting sharply with its pristine surroundings. When I went outside, after hurriedly washing up and dressing, I found a world totally quiet and at peace with itself. Not a sound by man or beast spoiled this perfect moment, Christmas day, 1950. I went into the street and walked through the snow, kicking at it at times in youthful exuberance. I was happy. Later that day all three of us played in the snow like little children, Leo dressed in his blue air force uniform. The light snow didn't lend itself to making snowballs or a snowman. My mother squealed with childish delight, throwing snow into my face, into Leo's face, laughing like I had not heard her laugh in many years.

I had not registered with the police in Fürstenfeldbruck upon my arrival because I thought we would be leaving soon. But in early January we were still there, with no idea when Leo would receive his travel orders. All three of us lived in that one little room at Frau Buck's, who became uncomfortable about my registration status. She confronted Hedy in the hall, insisting that she register my presence with the police. "*Es gehört sich so*," Frau Buck said apologetically; it is the proper thing to do and must be done. "I don't want to get into trouble with the *Polizei*, Frau Ferguson. You understand, don't you?" It was the first time I heard anyone address my mother as Frau Ferguson, her new name.

Before I left Hannover, I had made a quick trip to the *Polizei* late on the afternoon of December 4 to register my departure. After work I cleaned up as quickly as I could and ran to the nearest police station on Königstrasse. I got there just after they locked the doors for the day. I pounded on the door until an irate police sergeant opened the door. Before he could say anything, words spewed out of my mouth in rapid order, explaining my predicament, begging him to please, please give me the necessary papers— or I wouldn't be able to go to America. The sergeant stood there listening to my wild babbling, then told me to calm myself and follow him. He went over to a desk, signed me out, and gave me the necessary papers, all properly signed and stamped, to take to my next place of residence. He even smiled when I shook his hand and wished me the best of luck in America. On January 10, presenting my papers from Hannover, I registered my presence at the Fürstenfeldbruck police station, and Frau Buck signed a registration form attesting that I lived in her house only temporarily. I was given a temporary residence permit, pending emigration to the United States. Officially, no one could move anywhere in Germany without permission from proper authority—that authority, as in the old days, being the police. The restriction implemented by the Allied Control Council a number of years earlier was frequently violated, even though the police and local government could make life miserable for those not in compliance with rules and regulations. I knew we Germans liked things to be orderly. Being orderly meant following the rules, and that was all Frau Buck was doing when she insisted that I register with the police.

A week later Leo came home, his face beaming, waving a thick sheaf of papers into Hedy's face. "I have our travel orders," he announced gleefully. Leo's happiness was contagious, and I couldn't wait to take a look. He handed me a copy, saying, "It's yours." I sat down and tried to read every word, every line—an impossible task. Not only were all instructions in English, but much of it was abbreviated military jargon. I could make out some things: Special Order Number 8 issued by Headquarters 36th Maintenance and Supply Group, to which Leo was assigned, directing "Sergeant Leo B. Ferguson, accompanied by his German-national wife Hedwig and his stepson Wolfgang, also a German national, to report to the port of Bremerhaven not later than January 21 for further movement by first available surface transportation to the United States. By order of Lieutenant Colonel Hartwig." I read and reread that last sentence several times, "for further movement by first available transportation to the United States" and ran my finger over those lines of print. I couldn't quite grasp the enormity of the event, that it was really true that I, a lowly refugee boy not wanted by anyone, a baker's apprentice, a boy with only an eighth-grade education, maybe less, was going to America.

In years to come, at the height of the Cold War, I was to fly with the 36th Tactical Fighter Wing, the same wing that my stepfather Leo once was assigned to in 1950. By 1970, when I arrived after a combat tour of duty in Thailand, the wing had relocated from Fürstenfeldbruck to Bitburg air base in the Eifel mountains of Germany. Then in the late 1980s, in the final years of the Cold War, my son Charles would fly his A-10 attack jet out of Bitburg as well.

Late Saturday morning, January 20, 1951, Leo, Hedy, and I said *auf Wiedersehen* to the Bucks. We took a taxi to the train station and boarded a slow *Personenzug* to Munich. At the Munich railroad station we changed to a waiting American army train which would take us overnight to the port city of Bremerhaven, just over 600 kilometers north of Munich. We were assigned a private compartment for the three of us, and three beds in a sleeper car. At four o'clock in the afternoon the train slowly pulled out of the station. It was still light outside, and I watched the wounded city glide by from my window in the dining car. I had never traveled in such luxury before: eating in a dining car served by a white-jacketed waiter who bowed ever so slightly every time he addressed Hedy and Leo. In years past, when I traveled with my grandfather Samuel, we always took sandwiches with us on our trips. Opa would put them in his briefcase, and when we got hungry, we ate them right there in our compartment in front of everyone. The train crossed a small overpass. Just then a new American car, a Chevrolet, emerged from under the bridge. I followed the car's red taillights until it was out of sight. I wondered if we would have a car like that when we got to America.

After dinner we returned to our compartment. The creaking coach, the whoosh of the wind, the occasional hooting of the engine, and the clickety-clack of the wheels were familiar and soothing sounds. It was a train just like the one we took from Sagan in January 1945 to escape to Berlin, but this time there were no Russian tanks threatening, or bombers dropping bombs, or anti-aircraft shrapnel bouncing off the roof of the coach. For once, I felt secure, more secure than I had felt for the past six years of my life. I fell into a totally relaxing sleep without dreaming of anything. When I briefly awoke in the middle of the night, I was stretched out on the upholstered bench in our compartment, a blanket pulled over me. I looked up at the dim ceiling light and felt this incredible sense of happiness. I closed my eyes and went back to sleep.

We arrived in Bremerhaven early the next morning. At the station we were met by American army buses, and along with many other families, driven to a hotel in an army compound and assigned two nicely furnished rooms. Because of my age, I had a room all to myself, including my own bathroom. When I was alone, I threw myself on the soft bed and stretched out my arms and legs the way I used to do as a little boy when I made snow angels. It was a big bed meant for two. I had it all to myself. I felt totally unconstrained. Happy. Freed of the burdens I carried for so long. I had food, a warm bed, an entire room with adjoining bathroom. I had a family and a future to look forward to. I didn't have to worry about a leaking roof, about getting wood for the winter, begging strangers for food, or planting a garden to supplement meager rations. I was no longer a baker's apprentice living in a moldering house ruin. The past and future ran through my mind like alternating streaks of darkness and light. The light prevailed and the darkness faded.

We ate our meals in a large dining room for transiting families, and had a permanent table assigned where we ate breakfast, lunch, and dinner at the same times each morning, noon, and evening. Freshly cut flowers adorned the table every day, set with a spotless white linen tablecloth, fresh linen napkins, and silverware laid out in the proper manner, the way I had been taught by Mutti as a little boy—knife on the right with the sharp side toward the plate, dinner and salad forks on the left, dessert spoon horizontally above the dinner plate. Table manners, eating properly with knife and fork, knowing how to set a table, those were things important to my mother, and she had taught them to me at the early age of five. When she gave dinner parties in Sagan, she took great pride in having her little boy at the table, dressed in his best suit, standing patiently behind his chair until all the adults had been seated, using his knife and fork as adeptly as any of them, which invariably elicited praise of Hedy's child-rearing skills. I was bored stiff by her all too frequent dinner parties and couldn't get out of there fast enough to change into something comfortable and run outside and play with my friends. But before I could do so, I had to ask her permission to leave the table. When I did, I rose unhurriedly, knowing that everyone was watching, pushed my chair back under the table, and bade everyone goodbye, bowing slightly toward the guests before exiting and closing the door, never turning my back on them. Such were the things once so important to my mother. All that had changed.

Dinner was served by a friendly German waiter in a white coat who carried a white linen serving towel over his left arm. "Where are you going?" he asked Hedy the first evening.

"Colorado," she replied.

"You will never want to leave Colorado once you get there," the waiter replied to my great surprise. "It is such a beautiful place. I was there for over three years as a prisoner-of-war in a camp south of Denver, near Colorado Springs. I enjoyed every day of my stay. Wait and see, you will just love it in Colorado. You will never want to leave. They'll have to drive you out with a stick." He gave her a broad smile. "I would have stayed if they had let me," he said. I smiled at Mutti. Maybe now she wouldn't worry anymore.

Last September, when I came to visit her in Fürstenfeldbruck, she asked me if I would accompany her to the United States once she and Leo got married. Then she pulled a picture from her purse and handed it to me. "What do you think?" she asked. The picture showed a family standing in front of what looked like the basement of a house. But there was no house on top of the basement, only tar paper.

"I don't know what to think," I told her. "Who are these people?"

"Leo's brother Raymond, his wife, and their three children. Look at that house! I won't live in anything like that, Wolfgang. Never, never, never. I don't know if I want to go to America." Her eyes reflected her feelings, showing emotions I had never seen before—fear and indecision. I took her hands in mine and tried to assure her that she didn't have to live like that, that she would make her own life with Leo once she got to America. "Let's forget the picture and put it away," I finally told her. "America is much more beautiful than what you see here in this photograph. We will love it there. Just wait and see."

"Oh, Wolfgang," she said, and the smile was back in her voice and on her face, "you always see everything through rose colored glasses." She stroked my hair back the way she used to when I was really little. "That's what makes you so loveable. I am glad you are coming with me." The subject was closed. But I knew she wouldn't forget. She never forgot anything. And the first thing she would do once we got to America was to make sure that there was no basement house in her future. After life in the barracks she never again wanted to live like that, or in anything that reminded her of those terrible days of poverty, degradation, cold, hunger, and want.

Our ship was the USNS *George W. Goethals*, a Liberty Ship sailing on a regularly scheduled run between the east coast of the United States and European ports, carrying military dependents, troops, and miscellaneous cargo. In later years I learned that the ship was named in honor of Major General George Washington Goethals who oversaw the construction of the Panama Canal. The *Goethals* entered service in 1943, number 599 of a total of 2,751 Liberty Ships built to a standardized, mass-produced design. The 12,000-ton ship had a length of 489 feet, and its original design allowed it to carry up to nearly two thousand troops at a speed of seventeen knots. In 1946, the *Goethals* accommodated military families as well.

We boarded on Wednesday, January 24, 1951, and were assigned a cabin amidship with other American families returning to the United States. The family area was roped off and had "off limits" signs posted for the troops who were quartered in the belly of the *Goethals*. I had never seen a ship before as large as the *Goethals* and had never been on a ship of any size. After we boarded and settled into our cabin, I excused myself and went outside to the ship's railing to see what was going on. There were hundreds of soldiers coming on board. So many I couldn't count them all. The soldiers wore dress uniforms, overseas caps neatly tucked under the right shoulder epaulet, trousers bloused over high-laced paratrooper boots. I thought they looked like real combat soldiers, each carrying his duffel bag over a sagging left shoulder. The soldiers stood patiently in two long lines, inching their way up two narrow gangways into the belly of the ship. When all were on board, the gangways were unhooked and stowed on the dock. Then the dock became very quiet.

It was late afternoon, the sky overcast, with a low-lying blanket of lead-gray clouds stretching from horizon to horizon, typical for the north of Germany that time of year. A light, cold breeze blew off the water. I pulled my new overcoat tightly around me. On the other side of the *Goethals* two tugs pushed us away from the dock. I perceived movement and a rumble within the ship. I felt the ship's engines come to life through the wooden deck planks under my feet. On the pier below several people stood watching. One figure, a man, standing apart from the rest, waved his right arm in a slow *auf Wiedersehen*. I looked around me but saw no one else. Only I was still standing at the railing; everyone else had gone to their cabins. I wondered who the man was waving to. I waved back. I waved at the man on the pier until he stopped waving. Then he just stood there watching the ship pull away from the dock. I noticed the man wore an overcoat like my father Willie's and a hat with the brim pulled into his face, the way my father always wore his hat. Could he be my father? I couldn't tell. I stood too high up and the ship was too far away from the dock. Maybe he had come to say goodbye in his own way. He was like that. Certain things were important to my father, and for those things he would make any sacrifice.

The docks slowly receded from view. Then there was mostly water and land barely above sea level. I felt a deep sadness come over me. I was only fifteen and never really had the opportunity to get to know the land of my ancestors. Now I was leaving, perhaps never to return, never to see my dear grandparents again. Only six years earlier to the day, on January 24, 1945, I had been a happy nine-year-old boy living in a small, unimportant town in the east of Germany. There I went eagerly to school and, like all young children, learned to read and write, learned my numbers—how to add and subtract, multiply and divide. In winter we boys constructed elaborate snow forts, built snowmen, had snowball fights, and on the way home from school tried to catch the girls and rub snow in their faces. It was a wonderful time. Then suddenly war was upon us, and I never again played the games of childhood. I lost my home. My family broke apart. We became refugees, unwanted strangers in our own land. Many in my family died. My grandfather Grapentin was beaten to death by German

Communists. My aunt Marie and my cousin Vera were raped by Russian soldiers for days on end, and Mutti's sister died of typhus fever, the same disease that nearly killed Mutti as well in the summer of 1945. My mother was raped and shot by an enraged Russian army major. What was it my family had done to deserve such awful punishment? It was no use to look back. I needed to look forward to the future.

I tried hard to keep the shore in sight. Then suddenly it disappeared, dropping away as if it had fallen off a table, and all that remained was water and sea gulls floating across the horizon. The ship stopped briefly to discharge the pilot, who clambered down its side on a rope ladder and jumped into a pitching motor boat that had come to take him back to Bremerhaven. Then the USNS *George W. Goethals* strained mightily and moved swiftly into the cold, gray waters of the North Sea. The masts of ships sunk long ago rose from their shallow graves, stark reminders of the recent war. I stayed at the ship's railing until dark, until I could see no more and could only feel the movement of the ship beneath my feet as it headed out into the Atlantic to deeper water. My sadness lessened. Tomorrow I would be back on deck, I decided, as I turned toward our cabin, to stand at the railing and look to the west—toward my new country.

CHAPTER 4

USNS *George W. Goethals*

Ashiver ran through my body as I stood on the windswept platform in Sagan, waiting for the train from Liegnitz. Daylight had come and gone. I felt cold, tired, and hungry. I remembered my mother saying this was the last train; there wouldn't be another. I was afraid the Russian tanks would get here first. I stomped my feet on the concrete platform to get warm. It didn't help. It was January 24, 1945, and one of the coldest winters on record. Suddenly, there it was, speeding around the bend, brakes screeching loudly. Clouds of steam and coal dust settled onto the anxious crowd as the engine roared past, coming to a halt slowly, noisily far down the track. My mother hurried off to find a place on the train for us, pulling Ingrid behind her, leaving me to guard our suitcases, hurriedly packed the night before. I stood there obediently, watching, waiting for a sign from my mother. Then I saw her at a coach window, beckoning with her hand. She looked happy, smiled. Ingrid was beside her. I wondered how they had gotten on the train so quickly. I stood at my place, surrounded by a sea of frantic, pushing, shouting humanity. As I tried to walk toward her coach, my feet wouldn't move. No matter how hard I tried, my feet would not move. I heard a faint whistle in the distance, then the engine's hooting reply. Slowly the train began to move. Didn't she know I couldn't move my feet? Why didn't she get off the train to help me? I tried to call out to her that I needed help, but no sound passed my lips. No matter how hard I tried, I could not make a sound, and I couldn't move my feet. My mother kept beckoning with her hand, kept smiling at me as if everything was alright. Then I knew I would never see her again. I stretched out my arms toward her in one last futile gesture, and using all my strength, a scream finally broke through my lips, "Mutti, don't leave me!"

I sat up straight in bed, my scream echoing in my ears. Bathed in sweat, I gasped for air. My chest hurt. I couldn't breathe. Hedy had her arms around me, talking softly, soothingly, saying words I didn't comprehend. She stroked my hair, gave me a kiss on the temple, put her cheek up against mine. My heart pounded wildly. "It's all right, Wolfgang," she whispered, "there is nothing to be afraid of, my dear boy. I am right here with you. Go back to sleep. We are on a ship taking us to America, don't you remember?

There is no war in America. No war." Gradually I began to understand that there were no Russian tanks coming to kill me, and no one was taking my mother away from me. She was right there beside me. I don't know if it was her words, the tone of her voice, her touch, or just her presence that was so calming. As my nightmare faded to where it came from in some deep recess of my mind, the pressure in my chest diminished, I could breathe again, the terror passed, and I drifted back to sleep.

There were times when I dreaded going to sleep, fearing where my dreams might take me. Either I was falling into a deep, dark chasm, knowing that when I hit bottom I would die; or I was standing on that cold train platform in Sagan being left behind by my mother. A third nightmare took me to a field of horrors filled with dead people who looked at me accusingly as if I should be one of them. There were times when I felt I was at the precipice of death, the dream my reality, waking an unexpected, last second escape from the netherworld.

The next morning, as we were going through a lifeboat drill, Hedy leaned over and whispered, "Leo is a sound sleeper. Hardly anything wakes him. He wouldn't wake if the ship was sinking." She laughed her happy laugh. Looking me in the eye she added, "He didn't hear a thing last night. Are you all right?"

"Yes, Mutti, I am fine."

"Leo sleeps like a man with an untroubled soul," she continued. "We make up for him, don't we, Wolfgang?" I nodded my head. The evacuation drill over, we took off our vests. Hedy and Leo went back to the cabin. I stayed behind on deck, as far forward as I could go, to watch the waves break against the ship's bow, to feel the wind in my hair and against my face, to look for America.

Hedy and I had been together since that night in January 1945 when we fled Sagan from approaching Russian tanks. We shared the many horrors and hardships that came our way in the years that followed. I cared for her when she lay near death from a Russian bullet. It was I she talked to when she learned of her father's horrible death. We shared nearly every moment of our lives for three long years, and together we survived. Our bond was deep and went far beyond that of mother and son.

The *Goethals* stopped at the port of Southampton on the southern coast of England to pick up another group of GIs and several families. A week into our voyage we were battling heavy seas off Iceland. The *Goethals* lost some of its forward railing and suffered minor damage to its superstructure in a pounding storm. We had left Bremerhaven on January 24, expecting to arrive in New York on the second of February, my sixteenth birthday. But the encounter with the Noreaster, as the ship's captain referred to the raging storm which blew up unexpectedly, added a couple of days to an already lengthy voyage. It didn't matter. For me, the ship was home. Home was where Hedy was. Unique about this particular home was that the ship was a world unto itself, totally secure from my perspective, without any apparent threats to my safety. The storm, although fierce, didn't inspire fear. It was just nature being itself, and I understood the ways of nature. For the first time since 1945, I felt no need to be on guard. No need to be afraid of anyone or anything.

Aside from this liberating feeling of personal safety, first and foremost among my new experiences was the ship's food. I looked forward to every meal—breakfast, lunch, and dinner. Only briefly on the first and second day did I feel a slight discomfort as a result of high seas; then I settled down, and when the seas were rough, I began to anticipate the roll and pitch of the ship as I walked around deck. One sailor kidded me about my sea legs and asked if I wanted to sign on for the next voyage. He spoke a little German and exchanged greetings with me whenever he saw me. Often, I was the only one in the dining room, other passengers apparently too seasick to eat. I wouldn't think of missing a meal. In the immediate postwar years I had gone with little or no food too often not to be tantalized by the bonanza that awaited me every time I entered the ship's mess. The ship's kitchen was the proverbial *Schlaraffenland*, a mythical German heaven where food of all kinds was plentiful and if you were lazy and slothful you didn't even have to put the food on your plate as the roast ducks and chickens would fly right into your mouth. The servers, standing idly behind a long line of steam-heated trays filled with enough food to feed all the passengers, smiled when they saw me coming. They probably thought, "Here comes that crazy German kid again who eats enough for an army." They generously filled my plate with scrambled eggs, golden brown pancakes, crispy bacon, fried potatoes, fried sausages, and ham. At first, I was timid about getting a second helping, but as the days passed and the servers and I became familiar enough to exchange smiles and laugh at one another, my reservations vanished. I ate until my belly hurt. All of us hungry German children had at one time or another wished for our bellies to hurt from overeating, a feeling we could only imagine. The hurt we knew came from an empty stomach, which we cured by pulling our belts just a little tighter. On the *Goethals* I could indulge myself by overeating, always having at least two full helpings, three occasionally, a fourth when there was an especially tantalizing dessert. After a large breakfast, I soon was hungry again for lunch, and again in time for dinner.

The family dining area was roped off, but I could see the soldiers eating on the other side. Their faces were young, not much older than I. Their numbers diminished at meal time as the days passed and the waves remained high. My mother never recovered from her initial bout of seasickness after we left Southampton, and I don't recall if and when she ate. I stayed on deck most of the time, or in the passenger lounge if the seas were too rough and we were prohibited from going outside. The minute the dining room opened though—I was there.

The food was served on heavy china plates, nearly as durable as the metal trays the soldiers used for their meals. At breakfast I especially loved the scrambled eggs and always took a generous helping. The eggs were soft and moist and reminded me of the time in 1945 when a compassionate farm woman gave me three eggs for my mother who lay near death, shot through the neck by a raging Russian officer whose advances she had refused. My grandmother Grapentin carefully prepared the three eggs for Hedy, but Hedy was delirious, and Oma was only able to get a little of the precious eggs into her mouth and down her throat. We three—Ingrid, Oma Grapentin, and I—shared what was left. I could still recall the heavenly taste of those eggs. On the ship, before me at breakfast every day were all the eggs I could possibly want to eat. There was always a huge quantity of deliciously smelling, very crispy bacon in the tray next to the eggs. I had never tasted bacon prepared like that. German bacon was thick and fatty, while this bacon was thinly sliced and most of the fat had been baked out of it. I took plenty of the bacon along with my eggs, slices of ham, and several delicious pork sausages as well—sausages like my grandfather Samuel used to make when he killed a pig. Breakfast remained my favorite meal throughout our voyage. After breakfast I usually went on deck, pulled a chair to a sheltered spot, listened to the waves crushing against the hull of the ship, and watched the ever-present seagulls who didn't seem to be affected by any kind of weather.

After lunch a sailor showed cartoons in the ship's family lounge. I didn't understand a word of what the talking cartoon animals were saying, but it really wasn't necessary to understand Woody Woodpecker and Daffy Duck. I think I laughed a little too loudly. I was nearly sixteen, and the oldest child among those watching. The other children, younger than I, stared at me when I laughed, as if I were some creature that didn't belong in the room. Maybe I laughed at the wrong times as well. Eventually they got used to my presence and began laughing along with me. I accepted uncritically everything new I encountered—new smells, new foods, the sounds and sights of an emerging American world. After my nightmare on the first night, I slept soundly for the remainder of our voyage.

Overcome by severe seasickness, Hedy's complexion turned a shade of gray and never returned to its natural color until we got off the ship in New York. Hedy was amazed at my robust appetite. When she saw me patting my stomach, she just shook her head and smiled in disbelief. I loved putting on an act for her. Unlike some of the other women passengers who remained in their cabins throughout the voyage, Hedy accompanied Leo on deck every day. He set up a lounge chair for her on the sheltered side of the ship, wrapped her in several blankets, and then went to talk with other male passengers taking in the fresh sea air. Leo always dressed in his uniform. When on deck he wore a winter coat, hat, and gloves. Like me, he didn't get seasick.

I believe my mother was pleased to see me relax and enjoy the voyage. Occasionally though I noticed a fleeting shadow cross her face. Hedy knew, I didn't, that the future would be hard for us in our new country.

I had few expectations. Perhaps I would go back to school. I didn't consider that I couldn't speak, read, or write English, nor what grade I might enter should I have the opportunity to return to school. At age sixteen, I should enter the eleventh grade, but in Germany I progressed only to the eighth, and some of those eight years hardly qualified as education. When we escaped Sagan in January 1945, I was in the fourth grade and didn't return to school again until that September. We lived in the Russian zone then, and the Communist teachers had little interest in conveying knowledge to us children, but focused instead on teaching the ideology of the proletariat. I didn't take well to that, rebelled, and was beaten by my classmates for being unlike them. I didn't enter a real school again until January 1947 in Fassberg, after fleeing the Russian zone in December of 1946. How much schooling did I really have? I had far too little.

I watched Leo talking animatedly to a Red Cross official who was returning to the United States after a tour of duty in Germany. Leo was, of course, smoking a cigarette, a sign that he was having a good time. For Leo, good times and cigarettes were synonymous. Leo was a career soldier who escaped the poverty of his own youth by joining the army in the early '30s. He first served in the field artillery in Hawaii, then transferred to the Army Air Corps and returned to Lowry Field, near Denver, Colorado, his hometown. There, late in the war, Leo met Alice. Within days of their meeting they went to a Justice of the Peace and got married. A spur of the moment decision, Leo told Hedy, which at the time seemed the right thing to do. Alice had a little boy which Leo adopted. Alice soon confessed to having second thoughts about their marriage and wanted more time to think things through. For Leo, the only difference between before and after was that suddenly he was sending a monthly check to a woman who was his wife in name only. In 1948 Leo shipped out to Germany at the start of the Berlin blockade by the Soviets. When Leo met Hedy, Alice agreed to a divorce, as long as he continued to pay child support until her boy was eighteen. I didn't know about the money issues confronting Hedy and Leo. I was blissfully ignorant of that aspect of our future, instead stuffing myself three times a day at the ship's richly set table.

On February 4, 1951, after eleven storm-tossed days, a battered USNS *George W. Goethals* sailed into New York harbor, two days past my sixteenth birthday. The three of us stood together at the ship's railing—Leo excitedly anticipating the moment when he would again step on American soil, me taking in the panorama of New York City and its incredible skyline, Hedy somewhat pensive, her eyes steady, her face revealing none of the turmoil she may have felt within—possibly thinking of Leo's brother's basement house and how they were going to manage on Leo's small salary. As we passed the Statue of Liberty, Leo tried to explain to me what it was and what it meant to Americans. I couldn't figure out what he was trying to tell me, couldn't grasp the symbolism of that strange-looking woman of bronze holding a torch at the harbor's entrance. I thought it was a fancy lighthouse. I didn't want to hurt Leo's feelings, so I looked attentive, smiled, and nodded my head when I thought it appropriate. I figured I would be doing a lot of that in the coming year, in a world where I understood hardly anything others said.

The day of our arrival in New York was similar to the day we left Bremerhaven, only the clouds weren't hanging quite as low, and the wind wasn't blowing as fiercely. But it was quite cold, and I was glad I had a warm overcoat. I began to understand that our voyage was at an end, that we would have to leave the ship which had become my home, the provider of all my needs and the source of a precious feeling of safety and security. As I walked down the gangplank, deep insecurity flooded my body, a hot wave of fear rushing from my gut to my face. Sweat pearled at my hairline. I wanted to turn around and run back up the gangplank and hide on the ship. But I knew that wasn't an option. My feet kept moving forward until I reached the firm concrete of the dock below—America. I looked at my mother walking ahead of me and picked up my pace to be near her. Being near her made me feel better. Everything would be all right as long as she was there.

CHAPTER 5

Coming to Colorado

The dingy pier with its rusting steel pillars had been crowded a few years back with thousands of American soldiers loading on ships to invade Hitler's Europe. Five years after war's end it was empty, except for a string of army buses lined up nose to tail waiting for passengers from the just arrived USNS *Goethals*. Families boarded the first two buses; the soldiers, who spent their voyage in the belly of the ship, boarded the others. While we strolled down the gangplank in haphazard family groups, the soldiers exited the ship the way they had boarded—orderly and disciplined.

Our bus took us through an aging part of New York City, not a scene that matched the vision I harbored in my mind of the land of the Mohicans. As we rode along, my disappointment deepened, as did my melancholy. I closed my eyes, let my new world pass unseen. Everything looked too much like what I had left behind—old, grimy, dirty. When the bus stopped and I opened my eyes again, we were inside a large court-yard at Fort Hamilton, an old army post in Brooklyn across the Verrazano Narrows Bridge from Staten Island. We were assigned one room for the three of us in on-post quarters, a room which smelled of the hundreds or thousands of people who must have slept here over the years, each leaving behind a little of themselves. The room had seen neither paint nor paper in many years, its furniture dark, functional, nondescript, appearing in search of a junk pile or a fireplace. I sensed the ghosts of the past, smelled their presence, couldn't breathe, and ran outside into the courtyard, leaving behind a startled Hedy and Leo. The feelings the room aroused in me were dark, oppressive, and terrifying. It all smelled too much like a prison, and I dreaded the night because I feared I would have one of my nightmares. But that night I slept soundly and had no dreams.

The first hours in this new land, my land, were bleak and forbidding. I was glad when the afternoon sun broke through the gray layer of cloud, instantly raising my spirits. Even the weathered red brick buildings of the old fort assumed a more hospitable aura under the bright, if cold, rays of the New York winter sun. Nothing changed just because the sun emerged for a brief moment, yet it brightened my spirits. It was a trick played on the mind, and I welcomed it.

After Leo received his orders assigning him to Lowry Air Force Base in Denver, Colorado, he and Hedy joined two other couples, friends from "Fürsty," and we all went into New York City—to Times Square. Lots of people strolled around the square which wasn't square at all. The lights were bright and dazzling. Huge signs flashed messages into the fading daylight. Small shops displayed their wares in the open, in front of their doors. Seeing this, my anxiety faded. Again Leo acted strangely, at least I thought he did, as he had earlier in the day when we first came off the ship and stepped onto the dock at the Brooklyn Navy Yard. There he touched the ground, concrete, with his gloved right hand. I understood that was his way of saying he was glad to be back in America. I thought it was a childish gesture. He acted as if Times Square was something special as well. I couldn't follow Leo's exuberant explanation but acted interested, smiled, and nodded my head as I always did when people spoke excitedly and I felt that they wanted me to share their enthusiasm.

Hedy spoke English well. The one-time German farm girl had a natural facility for languages. When we still lived in the Russian zone in 1945 and 1946, she quickly learned enough Russian to enable her to trade on the black market with Russian officers. She only had to hear a word once and it became a part of her vocabulary. In the English zone, Hedy found a job in the British NAAFE at the Fassberg airfield, the English equivalent of the American Base Exchange and Commissary, and soon began speaking English. I, on the other hand, could count the English words I knew on the fingers of my hands. English was offered in school in Fassberg, but when I arrived in January 1947, I was told that my year group was already too far along. I wouldn't be able to catch up. No one thought of entering me the following year in a class junior to my own, or finding out if I was willing to work a little harder to catch up with my classmates. It just wasn't done that way in a German school. So I didn't get to take English. Now I wished I had.

We found a table in a second-floor restaurant overlooking Times Square. The waitress thrust a menu into my hands. I didn't know what to do with it. I had never ordered food from a menu, much less an American menu. As I looked through the strange words, I recognized the word "steak." The German detective magazine I bought every other week when I was still at school in Fassberg was about a Manhattan detective named Kenney. Kenney not only always got his man, but he also had some peculiar personal habits, which as a young boy I thought showed how tough he was. Kenney lit a cigarette first thing in the morning after getting out of bed, inhaled deeply, then had a shot of whiskey. After that ritual, Kenney settled down to a breakfast of very strong, black coffee. Of course Kenney only ate bloody steaks—very, very rare, barely cooked at all. When it was my turn to place my order, I rounded up all the courage I could muster and blurted out, "Steek, please."

The waitress gave me a puzzled look, laughed, and turned to the others looking for an explanation. "What is he talking about?" she said in a condescending tone of voice. "Can anybody tell me what steek is?" Everyone laughed. I didn't really know what she said nor why they were laughing. When I realized the laughter around the table was at my expense, I was deeply embarrassed over my first failed attempt at using the English language.

Hedy quickly intervened, asked me in German, "How do you want your steak cooked, Wolfgang?"

"All the way through. Not bloody."

"Well done," Leo said to the waitress. Whatever that meant. The waitress turned away scribbling on her order pad, probably wondering what all these foreigners were doing here anyway. Only a few years ago the place must have been filled with GIs celebrating the end of the war. The same GIs were now showing up with German women and their kids. I saw the waitress shaking her head as she disappeared around a corner. My steak was thin and well done. I had a hard time chewing the tough, dry meat. It wasn't nearly as good as I imagined it to be, not even close to the wonderful food I had become accustomed to on the *Goethals*.

I wanted to get out of New York City, go to Colorado. New York City reminded me all too much of where I came from. I wanted to get to the America of my dreams, and we weren't there yet. We stayed one night at Fort Hamilton. The following evening Leo and his friends hired a couple of taxis and we all piled in and rode to a Greyhound bus terminal. Leo wanted to take a train to Denver, but when we got to Grand Central Station to buy tickets, the huge hall was filled with marching people carrying placards.

"They are on strike," Hedy explained to me. "There are no trains running. Leo says we have to take a bus to Denver." It was all the same to me. Train or bus, I had no preference. Just get me to Colorado. I didn't know what a strike was. Apparently it meant that people refused to go to work. In Germany people thought themselves lucky to have a job, any job, that paid real money. I couldn't understand why people would refuse to go to work when they had jobs and were getting paid. I had no concept that workers might feel they were not getting paid enough for their labors.

Leo was unhappy about us having to take a bus to Denver. I took a window seat and with the help of two pillows made myself comfortable. I had never ridden on a bus for any distance and was pleasantly surprised. I couldn't understand why Leo didn't want to ride on a bus that offered such luxurious seats. I began to look forward to the trip. From my geography lessons I recalled that New York was on the east coast of America. I knew Denver was somewhere in the middle, but had no concept of the distance we would cover over the next several days to get to Denver. We left late that evening and for the first hour or two the bus passed through township after township. Everywhere I looked there was light. Used car lots were especially brightly lit, with strings of light bulbs strung around each lot like Christmas ornaments, making the cars shine and look like new. I came from a land of darkness, a land without streetlights. Once daylight passed, darkness ruled, interrupted only by the occasional low wattage light bulb turned on by a frugal apartment dweller who turned it off as soon as the need for light was no longer there. Europe had no lights just for the sake of light. Europe was a dark place, as dark as its recent past.

The second thing that caught my attention as we drove through the seemingly endless city of New York were the many automobiles. Not the hundreds of cars being driven on the streets, but the hundreds of cars sitting idly in brightly lit lots. Why would thousands of automobiles just be sitting around? Why weren't they being used? In Germany every car and truck I saw was in use, and there weren't all that many. I moved over to Leo's seat and pulled his sleeve. "Come," I said. Leo followed. I pointed at a car lot we were passing and attempted to ask him why all those automobiles were just sitting on those brightly lit lots. Why was no one using them? Leo tried to understand my question, but in the end he couldn't.

"Used cars," he said. "Just old, used cars, Wolfgang." I didn't understand, and the car mystery remained a mystery. We traveled for three days and nights across America. On the first morning I was captured by seemingly endless fields and forests, by the small towns we stopped in and the villages we passed through. As we drove on and on, I began to comprehend the size of the land, and I was awed. I never imagined America could be that big. Occasionally the bus pulled into a station, and we got off, ate a quick meal in a nearby cafeteria or sandwich shop, and moved on. Whenever we changed buses I sat alone, away from Hedy and Leo. I wanted no interruptions as I watched *my* new land pass by me. I wanted to take in everything, didn't want to miss anything.

The farther we traveled into the heart of America the more I began to feel that it was my country, that this was where I belonged. New York City and Fort Hamilton were all but forgotten. Although I spoke very little English, I began to look at myself as an American. It was a perception of myself that evolved as naturally as daylight follows night. I could not be both—a German boy and an American boy. I had to be one or the other. Traveling across America on a Greyhound bus, I became an American boy.

On our second day of travel we stopped early in the afternoon in the square of a small town. A real square, with a small park in the middle and a monument of sorts. I guessed the monument was built to honor the dead of some war, similar to monuments all over Germany. It was a warm, sunny, blue-sky day, like I had seldom experienced in the north of Germany this time of year. Well-dressed people walked by our bus, their eyes and movements open and unguarded. There was no fear that I could detect either in the way they looked at their world or in the way they moved through it. Teenagers walked past my bus carrying books under their arms. I watched them wistfully as they walked past, laughing and talking. I wondered if I would be able to go back to school, to learn and become one of them.

A girl caught my attention crossing the square in front of the bus. She carried her books like the others, in her left hand, a jacket under her arm as well. She walked slowly, confidently. To me her appearance was crisp and clean—the blouse, the belt, the wide skirt, bobby sox, and saddle shoes. She was so beautiful, I thought. Her hair was neatly combed and held together in back by a ribbon. She wore a skirt which came down to mid-calf with petticoats blousing it out, like something I had seen in the movies. Her white blouse and wide, black leather belt accented her blossoming womanhood, and I was suddenly overcome with strange and confusing feelings. I watched the girl intently until she vanished from view. What was it about the girl that made her seem so special? Her fluid, confident stride? The skirt which made her look like a princess? The vision of that first American schoolgirl stayed with me for a long time. Actually, it never faded, remaining with me throughout life like other seemingly unimportant things my mind tended to latch onto and not let go of.

After crossing the Mississippi River at St. Louis, Missouri, the character of the land changed rapidly. Slowly the landscape began to look more like my vision of the American west, a vision formed by reading books written by Karl May, the prolific German adventure writer whose tales of Winnetou, the noble Apache chief, and his German blood-brother, Old Shatterhand, enthralled generations of German youngsters. Before me stretched undulating plains covered with a light dusting of snow. Clumps of dried grass stuck out of the blanket of white—not a tree or bush in sight. As our bus crested the next line of hills, there was more of the same, more snow-covered plains, more gently sloping hills, broken by a sandstone cliff here and there. Trees grew along rivers and in towns, but not out on the open plains. There were no more forests, only the vastness of the American prairie. The trip became mind numbingly boring; even the automobile traffic became sparse. I drifted off to sleep, my forehead pressed against the window pane. Nothing had changed when I awoke again. We drove on into the night, at times not a light to be seen for miles around; lights, so prolific and abundant in the east, were scattered and sparse in the west.

From Missouri we drove across Kansas and finally crossed into Colorado. Colorado seemed even flatter than Kansas, with no hint of mountains. I had thought Colorado was all mountain country. The small towns we stopped in lay far apart, with few people to be seen. The only constants, aside from the seemingly endless plains, were the highway, often a straight line from horizon to horizon, railroad tracks frequently paralleling the road, and equally endless telephone lines. Occasionally we passed an abandoned ranch house with a shed or two and rusting farm implements scattered about. Then it was back to the same monotony as before.

We arrived in Denver on the evening of the third day. I was very, very tired, ready to stretch out on a real bed and sleep for eighteen hours straight, the way I slept in January 1945 when we fled from Sagan to Berlin. When Hedy, Ingrid, and I arrived in Berlin after our harrowing escape from Sagan, we trudged through the dark city for several hours before arriving at our destination, an apartment house where we stayed with kind and generous strangers. There, I slept for eighteen hours straight without changing position—slept through three air raids that night into the following day. Hedy told me she did not have the heart to wake me, figuring that since the house we stayed in had survived so far, it would survive another day. My mother later confided to me that after the second air raid she looked in on me and became worried that maybe I had died since I hadn't moved since she put me to bed, and she couldn't hear or see me breathing. She put a small mirror she carried in her purse to my nose and mouth, and to her relief my shallow breathing fogged the mirror. It was January 1945, the bedroom was unheated and cold, but the featherbed was warm and comfortable. Maybe I could sleep that long again in Denver, not in a feather bed, but in a bed where I could stretch out to my full length. I finally understood why Leo was not pleased that we had to take a bus to Colorado.

We took a room in an old brownstone hotel near the Greyhound bus depot. I didn't notice much before falling asleep except that there was a coin-operated radio in the room—I had never seen anything like it before. The room had one sink and no bathroom. The lavatory was down the hall. When I awoke the next morning, the bright sunlight was filtering into the room around the edges of the heavy drapes covering two windows looking out onto Fourteenth Street. I felt rested. I rose quietly, washed my face in cold water, and dressed. I sat for a few minutes on a lone chair stashed in one corner of the room, its seat covered with a reddish, velvety material, nearly worn smooth from years of use. I waited for Hedy or Leo to wake, but their breathing was regular and deep. I quietly stepped out of the room into the dimly lit hallway, used the lavatory, then went down the narrow flight of stairs and stepped outside into my new world.

Fourteenth Street was lined with small shops and restaurants on the ground floors of aging four-story buildings, some with false fronts which made them seem taller than they really were. When I looked west, there, in the early morning light, rose the snow-capped peaks of the Rocky Mountains. It was a stunning sight marred only by the ugly power lines strung between equally ugly poles running down one side of the street. I didn't recall ever seeing power lines strung out on streets like that before; they should be buried underground I thought, but then they did things differently in America. I took another long look at the mountains. Their beauty far exceeded my expectations. A deep snow pack covered the peaks down to a lower elevation where the snow suddenly appeared to stop, as if a straight line had been drawn across the mountain range with a ruler and someone had decreed that there would be no snow below that line. The peaks glistened brightly in the morning sun. The air was still and clear, cool and refreshing against my face. My stomach growled, having become accustomed to the large helpings on the *Goethals*. Out of long habit I pulled my belt a little tighter. I looked at the height of the sun in the crisp, clear morning sky and figured it must still be very early. I had left my watch in the room. The oversight annoyed me. I never went anywhere without my watch. I bought it in Fassberg from money I made selling rather than eating candy bars and chewing gum American airlift soldiers gave me for running their errands, like getting beer from a *Gasthaus*. I was very proud of my watch, the very first thing I ever bought for myself with money I earned on my own. Now and then a car came down the street. Occasionally a pedestrian passed on some early morning errand. Other than that the city was absolutely quiet, like the silence in a deep forest where an occasional sound only served to accentuate its absence.

We ate breakfast in a simple restaurant across from the hotel. Leo ordered eggs over easy, hash-brown potatoes, toast, and coffee. I had the same, except for the coffee. Coffee was expensive in Germany, and my grandmother always cautioned me that it wasn't good for children. I still considered myself a child, so I didn't drink coffee. Hedy and Leo looked somber, neither smiling. Maybe they were still tired. I stayed quiet throughout the meal. The food was very good, and I could have all the jam I wanted. Leo's younger sister Juanita arrived before we finished eating. She parked her new Chevrolet in front of the restaurant, a car just like the one I observed from the train window as we left Munich for Bremerhaven. Leo must have called her while I was out on the street earlier that morning, because I didn't remember him making a phone call. Juanita was to take us to their parents' home in Derby, a minuscule village just north of the Denver city limits. Juanita's greeting seemed perfunctory, as if she was there against her will. I was surprised at her near open hostility toward Hedy and me. She was a small woman, talking incessantly to Leo, ignoring both Hedy and me, as if we didn't exist. Leo looked apologetic. He was a courteous and gentle man and obviously offended by his sister's behavior, but unable to do anything about it. Leo stowed our luggage in the spacious trunk of Juanita's new car, Juanita cautioning him to be careful and not to scratch the car. "It's expensive," she reminded him. "We are still paying for it." We got into the car—Leo in front, next to his talkative sister, Hedy and I in back. It could have been a pleasant drive if only Juanita had stopped talking.

The part of Denver we drove through seemed old and rather run-down. We passed the grain silos of the Purina Chow Company, its logo prominently painted on one of the tall silos. The sulfurous smell of a small oil refinery intruded, even though we had the windows of the car rolled up. It was all interesting to me. I had never been near a refinery before. When we arrived at Leo's father's house, Juanita helped to unload our bags, set them by the side of the road, and immediately drove off without saying goodbye to anyone, nor greeting her father. I had been taught to be polite by my parents and grandparents, especially to strangers, even if I didn't like them. I thought Juanita's behavior was rude. What had Hedy or I done to offend her?

Down a narrow concrete walk sat a very small, one-story clapboard house with a steep roof and peeling white paint. Its windows looked as if they had never been washed, and sagging drapes and untidy curtains were visible from where I stood. A few feet to the left of the small cottage stood a basement-like structure with a flat, tar paper roof. Concrete steps lead down to a door. I recognized it immediately as the house in the picture Hedy showed me in Fürstenfeldbruck, the picture which had upset her so much. Between and behind the two houses sat an array of rusting, broken-down cars, all Hudsons as I discovered the following day. Two broken washing machines, car wheels, worn tires, dead batteries, and an assortment of discarded furniture lay scattered in the dry grass. If it hadn't been for the brilliant sunshine, the untrammeled blue sky, the crisp and refreshing dry air, and the beautiful, majestic snow-clad mountains in the distance, the sight of Leo's parents' home would have been totally dispiriting. Not too long ago we lived in a rotting and neglected barracks not much different than this place—but there were no mountains there, only brooding pine forests. The air had been damp and cold in February, and the low gray cloud deck remained overhead for weeks at a time. Colorado was different. I only saw the beauty of the land, sensed its residual wildness, and that excited me. I had finally arrived in the land of the Mohicans, or whatever Indians once roamed across these lands.

An old man came hobbling up the concrete walk using a cane for support. Pop, as Leo referred to his father, had gray hair that looked like it had never known a comb, nor had he shaved this morning, or yesterday morning for that matter. His sweater was a bit too large and his pants looked like they'd never been new. His right cheek was puffed out, and just before he reached us he spit out a concisely aimed stream of brown tobacco juice. In contrast to Juanita though, Pop was plainly overjoyed to see his son Leo again, and gave Hedy and me a warm welcome. My mother had regained her composure and was smiling again. I knew she saw what I saw, and if I understood her correctly she was probably thinking how best to fit into her new world. Returning to Germany was not an option for either of us.

"Leo," Pop croaked, putting an arm affectionately around his son. Leo was dressed in his usual impeccably pressed blue uniform, looking as if he stepped out of an air force recruiting poster. He hugged his father. "Pop," he replied. That's all they needed to say to show their deep affection for one another. There was no embarrassment on Leo's part, no excuses offered for the obviously humble place that once had been his home. Then, turning toward Hedy, Leo said proudly, "Pop, this is my new German bride Hedy and my stepson, Wolfgang." Pop shifted the wad of tobacco from one side of his mouth to the other, spit a stream of brown tobacco juice into the dry grass, shifted his cane to his left hand, and held out his right to greet Hedy. She grabbed the old man's hand firmly and shook it.

"I am so happy to meet you," Pop said. I moved toward him and shook his hand as well. It was an old hand, just like my grandfather Samuel's, strong and gnarled from years of hard physical labor. Pop's crooked smile was warm and affectionate, without prejudice toward us.

"Come on in," he said, speaking to all of us, "you are very welcome." Leo and I grabbed our bags and followed the old man into the house. "You and Hedy take the bedroom to the right, the boy can sleep with me in the other room." On a couch in the living room, the only other rooms in the house a small kitchen and an even smaller bathroom, lay a large woman covered with a quilt. She didn't move when we entered, staring emptily into space. "Mom had a stroke," Pop said matter-of-factly. "She can hear you, Leo, but she can't speak or move. She can bat her eyes to let you know that she understands what you are saying." Leo was visibly shaken. Juanita apparently had not apprised him of the situation. Tears ran down his cheeks as he knelt by his mother's side, holding her hand. He cried and put his head on her shoulder.

"Come on, Leo," Pop said gruffly, his blue eyes soft and understanding, "it's the Lord's will. Audrey and I had many good years together." Leo rose, wiped the tears from his eyes with the back of his hands, and carried our suitcases into the small bedroom Pop had assigned to him and Hedy. My mother closed the door, and when she emerged, she had changed clothes. Without saying a word she began to clean the house, which was in dire need of attention. Pop was impressed by Hedy's industriousness, following her around all afternoon like a puppy, but staying out of her way. By evening the little house looked tidy and neat. Hedy and Pop were good friends by then, laughing about things they said to each other. Hedy cooked a quick meal from things she found in the kitchen, a meal which Pop seemed to enjoy more than the rest of us. He probably hadn't had a home-cooked meal in a long time. I wondered as we sat down to eat if Pop would take his wad of tobacco out of his mouth. He did. I liked the old man.

Raymond, Leo's younger brother, who lived in the basement house next door, came over after work to meet Hedy and shake hands. Raymond wasn't quite as tall as Leo. His hands were strong though, bony and rough. And even though Raymond was two years younger than Leo, he looked not only older, but somehow worn out, like a man who had worked too hard for too long. When Raymond walked, he never totally straightened up, as if he was bending under a heavy load he couldn't put down. Later I learned that Raymond worked in a meat packing plant and gutted cows all day long. Like Pop, Raymond didn't seem to be able to keep his hair in place, and his clothes looked worn and disheveled. But in contrast to his sister Juanita's almost hostile welcome, Raymond had a quick, warm smile for his new sister-in-law, between hurried puffs on an ever-present cigarette. He vigorously shook Hedy's and my hands. I understood little Raymond said, but I knew his words were generous and given with warmth and respect.

When I looked at Leo, I noted that he was just the opposite of Raymond. He stood straight, his clothes clean and pressed, his wavy brown hair meticulously combed. Leo smoked his cigarettes slowly and deliberately. Raymond took short, hurried drags. I kept a close eye on my mother, a little worried about how she would take to all this. I wasn't fooled by her burst of activity earlier in the day. I suspected that was as much to get her mind off the situation as it was to deal with an obvious housekeeping problem. But I saw no indication that she was unable or unwilling to cope with her new world. The following evening friends and family of Leo's came to celebrate his return from Germany and meet his new German wife. I was surprised how large his family was. Beside Raymond and Juanita, Leo had two more sisters, Marie and Audrey, and two additional brothers. Charlie was a railroad engineer with the Union Pacific and lived in Sacramento, California; Fred was a prison guard in Canyon City, Colorado. Neither was there—it was just too far for them to come. All the others came, except for Juanita, bringing food and drink. They partied in the same room where Leo's mother Audrey lay immobile on the couch, staring up at the ceiling. They wanted her presence. Now and then I saw people stop by her side, take her hand, stroke her cheek, or just talk to her. I stayed in the kitchen watching, drinking a Coke. It was a festive occasion with lots of beer, food, cigarettes, and laughter.

"My name is Sue," a tall, thin woman dressed in tight blue jeans and a clinging and revealing white blouse introduced herself to me in a melodic voice. Startled, I took her hand and returned her smile. "How old are you?" she inquired. I figured out what she meant and said, "*Sechzehn*." I held up both of my hands, then six fingers. She nodded her head and lit a cigarette. "Wolfgang is such a lovely name," she continued our one-sided conversation, "and at age sixteen you need a girl, don't you? You look so lonely standing there all by yourself. Let me get you a nice-looking girl who'll help you enjoy the evening." I wasn't sure what she was proposing, but I understood the word girl and putting two and two together, I figured she was going to fix me up with one of three young women present. They were a little older than I but close enough, and as she said, nice looking—the way American girls looked, different from German girls. I politely nodded my head, and Sue was about to go and make good on her offer when Hedy put an end to it all. My mother had apparently overheard Sue's proposal.

"He's too young for that sort of thing, Sue," she said. "Thank you for wanting to help. The boy is just fine. He doesn't know about girls yet."

"If you change your mind, Hedy, just let me know," Sue replied, grabbing a beer from a nearby cooler, cigarette dangling from the corner of her mouth, "and I'll fix him up in a jiff. A good-looking boy his age needs a girl, Hedy, you know that." Sue smiled at me, then rejoined the constantly moving, churning crowd in the small living room. My mother explained the situation to me, and I found that I had correctly understood what the woman called Sue had tried to do for me. For the briefest moment I felt a rush of excitement coursing through my body. I didn't think much about girls, didn't know anything about girls. Although I had suppressed it for a long time, girls held an ever-increasing attraction for me.

The following week we moved in with Marie, Leo's sister, who lived up the hill from Pop's house with her husband Tom and their only son Leroy. Leroy was three or four years younger than I. I never saw much of him. He went to school early in the day, and when he came home, he spent most of his time with his friends. Marie's house was a small, two-bedroom house. In contrast to Pop's, it was new and furnished with modern appliances and simple but comfortable furniture. The living room had a large picture window looking out on the splendor of the Rocky Mountains. Marie's house sat alone on top of a hill surrounded by cornfields, which at that time of year exhibited only the stubble of last autumn's harvest. Marie worked as a bartender at a nearby bar from noon until early evening; Tom, her husband, worked in Denver as an auto mechanic.

Leo, whose new assignment was at Lowry Air Force Base, to the east of Denver, applied for on-base housing soon after our arrival. He was told that it would take several weeks before a house would become available. Until then we would live with Marie and Tom. Leo found another air force sergeant who lived nearby and commuted to work with him. We didn't have a car yet, and I understood we wouldn't have one for some time to come. Leo had no savings, only debts and obligations, and his air force salary was small. A car for us was somewhere in the distant future and, according to my mother, not a high priority. Saving for a house was Hedy's first priority, and Leo agreed.

During the day, when everybody else was away, Hedy and I had time to talk. Hedy decided it was high time for me to learn English. She insisted that I wouldn't learn the language unless I began to speak it. "I am no longer going to speak to you in German," she advised me. "You have to learn English. It is your language now. And the best way to learn is by doing. That's how I learned. So listen up, imitate others. Don't worry about making mistakes. I don't mean to be mean to you, Wolfgang,

I love you my son, you know that. That's why I am doing this." In the days after Hedy issued her "speak only English" decree, our conversations dried up. I had to figure out what she was trying to tell me.

Opportunities soon arose for me to interact with others my age. A friend of Leo's drove up early one evening accompanied by his sixteen-year-old daughter. I heard them talking outside before coming into the house. "Wolfgang," Leo called out, "you need to get out and have a little fun. There is a young girl here, very pretty, and she is inviting you to join her and her friends to go roller skating. Would you like to do that?" Leo had obviously said things about me to his friend which got his daughter interested in meeting the new "German boy." Hedy broke her vow of only speaking English and explained what was going on. "Go ahead," she said, "have a little fun. You deserve it. You've been sitting in this house far too long." I asked my mother to tell them that I couldn't speak a word of English, nor could I understand anything they were saying. "Tell them, Mutti. They need to know." Hedy smiled and walked me to the car, a shiny new Mercury.

Peggy sat in the back seat and was intimidatingly pretty, that fresh, clean-cut American girl prettiness. Maybe it was her self-confidence, the way she fixed her hair, or the suggestion of makeup she wore which made my knees feel wobbly. She welcomed me with an outstretched hand, giving me a generous smile. I was glad I was sitting down. She sat in the middle, close to me, her elbow occasionally touching mine; a friend of hers sat to her right. I was getting hot, perspiration forming on my forehead even though it was a cool February evening. Leo was still talking to his friend, a former air force sergeant who had recently retired and gone to work at Lowry as a civilian. They were admiring the new Mercury. After another five minutes they finally said goodbye to each other, and we drove off to the skating rink. I sat quietly next to Peggy, not moving a muscle.

The roller rink smelled of sweat. Loud music blared from several speakers, music unlike any I heard in Germany, except around Americans. They played the *Tennessee Waltz* and *Mockin' Bird Hill*. *Goodnight Irene* I remembered hearing at the NCO Club in Fürstenfeldbruck. I had always liked that song, but then I liked most American music. To me, American music was open, inclusive, varied, warm, and human, in contrast to most German music which sounded largely the same—the same beat and rhythm for nearly every song. To my ear at least, American music was all over the place, as varied as the land and its people, and it captured me the same way the Colorado Rockies did. They played the *Tennessee Waltz* several times. I liked the tune and tried to mouth the words, but not loud enough for anyone to hear.

Peggy had an open, uninhibited manner and tried several times to talk to me on our way to the rink. Once there, she helped me pick out a pair of skates and introduced me to her many girlfriends. The girls surrounded me, chattering excitedly, giving me looks, smiling, and laughing. I quickly sensed that Peggy was showing me off like someone showed off a new dress or a new gadget. But as the evening wore on, the novelty of the German boy wore off. My inability to speak or understand English became all too much work for the girls. I was relieved when Peggy's father showed up at ten o'clock and drove me home. Peggy just nodded her head when I exited the car. I knew I wouldn't see her again. Although my first social outing in my new country was a failure, I didn't feel discouraged. I thought the adults were pushing me too quickly into new situations. I needed time to work things out on my own.

Hedy asked Tom if he knew of a job for me to make a little money. Tom took me to a nearby private airfield and spoke to the manager. Both looked at me as they talked. Then Tom said goodbye and drove off. The manager gave me a broom, pointed to some buckets, soap, and a hose, and motioned for me to clean the hangar. I rolled up my sleeves and went to work. It wasn't yet eight o'clock in the morning. I worked the way I worked in the bakery in Germany, without let up. By two o'clock that afternoon I finished. When I went over to the manager and indicated to him that I was done, pointing to the clean hangar floor, he seemed amazed at how quickly I had done my job. He walked around the hangar inspecting this and that, then nodded his head approvingly, said a few complimentary words, dug around in his pocket, and counted out several dollar bills and some change which he pressed into my hand. Then he spoke to me, gave me a wave of the hand, and walked back to his office. I didn't understand everything he said, but from his gestures and actions I presumed I was through for the day and walked home. I counted the money and figured that he paid me one dollar an hour, a total of six dollars and fifty cents—the first money I made in my new country. I handed it over to my mother.

Leo's sergeant friend, with whom he rode to work every morning, dropped him off in late afternoon at the bar where Marie worked. Hedy and I walked there to meet him. After a beer and some socializing, Leo then drove us home in Marie's car. Marie came home with her husband Tom, who stopped by after work and stayed until her shift ended around eight. There was always a lively crowd in the bar, a neighborhood kind of place where everyone seemed to know one another. The bar patrons all wanted to meet the woman and the boy from Germany, and in time I shook everyone's hand and listened to each one, looking attentive, even though I understood little of what was said. One afternoon I noticed one particular man who kept looking at me and smiling while he drank his beer and smoked his cigarette. He wore an off-white suit and a yellowing straw hat with a wide brim. Hedy came over and said, "Mr. Jones knows a German lady. He thought you might enjoy meeting her. She is an old lady and probably would appreciate your coming by and talking to her. Would you do that for me?" Only at times like that, when she needed something from me, would Hedy speak to me in German. Mr. Jones doffed his hat, then came over, and we shook hands. "Go on," Hedy said, smiling, as she turned away to rejoin Leo. Mr. Jones held the door for me, and I followed him to his car. It wasn't a long drive. We stopped in front of an old Victorian house, shaded by large cottonwoods. He motioned for me to follow him, smiling. We climbed the few steps to the front porch, and Mr. Jones knocked firmly on the door. There was no bell or knocker. He knocked again, this time louder. Soon I heard the shuffle of feet, bolts being pushed aside, and the door opened.

A slightly bent, prim-looking woman emerged from the house. Small in stature, like my grandmother Samuel, she must have been in her late eighties, her gray hair pulled back tightly into a bun. She blinked in the bright afternoon sunshine the way people do who spend most of their time in dark rooms. Mr. Jones greeted her respectfully, doffed his hat, then motioned toward me, explaining something to her. When he stopped talking, the woman stared at me for a considerable time. Her look was slightly annoyed, I thought, emotionless at best, as if whatever Mr. Jones tried to do was an imposition. The old woman said something to me which I couldn't understand. I knew it wasn't English though. I reached out to shake her hand. She ignored my hand, continuing to hold onto the door knob instead. Speaking in German I said, "*Guten Abend*. I just came from Germany and don't speak English yet. Where do you come from in Germany?" The woman gave me a strange look, her eyes seemed to turn colder, hostile. She turned to Mr. Jones, spoke to him in a rapid, excited voice. When she finished, she turned around and slammed the door shut—bolts rattled as they were forced back into hasps. Mr. Jones gave me an apologetic look, shrugged his shoulders, and motioned toward his car. Obviously something had gone wrong.

"How did it go?" Hedy asked when she saw us walking through the door. Mr. Jones explained. Hedy and all the patrons within hearing broke into loud laughter.

"Why are they laughing, Mutti?" I asked her. "What's so funny? Please, tell me."

"Oh, the old woman said to Mr. Jones that you didn't speak German. She didn't know what it was you were saying to her, but she knew it wasn't German. She didn't want to speak to someone like you, an impostor, and told Mr. Jones not to bring you back again. You are in real trouble, Wolfgang," Hedy said between laughs. "Not only don't you know how to speak English, you can't even speak German anymore." Everyone in the bar laughed loudly, lifting their glasses toward me in a mock toast. Later, Hedy put her arm around my shoulders and said, "You have to remember this is 1951. The old woman probably came to this country as a young child many years ago and things have changed. It's not your fault or her fault. Don't feel bad about it. Mr. Jones tried to be helpful, and you tried to do your part. It just didn't work out."

What stayed with me from that strange episode was how helpful Americans were, how understanding, and ready to laugh. Mostly, how much everyone tried to make us a part of their community.

CHAPTER 6

Emily Griffith
Opportunity School

Over dinner Hedy mentioned to Leo that a bar patron had arranged a job interview for me at a nearby bakery, a large factory-like building down the street from the bar where Marie worked. "The man heard you say that Wolfgang apprenticed as a baker in Germany. He works at the bakery and told me they are always looking for good people. They pay one dollar and seventy-five cents an hour to start. A good wage, he assured me." Leo listened patiently to Hedy, as he always did. It was the first I heard of the job offer, and I wasn't sure if the skills I acquired in a small, family-style bakery would be transferable to what I viewed as a huge bread factory. My initial cautionary feelings quickly gave way to a rapidly rising euphoria. I am a quick learner, I thought. I can do it. A bakery is a bakery. And wouldn't it be nice to make that much money? I did some quick figuring and realized I could make nearly three hundred dollars a month. A huge amount of money as I understood things. I had seen cars in used car lots for sale for around that much, maybe a little more. I could buy one of those large American cars, and then Leo wouldn't have to pay someone to get a ride to work. My initial reaction was to take the job to help my family. But the irony of the situation didn't escape me. I had come all the way to America only to be a baker once more.

Leo finished eating, laid down his fork deliberately, then turned to me and said, "What do you want to do, Wolfgang?" I wasn't sure I understood his question and hesitated. Hedy translated. Few people had ever asked me what I wanted to do. People usually told me what to do. I was taken by surprise.

"It's OK, Leo," I replied after a prolonged pause. I continued in German, "I can save my money, Mutti, and when I have enough I can buy us a car." Hedy translated. My reply reflected my whimsical thoughts on making money, our obvious need for a car, and our family financial situation in general. Leo shook his head vigorously.

"No," he said, determination coloring his voice, "the boy doesn't have to buy a car for us. He needs to go back to school and get a high school education. We'll buy our own car when we have the money. I didn't get my high school diploma, and I've regretted it all my life. I paid for that decision with the many bad jobs I had to take before I went into the army. Even in the army my lack of a high school education held me back. Wolfgang has to return to school, Hedy. It's the least we can do for him." Hedy and Leo continued talking, Hedy trying to persuade Leo that what they needed was the money I could bring in to help them get on their feet.

"Wolfgang can go to school later," she argued. "Right now he has to pitch in and help, just as I had to when I was a young girl." Hedy had gone through the eighth grade in a one-room schoolhouse in the small village of Neuensund where she was born, near the market town of Strasburg, about a hundred miles north of Berlin. She grew up in a feudal environment, her parents not much better off than serfs, living from hand to mouth. Hedy's logic was sound based on her own background, but it wasn't good logic in the year 1951 in America. Leo wouldn't hear of it. I listened attentively to their conversation, heard them use the word school frequently. Although Leo nearly always gave in to Hedy's wishes, on this occasion he remained adamant, "It's Wolfgang's future we are deciding, Hedy. Without a high school diploma he'll have a hard time getting anywhere in this country. Believe me. I know what I am talking about."

While I did not know it at the time, one of the most important decisions to affect my future was being made around that dinner table. I didn't know how seriously and conscientiously Leo Ferguson took his role as my stepfather. And I certainly didn't know the consequences that would accrue had I followed the path most easily traveled, the path my mother wanted me to take—to work at the bakery. Hedy then told me that Leo decided that I should go back to school. "No one in my family ever went to the Gymnasium," she added, "and we all did alright. I don't agree with Leo. It is up to you what you want to do, Wolfgang. I think you should go to work and help us get started. You can go to school later. But if you decide to go to school, then tomorrow morning you and Leo will ride into town with Tom on his way to work. Leo will take you to what he calls Opportunity School. He once went there as a teenager, but never finished. He says it is a high school for all ages, not just for children. What do you want to do? Go to school? Or go to work and help us get started?"

The evening turned out so differently from others. I didn't like the dissension this discussion brought into our small family. Leo and Hedy looked at me expectantly. I wasn't really prepared to render a thoughtful decision so soon after arriving in Colorado. I wanted to please my mother. I loved her and didn't want to disappoint her. She had made so many sacrifices for me. How could I deny her? I also wanted to carry my share of our family's burden. But going back to school was what I always thought I really wanted to do if I ever got another chance. Now that the opportunity presented itself I was intimidated by my own mother. I knew if I said that I wanted to go to work, Leo would not be able to prevail against her. But it wasn't only Hedy who made my decision so difficult. The fact that I couldn't read, write, or speak English was intimidating in itself. I knew only about ten words of English—cigarette, Coca-Cola, chewing gum, OK, yes, no, thank you, girl, school, car. If I thought real hard maybe another word or two would come to mind, but I couldn't form a coherent sentence in English, didn't understand most of what anyone said. I was a good guesser, but anything complex escaped my understanding. Hedy and Leo continued to stare at me. There was an uncomfortable silence around the table. Then I heard myself saying, "I want to go back to school." My voice sounded to me like someone else was saying the words. I was shocked at myself. In spite of the difficulties I anticipated facing, in spite of my mother's arguments and my deep feelings of loyalty toward her, in spite of all that, I opted for school. Hedy rose grim-faced from her chair, noisily cleared the table, and busied herself washing dishes, her back turned toward Leo and me.

Emily Griffith was born in 1868 in Cincinnati, Ohio, and began her career as a schoolteacher at age fourteen in a sod schoolhouse in Broken Bow, Nebraska. "It was here," notes the Opportunity School history, "that she first discovered that many of her students' parents did not know how to read, write, or figure their bills. Many were immigrants and did not know the English language. Her dream of a school for adults was born. Emily envisioned a school where students could attend classes day or night and receive as much education as they wanted or needed." In 1895, at age twenty-seven, Emily came to Denver and went to work for the Denver public schools. Her vision of providing educational opportunity to the unfortunate regardless of age never faltered, and in 1915 chance would have it that she met a *Denver Post* reporter to whom she confessed, "I want the limit for admission lifted and classes so organized that a boy or girl working in a bakery, store, laundry, or any kind of shop, who has an hour or two to spare, may come to my school and study what he or she wants to learn to make life more useful. I already have a name for the school," she added. "Opportunity." Talking to the reporter was Emily's break, and it became my break thirty-five years later. The *Denver Post* wrote about Emily's vision, and in September 1916, the Opportunity School opened its doors in a former school building at thirteenth and Welton Streets, signing up an amazing 1,400 students in its first week of existence. In 1933, the school was renamed Emily Griffith Opportunity School. I, an immigrant boy just off the boat in 1951, had the great luck to come to Denver, Colorado, and benefit from Emily's generous and farsighted efforts of many years ago—just the way she envisioned for things to work.

The following morning Tom dropped Leo and me off in front of the Emily Griffith Opportunity School, and I soon found myself sitting at the desk of Ms. Helen D. Redford, the school's principal. Ms. Redford gave me a welcoming smile which eased my tension. I had great doubts about my decision of the previous evening and was seriously thinking about walking back out to the street. Ms. Redford kept smiling, kept me in my chair, while Leo explained my situation. I obviously wasn't the first immigrant lacking language skills to come through the doors of her school. After the formalities were settled and Leo filled out the necessary forms, Ms. Redford walked him to the door of her office and told him that she would take care of the rest. "You can pick him up around four o'clock this afternoon," she told Leo, who then caught a bus to Lowry Air Force Base to go to work. With the assistance of a counselor, Ms. Redford prepared a class schedule for me which included algebra, social studies, English, American history, and typing. Within minutes I found myself entering a classroom. Ms. Redford introduced me to Ms. Beatrix Whitney, then excused herself and left the room. After directing me to a chair at a large round table, Ms. Whitney handed me a copy of the *Saturday Evening Post*, its cover depicting a baseball game in progress from a painting by Norman Rockwell. She then continued with her lesson where she had left off when I entered, explaining to the group of seven foreign adult students, and now to me as well, a German boy, one of America's great pastimes. From Ms. Whitney I learned about my new country's social customs, about baseball, football, and basketball, about picnics in the park and the voting rights of an American citizen—information essential to function effectively in the land that had taken me in, and that I adopted as my own.

The first few mornings I rode to school with Tom, but it was out of the way for him and an obvious inconvenience. I soon learned that a city bus stopped within twenty minutes walking distance of Tom and Marie's house. That bus took me to within a block of *Opportunity School*. My transportation problem solved, I could leave school at the time of my choosing rather than wait until five in the afternoon or later for Tom to come by to pick me up. The bus fare to and from school was thirteen cents each way, twenty-six cents a day which I didn't have and Hedy parted with reluctantly.

While my teachers proved to be adept and dedicated women who looked at each student as an individual challenge, with the best of will they couldn't provide me with a quick fix to remedy my English language deficiency. It would take time, patience, and hard work on my part, a deeply discouraging process on all too many occasions. All my teachers were women—kind, gentle, competent, persistent, insistent women. Maybe there were male teachers at the school as well, but I didn't have or see any. In English class I read aloud passages from my textbook to the rest of the class before the week was out. Nobody laughed. Most of the time I didn't understand what I was reading, but with every passing day it seemed that my horizon of comprehension expanded just a little. My comments in class were halting and tentative, but Ms. Whitney would urge me on with gestures of encouragement and nods of her head not to give up but to search for a word and keep on going. Although I added words to my vocabulary, I couldn't find the rhythm of the language.

Much of what people said remained an indecipherable babble. I listened to the radio whenever I could, as well as to people around me, hoping to find the key that would unlock the mystery—nothing seemed to work for me.

Algebra proved the easiest of all subjects; after all, numbers are an international language. I had never taken algebra before, never even heard of it. Ms. Gross, my algebra teacher, started me out with the simplest of problems and allowed me to advance at my own pace. There were no tests at Opportunity School; learning was a student-teacher cooperative effort, my teachers knowing exactly what I had learned and what I was having difficulty with. The process was interactive, and as I progressed from one level to the next, my teachers would expand my world of learning as rapidly as I was able to absorb new information. Ms. Winona Norton and Ms. Ruth Bigham were equally helpful teachers in other classes, always ready with an encouraging word, knowing instinctively when I needed assistance.

In typing class all of the students were women, except for me. I was also the youngest student in all of my classes. I quickly grasped the typing routines—the blank keyboard, finger positioning, memorization of the location of each letter and number. Soon I could find letters and numbers with my eyes closed. I typed words I didn't know the meaning of, just as I read words in English class I didn't understand. It didn't matter in typing. What mattered here was speed and accuracy. We were given speed tests regularly to measure our progress, and I was soon typing forty-five words per minute, doing dictation, and performing various other tasks expected of an office typist. Later in life it turned out that typing was one of the most valuable courses I took in high school, both at the Opportunity School and later at East High School. My typing skill was to provide future options and opportunities which significantly influenced the direction of my life. "Little things mean a lot," the fifties-era song proclaimed. It certainly held true for me with typing.

Happy moments at school came with tasks attempted and mastered, with making new friends, and with having a constructive routine once again. But there were many more moments of deep discouragement. My seeming inability to master my new language and the resulting daily challenges and frustrations were at times more than I thought I could bear. As long as I could not communicate with others, as long as I could not understand the world I wanted to be a part of, as long as that was true for me, I felt I wasn't a part of anything. Tolerated, yes. Accepted, no. I would remain an outsider, I felt, as long as I couldn't contribute. Although I kept smiling, acting as if everything was alright, nothing was alright with me. Some of my teachers, sensing my despair but unable to accelerate the process, counseled patience. "It will come, Wolfgang," they said. "It will come." Then they smiled. "Keep your chin up. Don't give up!"

A deep sense of failure began to settle over me as a result of what I perceived as my fundamental inability to learn the language of my new country. I didn't know exactly who I was anymore. I began to lose faith in myself and in my ability to cope with the new world that I had entered with such enthusiasm. My doubts went to the core of my being. Maybe I didn't belong here at all. Maybe I wasn't smart enough and should go to work in the bakery. Maybe Hedy was right all along. My identity crisis, not untypical of recent immigrants, was compounded by a deepening sense of sadness. Now that I lived in peace, with no more threats to my life, my past suddenly began to weigh me down. I thought about the many children I knew who died during that evil war as well as in the difficult postwar years. Why them? Why not me? The cries of the little girl in the red dress kept haunting me, kept echoing in my head, in my heart. She, like my friend Horst and others, died from drinking bad water in a filthy refugee camp in 1945. I remembered the dead baby in the basket near Woldegk when the Russian planes attacked and killed so many of us, the baby's dead mother leaning over the basket in a futile attempt to shield her baby with her body. Children like me—all dead. I felt very old at times, as if I had already lived my life. I didn't feel like a teenager and couldn't identify with others my age. American kids seemed always to be smiling, carefree, and relaxed. I felt tense, never totally relaxed, even in my sleep. Maybe I had seen too much sadness, lived too long on the edge of life and death. Whatever the cause, it was like a dark force pulling me down. Even the beloved Colorado sun could not banish the sorrow I felt in my heart, a darkness I couldn't share with anyone.

My increasing melancholy and inability to comprehend the language of my new country were burdens I found difficult to cope with. I wasn't sure I could explain myself to anyone who might want to listen sympathetically. I had no one I could turn to for help, not even Hedy. Knowing that my mother picked up effortlessly what eluded my best effort added to my feelings of inadequacy. The woman who had always given me strength, provided security and sustenance under the most difficult of circumstances, suddenly became a reminder of my own inadequacy. Her harsh rule to speak only English and her own success at learning the language made me feel stupid. Never before had I experienced such a darkness of spirit.

In spite of struggling with frustrations and my past, I continued with school. I told myself that maybe tomorrow would be the day when it all came together for me. Each day I looked forward to seeing my teachers. My experience at Opportunity School was very different from the Communist schools I attended in Strasburg from August 1945 to December 1946. We had no textbooks there, and the teachers taught mostly Communist dogma and never had a kind word for us children. I recall the terrible punishment inflicted on my classmates in 1946 when one day I incited them to join me in skipping a mandatory Russian class for a game of schoolyard soccer. We didn't have a ball, but kicked a small stone around. Boycotting Russian was my way of rebelling against teachers who were not teaching and who didn't care about us children, as well as against the Communists and the Russian occupiers. The consequences of my action were swift and brutal, something I had not anticipated. My classmates and I were summarily marched into the principal's office, and the Herr Rektor wasn't smiling when we entered. He was a short, stocky, balding man with the look of a bulldog. He planted himself in front of us, glowering, feet apart, hands on hips, screaming at the top of his lungs that no student would get away with challenging his authority. While berating us he looked me straight in the eye, knowing that I was the leader of the mini-rebellion. I stared back in open defiance. He screamed about the greatness of Communism, how he suffered under Hitler and escaped to his Russian comrades, and that now it was his turn and he was going to set things right. Part of setting things right apparently was that we Germans would learn the language of our Russian comrades. Then he added, lowering his voice, "No one is going to defy me and get away with it."

Then Herr Rektor lined us up, one behind the other. I stepped in front. I was the one responsible for the debacle and wanted to be the first to take whatever punishment he intended to hand out. He grabbed me by the shoulders and marched me to the rear of the line. Then, with his left hand, he grabbed the first student in line by the front of his shirt and with his right he slapped the boy's face. Back and forth—slap, slap, slap. Then he punched him in the face, hard, and in the stomach, until the boy bled from nose and mouth, crying pitifully for mercy. When the Herr Rektor finished with the first boy he roughly shoved him toward the door yelling, "Return to your class." Then he proceeded to beat the others in the same manner, stopping only when they bled and cried. I felt sorry for what I had done to my friends, but I was not afraid to face him. I would take my beating and not cry for mercy, I promised myself. I expected an especially severe beating. When my turn came, the Herr Rektor only rubbed his bloody hands together and stared me in the eye. After what seemed an eternity, he yelled, "Raus." I restrained myself and walked out with my head held high. But instead of returning to my Russian class I hid in a large waste barrel outside the classroom. I couldn't bear to go into the room without a mark on me. It would have looked as if I had sold out my classmates. When the bell rang, I remained in the barrel until the classroom emptied. Only then did I retrieve my pouch. After the beatings we students studied our Russian lessons diligently. Everyone, student and teacher alike, understood that the Communist regime was not to be challenged at any level. We never played schoolyard soccer again, and no one spoke of the incident.

We had very little money, so I carried my lunch to the Opportunity School in a brown paper bag and drank water from the fountain. During noon recess I stood by a window on the landing between the first and second floors, leaning against the wall, eating my sandwich and looking out the window at the street below. Evidently the word spread about the lonely German student who ate his lunch on the second floor landing. Soon many stopped to talk to me, only to be put off by my limited vocabulary. A young French woman from Strasbourg who spoke German stopped by nearly every noon for a few words of encouragement. Then one day a young navy veteran joined me on the landing. He too brought his lunch in a brown paper bag. We stood there, side by side, munching our sandwiches. He talked without let-up from the time he joined me until the bell rang and it was time to return to class. I nodded my head occasionally, smiled when I thought it appropriate, even said OK at times, but never joined in the conversation. I had no idea what the man was saying. At the end of each lunch break, the stranger shook my hand and walked away happily. Then one day words suddenly fell into place. I didn't even realize it when it happened, it came so naturally. All at once I could form whole sentences, and the one-time impenetrable English language assumed substance and meaning. My French friend no longer spoke to me in German, and I understood what my lunchtime companion in the navy uniform was saying. I continued my role as listener—nodding my head and laughing when appropriate. He talked about himself, about his service on ships he'd been on, about this and that. He apparently had no need to hear from me, never asked a question, nor inquired about my name.

When I began to understand what people were saying, when the English language suddenly became a coherent flow of sentences and complex thoughts, it was as if a light had suddenly been turned onto a darkened stage revealing the actors in a play only heard but never seen. It was as if sound was given to a pantomime, or the actors in a silent movie suddenly found their voices. Comprehension was thrilling. In my painful process of discovery I learned to listen carefully, and I knew that as an immigrant boy I would need to do a lot of listening in the future. One technique I picked up and found helpful was to sound out every new word I learned, even if some of its letters were silent and not pronounced, I gave them sound. That way, I remembered how to spell a word correctly rather than just trying to replicate the sound I heard. I also listened closely to those whom I thought spoke correct English—such as radio announcers and teachers. The spoken word came first, then the written word; finally, the rules followed.

CHAPTER 7

Hedwig Grapentin

A house finally became available in an air force housing project just outside the Lowry Air Force Base fence line, on the eastern edge of Denver's city limits. Beyond the air base, to the east, sprawled the small township of Aurora, and beyond Aurora, for hundreds of miles, stretched the barren high plains into windswept Kansas. Sixth Avenue, a four-lane, tree-shaded boulevard with a wide, grassy median strip, flanked by the sumptuous homes of Denver's social elite, ended at Lowry's main gate. North of Sixth Avenue, in the direction of East Colfax, then Denver's principal east-west thoroughfare, stood that humble air force housing project we were about to move into. On a Saturday morning we loaded our few belongings into Tom's car, and he drove us to 52 Jones Street, our first home in America. Hedy and Leo had been to the house on Jones Street earlier in the week to clean and arrange furniture Leo had checked out on loan from an air force family support center. Our new home was a modest, wartime built, temporary frame building, much like the barracks Hedy and I lived in as refugees in Germany, only this structure had been built specifically to house families, not soldiers. Our small duplex had two small bedrooms with hardwood floors, a carpeted living and dining area, a small kitchen, and a tiny bathroom. All houses on Jones Street looked alike—pink, with large black house numbers stenciled near their front doors. All residents of our small village were air force sergeants and their families.

Moving into our new home eased the strains which inevitably build up when too many people live together for too long in too little space, as we did in Marie and Tom's very small house. Hedy, Leo, Marie, and Tom parted as friends, but it was high time for us to move on. Later Marie confided to Hedy that she missed her German cooking, a small compensation for Marie and Tom's generosity. Although my mother never defined herself in terms of housewifely duties such as cleaning house, doing laundry, or cooking, she was in fact a very good cook. As the wife of a Luftwaffe officer she had put on many dinner parties in Sagan and prided herself on being an accomplished hostess.

Hedy applied for and obtained a job as a sales lady at the Base Exchange, the BX, at Lowry Field. During the Berlin airlift in 1949, she had worked in the BX at Fassberg, where she and Leo met. The BX was something familiar in a strange land, so Hedy thought of that job possibility first. It made good sense as well, since we lived in close proximity to the base. Finding a job for Hedy was not an option but a necessity. With Leo's limited income and the debts and obligations he brought into their marriage, she had to go to work if they ever wanted to get ahead, buy a car, own their own home. Here in America, in Denver, Colorado, Hedy no longer had to worry about her physical safety, being raped or shot, yet the struggle for economic survival was no less demanding. Stress remained a constant in her life.

Hedwig Grapentin was born on May 25, 1914, in Neuensund, a feudal village an hour's horse and wagon ride north of the small market town of Strasburg. Strasburg lay halfway between Pasewalk to the east and Woldegk to the west, in a region referred to as the Uckermark. The Uckermark, one of the poorest regions in Germany then and now, was not blessed with natural resources or anything else that might have attracted manufacturing or commerce. On top of that, the little town was built at a crossroads for warring armies, the remnants of its medieval town wall attesting to the futility of trying to stave off invaders from north, south, east, or west. In the seventeenth century, the soldiers of King Gustavus Adolphus of Sweden left their mark upon the town during the Thirty Years War—burning, raping, and looting on more than one occasion. A hundred and some years later, marauding Austrians and Russians chased remnants of Frederick the Great's Prussian army through the town after the battle of Kunersdorf during the Seven Years War. Napoleon's soldiers came through Strasburg on their victorious advance east toward Moscow and again in 1813 on their ragged retreat west, this time pursued by merciless Cossacks and revenge-seeking Prussians. No matter the invader's uniform, on foot or on horseback, Strasburg's residents were always left the poorer after each encounter, many of its women nine months later bearing the fruit of force and conquest. As it turned out, the year 1945 was a replay of a centuries-old tradition of violence. The army that swept through Strasburg in late April 1945 was composed largely of peoples from the far eastern reaches of the Soviet empire, Asians who burned, pillaged, and raped as other armies had before them. A monument depicting a weeping woman stands above a mass grave in Strasburg's cemetery, bearing mute testimony to the brutal storm the town barely survived in the waning days of World War II.

Strasburg, founded in the thirteenth century, sired numerous villages within an hour's wagon ride of its market place. It was to Strasburg where small farmers and large estate owners alike brought their product in horse-drawn wagons for hundreds of years, over a dense network of cobblestone-paved roads. By the time Hedwig Grapentin saw the light of day in May 1914 the world of feudalism she was born into was about to expire. The impending war would not only rearrange Europe's borders, but topple dynasties large and small, convulsively moving much of Europe, including the Uckermark, from the ways of its past, defined by the horse as the principal mode of transportation and agricultural power, into a technology-driven world with implications few understood.

Hedwig's father, Wilhelm, lived and worked on the estate of the von Arnims, a prominent Pomeranian family which for generations had fielded military leaders for Prussia's armies. Wilhelm was no more than a serf with few rights and privileges, living from hand to mouth, dependent on the largess of the von Arnims. The Neuensund village chronicle reveals that in 1892 the von Arnim estate comprised over a thousand acres and was home to "202 souls, 103 horses, 169 cattle, 1,185 sheep, 248 pigs, 25 goats and 12 beehives." By 1919, only months after the end of the Great War in which Wilhelm nearly lost his life in a gas attack at Verdun, the village of Neuensund had expanded to 260 souls, even though many of its young men had been killed in the Great War. In 1921 electricity arrived, the most profound change in the region since the coming of the railroad to Strasburg in the second half of the nineteenth century.

Until the arrival of electricity, Hedwig's life was pretty much determined by the diurnal cycles of the rising and setting sun—up by sunrise, to bed by sunset. After dark, an oil lamp was the sole source of light, and since oil cost money, the lamp wasn't lit very much. Even when an electric light fixture was installed in the ceiling of their kitchen, which was the family's living and dining area, routines remained much the same. Light remained a luxury. Hedy's days were filled with carrying water in buckets from the communal pump, washing clothes by hand on a simple washboard, helping her mother cook on a wood-fired stove, scrubbing the wooden floor of their small row house on her hands and knees, tending their tiny garden, and raising their small flock of chickens and geese. Hedy romanticized her humble upbringing to my sister Ingrid and me, telling us bedtime stories of when she as a little girl lay in the grass daydreaming while tending her family's flock. She told of her younger brother Ernst, who was always sickly, and of her older sister Marie, her father's favorite. Hedy, by her own account, was a spirited girl, frequently getting herself into trouble, not serious trouble, but the kind one can laugh about when looking back.

In spite of her impoverished beginnings Hedy had aspirations, dreams few other village girls seemed to share. Lying in the sun-drenched meadow tending her geese, she dreamed of becoming a fine lady, like the ones in beautiful silk dresses that she saw coming down the dusty village road in fancy horse-drawn carriages. When extra help was needed in the von Arnim manor house, Hedy volunteered, not only for the pittance she was paid, but for the opportunity to see how the beautiful people lived. She got to wear a black dress, a lacy white apron, and a little white cap, and found herself serving people who seemed to come from a world of luxury she could not easily picture for herself, but a world she was determined to be a part of someday.

The middle child of Wilhelm and Wilhelmine Grapentin, Hedy was given the formidable name of Hedwig Frieda Wilhelmine, which she changed to Hedy Frieda when she was naturalized an American citizen in Denver, Colorado, in July 1954. Most everyone in her village was named Wilhelm or Wilhelmine, after the kaiser and the empress. The two-bedroom row house in which Hedy grew up was built of *Findlinge*, the rounded granite stones left behind in abundance by retreating glaciers, making for a cold, damp house in both winter and summer. As a *Pferdeknecht* Hedy's father worked a team of horses on the von Arnim estate. His meager income was mostly in kind.

Hedy's sister Marie and brother Ernst appeared to have none of the dreams and ambitions that filled Hedy's head. They were satisfied with life as they knew it and would live and die in Strasburg. Marie died young, raped many times by gangs of marauding Russian soldiers in April and May 1945, dying that June of typhus fever. My grandfather fashioned a pine box for his beloved daughter Marie, dug her grave, and buried her himself in the Strasburg cemetery. Ernst was drafted into the Wehrmacht, served as an artillery gunner at a fort on the Cherbourg peninsula of France, and was reduced to eating rats before its commander surrendered to American forces in 1944. In 1946 Ernst was released from a British prisoner-of-war camp and returned to Strasburg, married his childhood sweetheart Lotte, and went to work on a collective farm as a *Pferdeknecht*, just as his father before him. I visited uncle Ernst once in 1946, when we still lived in Strasburg, in the Russian zone of occupation. I can still see him plowing a field, walking behind a horse, making sure his furrows were straight, a scene straight out of my fairytale books. The field Ernst plowed did not belong to him, and the simple apartment he occupied was owned by "the people." Nothing had changed for Ernst, living the same kind of life lived by his father.

By age fourteen Hedy decided she would never marry a local boy, have his children, and condemn herself to a life of hardship and poverty. She loved and respected her parents, but didn't want to live as they did. Hedy attended the one-room school in Neuensund like all other children of common laborers who worked on the von Arnim estate. Her eighth grade graduation certificate notes that her behavior was *Sehr gut*, worthy of an A, as were her reading skills and singing; her attendance was judged only *Gut*, a B, as were her notes for religion, German, arithmetic, history, drawing and nature studies. In geography and geometry Hedy received a *Fast gut*, a C. There was no such grade as a D, much less an F. What would have been the point? Eight years of school was all the village children were going to receive, regardless of their intellect. At age fourteen the children not only completed school but also passed into adulthood, signified by the act of confirmation and first communion. The boys were expected to go to work on the estate or on other nearby farms; the girls were expected to help their parents, help with the harvest, get married, and have children. Hedy wasn't buying into that tradition.

A large sugar refinery was built near the Strasburg railroad station in 1882, allowing for the economic processing and movement of large quantities of beets and molasses to and from the refinery. Sugar beets, rye, and potatoes were the three large cash crops in the Uckermark. The refinery brought Strasburg a modicum of prosperity, allowing field hands like my grandfather to exchange their lives of marginal subsistence and vassal-like dependence for a factory job. Wilhelm Grapentin finally succeeded in getting one of the coveted refinery jobs. It paid a weekly salary, which he received in a small, brown paper envelope, a *Lohntüte*, each Saturday noon, and promptly turned over to my grandmother. The new job allowed my grandfather to move his family out of Neuensund into a modest rental house in the tiny village of Louisfelde, just outside Strasburg on the road to Pasewalk. From Louisfelde, Wilhelm rode his bicycle to work.

Pasewalk was considerably larger than Strasburg with over ten thousand inhabitants and visibly more prosperous. The 6th Cavalry Regiment had its permanent barracks there, pumping money into the local economy and providing a never-ending stream of marriageable young men for eager town girls. In the spring of 1932, at the age of eighteen, Hedy and several of her girlfriends decided to go to a dance in Pasewalk. For the young village girls it was an exciting adventure. They set out on their hour-long walk from Louisfelde as soon as they finished their chores. Each sat timidly on a bench on one side of the dance hall, waiting for a young man sitting on the opposite side to ask her to dance. At that dance Hedy met Willie Samuel, a twenty-three-year-old cavalry soldier with an open smile and a natural wave in his thick brown hair. Willie not only was good-looking and charming, but could dance the shoes off Hedy's feet. Evidently, he danced himself right into her heart. That night Hedy and Willie were the last to leave, stopping only when the band packed up its instruments. Hedy's girlfriends had left earlier, after she insisted on having just one more dance, and then another. Willie persuaded Hedy to spend the night in his barracks. After all, it was after midnight and a long walk home, his roommate was on leave, and Willie assured Hedy he was a gentleman. Willie smuggled her into his room and evidently young love was not to be denied. Hedy knew she would have some explaining to do once she got home the next morning and was relieved when Willie insisted on accompanying her to Louisfelde. Once there, Willie quickly allayed Wilhelm's concerns. So Hedy and Willie became an "item," as we say today. Willie was the kind of man Hedy thought she was looking for—educated, a Gymnasium graduate; from a good family, his father a respected civil servant, a *Beamter*. Although she thought she was in love with Willie, she wasn't quite ready for something as permanent as marriage.

A year later, in 1933, Willie was transferred to the Berlin area after volunteering for service in the newly created Luftwaffe. Hedy, to be near her lover, found and accepted a position in Berlin as a maid. It was Hedy's big break, her way out of Strasburg, out of the seemingly perpetual cycle of poverty and servitude that had entrapped past generations of her family. For the first time in her life she had her own room, a bathroom with a flush commode, and a real bathtub with running hot and cold water. Her days were filled with dusting, vacuuming, cooking, flower arranging, shopping, and doing all the little things a personal servant does for her mistress, an old lady of a prominent and wealthy Berlin family. After serving lunch and dinner Hedy often watched her mistress through the keyhole in the dining room door to see how she ate. Hedy wanted to learn to do things "the right way." She carefully watched guests at dinner parties and afternoon teas—watched how they ate, how they used knife, fork, and spoon, how they held their coffee and tea cups, how they dressed, and most of all how they spoke. Hedy was a quick learner. Soon her country ways gave way to more sophisticated ways unwittingly taught her by Berlin's social elite. She promised herself that if she ever had children she would teach them the right way to speak and the correct table manners that signified a good upbringing in Germany—and that she did. Hedy's relationship with her mistress remained correct; however, the old lady taught her the intricacies of enhancing her looks with the subtle use of rouge, facial powder, eyebrow pencil, lipstick, and nail polish.

The city of Berlin captured Hedy's imagination as well. Walking on the *Kurfürstendam*, the *Kudam* as it was called by Berliners, or *Unter den Linden*, was an always exciting experience for her. She loved being among sophisticated, well-dressed people, liked the hustle and bustle of a busy sidewalk and automobiles in the streets. She studied the faces of movie stars on larger-than-life posters plastered on advertising kiosks, studied their hairstyles, makeup, even thought of walking into one of the many studios to try her hand at acting. An unexpected pregnancy kept Hedy from doing that, or surely she would have tried her hand in the movies. Hedy never tired of Berlin and retained a love for city lights for the rest of her life. Hedy's Berlin experience changed her life in ways not even she understood at the time, changed her perception of herself, and changed her aspirations. Berlin became Hedy's finishing school.

Hedy and Willie continued to meet whenever their schedules permitted. At one of those meetings, on August 26, 1933, Willie and Hedy exchanged silver engagement rings. They continued to keep their relationship secret from their parents and did not reveal their engagement until prompted by Hedy's pregnancy in the summer of 1934. They traveled by train to Schlawe, Pomerania, where Willie introduced her to his parents and asked them for their blessings in marriage. A trip to the Grapentins in Louisfelde followed. Then Willie applied to his commanding officer for permission to marry—which was denied. It proved the old adage, "If the army wanted you to have a wife, it would have issued you one." I was born out of wedlock in my grandparents' home in Louisfelde, on February 2, 1935. I was baptized in the ancient St. Marienkirche in Strasburg, and my birth was duly recorded in the *Kirchenbuch* as "illegitimate," my last name recorded as Grapentin, Hedy's maiden name. For eight months my name was Wolfgang Willi Eberhard Grapentin. In October 1935, eight months after my birth, the *Kirchenbuch* entry was amended to reflect that Willie Samuel recognized Wolfgang Grapentin as his legitimate son upon his marriage to Hedwig Grapentin, and my status was changed to "legitimate," my name to Samuel. The *Kirchenbücher* survived both war and Communists. I was able to review the original pen and ink entries and the subsequent changes, both in old German script, in 1995, while writing a family history.

Hedy and her young son Wolfgang followed Willie to several military assignments. In 1938 Willie was appointed a second lieutenant. That

November he was transferred to a military airfield near the small town of Sagan, about a hundred miles southeast of Berlin. Sagan became the site of an Allied prisoner-of-war camp, Stalag Luft III, made infamous in 1944 by the execution of sixty-six British and American flyers who were recaptured after a daring but unsuccessful escape. The event subsequently was made into a movie, *The Great Escape*, with Steve McQueen. We lived in a comfortable new housing development near the airfield built exclusively for military officers and higher ranking civil servants. Hedy made a beautiful home for her husband, acquired an equally beautiful wardrobe, and began to live the good life—small dinner parties, cigarettes, wine, movies, tennis, dancing, skiing. But here in Sagan her young marriage failed. While she was pregnant with my sister Ingrid, Willie had a blatant affair with his secretary, who also became pregnant. The breach was irreparable. Love died. Hedy asked for an immediate divorce but in the end agreed to wait until war's end. Hedy and Willie divorced in 1948.

In the summer of 1945 the Red Army caught up with us in spite of our best efforts. We passed from one refugee camp to another. A Russian officer, drunk and frustrated at Hedy's resistance to his sexual advances, pulled his gun and shot her through the neck. While recovering from her neck wound she came down with typhus fever as well and lapsed into a deep coma. Most gunshot victims soon died from infection; she didn't, even though on one occasion, while still in a coma, she stuck her left index finger with its long fingernail directly into the bullet hole in her neck. We watched in horror, but it happened so fast, we couldn't prevent it. Still, the wound didn't get infected and healed. After she was well enough to travel, we returned to Strasburg where her parents had moved in 1936.

Their house had been destroyed in the fighting. Her father Wilhelm soon was arrested by German Communists and vanished forever in one of their many prisons. With great difficulty Hedy learned that her beloved father was beaten to death, a fact she never revealed to her mother, who continued to wait for his return for many years. Life under Russian occupation became indescribably difficult. Hedy focused on keeping her two children alive. In the end she was forced to sell her body to Russian officers for food to keep Ingrid and me from starving to death. The young idealistic farm girl who had come so far so fast had fallen so low. Our escape to the British zone of occupation from Strasburg in the winter of 1946 ended the threat of rape and arbitrary arrest, but all other forms of deprivation continued until the summer of 1948. Hedy just kept on going, doing whatever the situation demanded, believing that some day she would be able to leave it all behind. In the process of trying to stay alive the young farm girl never let go of her dreams, and eventually made it all the way to America.

CHAPTER 8

Settling In

We lived close enough to Lowry Field that not having a car didn't present a significant problem. Hedy and Leo could walk to work if they had to, or take a bus; usually one of their many friends stopped by to give them a lift. Grocery shopping was another matter. We three went together to the Safeway supermarket, the closest store to our house, carrying our heavy bags of groceries from the store onto the bus, then trudging the rest of the way home, our arms threatening to fall off by the time we reached our doorstep. I continued to attend Opportunity School, only now I had a much longer bus ride down East Colfax Avenue to Broadway, where I changed to another bus which took me the rest of the way to the school on Welton Street. As my English improved, Hedy suggested I find a job after school. "I am so sorry, Wolfgang," she said to me one evening, "but Leo and I have to watch every penny. I can't afford to give you bus fare anymore to go to school. I don't mind you going to school, but you have to carry your load. You understand, don't you?"

I understood. I looked through the want ads in the *Denver Post* and the *Rocky Mountain News*, but jobs for young people were difficult to find in 1951. As a teenager, Leo briefly worked as a delivery truck driver for Gus's Bakery on Huron Street in south Denver. Leo checked the telephone book and found that the bakery was still in existence. He and I went to Gus's Bakery and spoke to Gus Jr., the current owner and operator, telling him about my experience as a baker's apprentice in Germany. Gus introduced me to his night foreman, Henry Sonnleitner. "Can you use him, Hank?" Gus asked. Hank was in his thirties, I figured when I looked at him closely, over six feet, slender, with an open, honest smile. I liked Hank immediately. Hank looked at me. His eyes sparkled, a smile played around his lips, and brushing back his thinning blond hair with his right hand, he said, "Yes, I can. I need someone to fold boxes for the evening cake run." I started work the next afternoon. The job involved folding jelly roll boxes and putting them on baking sheets. The tin sheets fit into roll-around racks holding forty sheets. Later at night a crew of women would fill the boxes with jelly rolls, wrap the boxed jelly rolls in cellophane, and by five o'clock in the morning the jelly rolls, along with various other cakes and breads, were delivered to city stores and supermarkets.

My job paid seventy-five cents an hour. I left home at six thirty in the morning to catch the seven o'clock bus into town. My first class was at eight. By four in the afternoon I caught a bus on South Broadway as far as Huron Street, then walked the remaining mile to the bakery. In the evenings I worked as long as possible, leaving just in time to catch the last bus, at ten o'clock, heading into town. I had to change buses at East Colfax Avenue and Broadway adjacent to the state capitol, then rode for another forty minutes to the end of the line. I usually got home around eleven thirty. A grueling routine evolved for me: ride the bus, go to school, ride the bus, go to work, ride the bus, go to bed, sleep five to six hours, get up and do the same all over again. Except for Saturdays and Sundays, every hour of my day was consumed by school, work, riding the bus, and sleeping. I woke up tired and went to bed tired. Nothing much had changed for me from the way things were back in Hannover at the Rheinische Bäckerei.

In the beginning Hedy made me hand over my meager earnings just as she had done with her parents when she was a child. Leo didn't like it. Hedy and Leo talked it over, and Leo reluctantly agreed that instead of Hedy just taking my money, I would pay for my necessities, from the toothpaste I used in the morning to the clothing I needed for school. While I understood our situation, it still disappointed me that the little money I earned for long hours of work seemed to vanish the instant I cashed my small paycheck. There were other compensations though. My enchantment with Colorado grew as the days grew longer and warmer. It might be cold in the mornings, but it was a pleasant crisp kind of cold without the bite of humid German air. By noon, the Colorado sun would invariably drive the temperatures into the fifties and sixties. I began to think of outside temperature in Fahrenheit rather than Centigrade, although like everything else in my life it took a little while before it became second nature.

Leo's younger brother Raymond asked me several times to accompany him on weekend drives into the mountains. What a thrill it was to finally see those magnificent mountains up close. Raymond was no hiker, fisherman, or hunter, but he drove up and down every road and gravel path, no matter its condition, down every canyon, up every dead-end, on occasion having to back up for a considerable distance because there was no room for him to turn around his coveted Hudson Hornet. Although Raymond worked hard for every dollar he earned at the slaughterhouse, on our Sunday trips he was generous beyond his means. Leo and Raymond were cut from the same cloth, overly generous, and not especially good money managers. Juanita, their sister, was very different in that respect. I understood Juanita and her drive to separate herself from the poverty of her youth and from all that reminded her of it, including her spendthrift brothers, but that didn't make her a nice person. Juanita, unlike the others, had a new car, a new house in the suburbs, and probably a bank account. She struck me as a person with a goal in life, which didn't include the family she grew up in or its lifestyle. I never again had any contact with her and never met her family.

Leo's youngest sister, Audrey, unlike the others, who tended toward the slim, was a heavy woman, well over two-hundred pounds, and married to an equally heavy man with two rotund children. They were exceedingly nice people, but prosperity was obviously not in Audrey's cards anymore than it was in Raymond's. Hedy was the one who bridled Leo's spending habits by taking control of the purse strings. In later years, when prosperity had come their way, Leo readily credited Hedy with that achievement.

Folding jelly roll boxes at Gus's was a brain-dead activity. I could fold boxes without thinking or looking, doing my homework in my head while my fingers picked up, manipulated, placed, and stacked boxes. I watched the women come in around eight in the evening and start up the cake line. Occasionally a young Mexican woman came over and retrieved the racks I had filled with the orange jelly roll boxes. She was attractive I thought, and I tried to talk to her, but she didn't speak much English, so we just smiled at each other.

Hank Sonnleitner looked after me like a big brother. He soon got me involved in things other than folding boxes for jelly rolls, taught me to measure and prepare the ingredients for yellow, white, and angel food cake. I filled containers with the dry mix for each cake variety, the number of containers varying each night depending on the number of cakes they intended to deliver the next morning. The bakers would take the containers filled with dry ingredients and mix each batch in large electric mixing bowls with the wet ingredients such as eggs, which came in large buckets, Crisco-like fats, and fruit, if fruit was part of the mix. Before I knew it, I was folding cake boxes, preparing the dry ingredients for cakes, and doing any number of other chores for Hank. Hank always smiled, encouraged me in my work, and never had a harsh word. He led by example and pulled people along in a good-natured way.

I got in a hurry once and forgot to put baking soda into the angel food mix. The cakes didn't rise and had to be thrown out. I only learned of my error by chance, because I had gone home by the time the cakes went into the ovens. When I confronted Hank, he smiled at me and said, "I knew it wasn't like you. It won't happen again. We all make a mistake sometime. I fixed it. Go back to work." It was a valuable lesson Hank taught me. Throughout my period at Gus's bakery Hank tried to get me a raise—just a nickel more an hour for all I did for him. But he wasn't successful. Gus Jr. didn't like paying out money to hired help anymore than Herr Krampe in Hannover. Both men were alike in that they tried to get as much as possible out of each employee at the lowest possible cost. Gus, like Krampe, seemed a cold, greedy man.

After I had been working at Gus's bakery for several weeks, an incident occurred which started me thinking about leaving. When I came to work, I went into a small locker room to change into my work clothes. A door led directly from the locker into the office where Gus had a large desk at the end of the room overlooking his staff. There were two wooden benches in the room. When I entered that day, two dollars of change lay on one of the benches in nickels, dimes, and quarters. It wasn't my money, so I let it be and used the other bench. When I opened the door leading into the office to punch the time clock, I nearly knocked Gus on his back. He had been watching me through a peep hole in the door. I didn't like to be set up as a thief, nor spied upon. I told Hank about the incident. Hank talked to Gus, who mumbled something about trying to catch thieves. Well, I wasn't a thief, and the way he went about trying to catch one was dishonest. Anybody could have innocently pocketed the change and still not be a thief. My instincts saved me from Gus's trap, but I felt I had to get out of there. Gus reminded me too much of people I left behind in Communist East Germany.

Hank was a devout Catholic and had a large and growing family. He invited me to his house on a Sunday afternoon. I played ball with his kids while he fixed hamburgers on a grill. Hank, like Raymond, loved the mountains. But in contrast to Raymond, who was strictly a sightseer, Hank was a hunter and fisherman. He invited me to accompany him on a weekend fishing trip into the Rockies. I couldn't wait to go. We left his house at four o'clock one Saturday morning, heading west toward Kremmling. I had no real idea where Kremmling was. We first stopped in Idaho Springs for breakfast, then drove up U.S. 40 over Berthoud Pass, a narrow, winding road. In one of the little towns along the way we passed a corral next to a small general store. On the corral fence sat a number of cowboys. Real cowboys. Like the ones I'd read about in my Karl May books back in Germany. Their faces were deeply tanned from the Colorado mountain sun and wind, their lean bodies clad in Levis and faded blue and gray long-sleeved shirts. They wore large, gray Stetson hats with sweat marks running in irregular patterns around the base of each hat. What really caught my eye though weren't the hats or the hand-rolled cigarettes hanging from the corners of their mouths, but their large, shiny silver belt buckles and the equally large and shiny silver spurs on scuffed cowboy boots with pointed toes. I never thought there were still men in Colorado who made their living that way. I did something Hedy taught me never to do, stare. The cowboys paid me no heed. Hank went into the store and came out with some fresh worms and salmon eggs. He smiled when he saw my wonderment. "They are real all right," he said quietly. "People work hard up here to make their living."

We drove past the large mesa near Kremmling and then deeper into the mountains until the forest swallowed us up. Hank parked the car under a large spruce, where it would be difficult to see from the dirt road, then shielded it with branches. We got our gear and headed up a rushing mountain stream to a lake at the foot of steeply rising cliffs. Hank prepared my rod, tested the line, and baited the hook with salmon eggs. Then we fished. I had fished before in Strasburg after the war to help supplement our diet at a time when food was very scarce, but not since then. By evening Hank had caught both of our limits in trout, letting go many smaller fish. I hadn't caught a thing. He made a fire and fried some of the fish in an iron skillet he had brought along. I was really hungry, starved. I guess it was the mountain air. I was still hungry when we zipped into our sleeping bags that night. There was an abandoned cowboy shack near the edge of the forest looking out on the lake. The shack was very low, only three feet high, just high enough for a man to crawl into. That's where we spent the night. I awoke in the middle of the night, my teeth chattering. I was very, very cold. I moved close to Hank and pushed up against him to gain just a little more warmth and went back to sleep. We rose very early in the morning, before sunrise. There was a large beaver lodge at one end of the lake, and when I looked to the other side of the lodge, a large cat-like animal emerged from among the trees and slowly slunk along the edge of the lake, ignoring our presence. I looked at Hank. "Mountain lion," Hank said, smiling.

"Mountain lion?" Colorado was everything I ever imagined it to be. I loved every breath of air I took, loved the sense of freedom flowing from the untended wilderness, loved the cowboys, the fish, the beavers, the mountain lion. I felt a part of it all, a part of Colorado. If I could only stay here. When we got back to Denver late Sunday afternoon, my parting question to Hank was, "When do we go again?" Hank didn't fish for the sport of it. He fished and hunted to stock his family's freezer. He had many mouths to feed. In season he went hunting for deer and elk, goose and duck. While I couldn't kill and never went hunting with Hank, we fished again many times. It was Hank who gave me Colorado.

Although my new world kept slowly revealing itself, my grasp of the English language was decidedly still a work in progress. Not only was my vocabulary limited, I discovered contextual problems as well. I learned that words may have different meanings depending on how I used them. Some words which sounded alike were spelled differently as well. English proved to be both simple and complex at the same time. But after only four months in America I was speaking, reading, and writing the language of my new country. However inadequate my efforts, it was something I was proud of. My teachers at Opportunity School spoke a refined English; they were women who valued the meaning of words and the coherent structure of sentences. I listened to them carefully and silently attempted to emulate their patterns of speech. What I heard spoken on the street, on the bus, and at the bakery was a different kind of English with an occasional profanity mixed into a sentence, almost as if it were an ordinary part of speech. I quickly learned to recognize the NO words and filtered them out. At the bakery, the women workers were all of Mexican heritage, many of them recent immigrants such as myself. They spoke only Spanish among themselves and appeared to make no effort to learn English. The bakers were not much different. Nearly all of them were of European heritage, recent immigrants or first generation Americans. Some spoke with an Italian lilt, which I liked listening to, but all spoke a rough English with little or no sophistication. Hank Sonnleitner and another supervisor I worked with occasionally were the exceptions, speaking what I thought of as correct if not sophisticated English. I learned by carefully listening to the different worlds I moved through and within.

Although I had little time or opportunity to make many friends at school or work, I did meet two wonderful girls about my age at Opportunity School. Both were in their senior year of high school, getting ready to go to college that fall. They were working girls, saving their money, picking up high school credits at convenient hours. Before I knew it we three were the best of friends. We met between classes, sat together in the cafeteria, and after class occasionally got together for a few minutes of talk and laughter. Leila Yamamoto had a warm, inclusive smile, and beautiful raven black hair. She was American by birth—a Nisei, as she referred to herself. Dolores Lopez was also American born and proud of her Spanish heritage. Her carefully combed, beautiful reddish brown hair flowed to her waist like a cascading waterfall. She was an inch or two taller than I, five foot ten or eleven. Hair, height, and impeccable posture gave her a regal look that caused both students and teachers to stop in the hallway to watch her walk by.

Our backgrounds were different yet similar, and this was what brought us together—a German boy, a girl of Japanese ancestry, and a proud Castilian. Wolfgang, Leila, and Dolores. Leila's family had been long-time

Colorado residents when they were evicted from their home soon after the Japanese attack on Pearl Harbor and banished to a camp in the western desert. Accused of being Japanese spies, they lost all their possessions and property. Leila lowered her eyes when she told me her story, but not before revealing the depth of her pain. I recognized that look of the violated, having seen it in my own mother's eyes after she was raped by Russian soldiers, and in the eyes of other German women who suffered the same fate. Leila never told me where her family was taken, or for how long, nor did she ever again bring up the subject of her internment. I felt bad for her and did not pressure her for information. I was horrified to learn that my new country had done such things. I never asked Leo the questions Leila raised in my mind, and although I looked hard, I couldn't find anything on Japanese detention camps in my history text. I looked forward to seeing Leila Yamamoto every day, to hearing her laugh, seeing her smile, and feeling the all inclusive warmth of her humanity.

Dolores Lopez was scarred on the left side of her face from an early childhood fire. She didn't talk about it, and I asked no questions. What I learned of her accident came from bits of information she dropped in casual conversation. Like Leila, Dolores had a ready smile for everyone, and her laughter was unconstrained. All three of us had lived through painful events. I believe that's what brought and bound us together.

I was paid every other week at Gus's Bakery, and on one payday my check was especially large because I had worked extra hours on weekends. I felt this was an occasion to celebrate. I invited Leila and Dolores to be my guests for lunch on Saturday. We found a small restaurant on Capitol Hill and splurged on thick, juicy cheeseburgers, french fries, and banana splits. Our banana splits cost forty cents, Cokes were a nickel, and the cheeseburgers were thirty-five cents each. We laughed a lot, knowing in our hearts we were the best of friends and needed to hide nothing from one another. When I got home late that afternoon, Hedy looked at my check stub and frowned. She was not pleased over my spending extravaganza. Other than a movie now and then, or a trip to the zoo or a museum, which was free, I had no social life of my own. It was all work, school, riding the bus, and sleeping.

CHAPTER 9

East High School

Between classes at Opportunity School I met an older German man. We greeted each other in the hallways, exchanged a few words now and then, but never stopped to really talk. One day he stopped me and asked my name and where I lived. "I have a son your age," he said. "He goes to North High School. Why are you here? You should be going to East High School."

"I don't know," I said. "I will check it out." At lunch time I went to see Ms. Redford and asked her if I shouldn't be going to East High School instead of Opportunity School. She smiled and said, "Wolfgang, you are not quite ready. I will tell you when." With that she got up from behind her desk and ushered me out of her office. "You will be ready soon," she said, as she held the door for me, "soon."

Summer came. I continued to attend classes at Opportunity School. One day Ms. Redford called me to her office and informed me that she thought I was ready to transfer to East High School. "I've spoken to all of your teachers, and they agree that you should enter a regular high school this fall. I will miss you, Wolfgang. We will all miss you. But it is time for you to be with youngsters your own age." I was both thrilled and saddened to leave, especially my kind and generous teachers.

It was customary in Germany when leaving one place for another to have classmates and admired teachers sign their names in an autograph book, usually accompanied by a verse of poetry, a custom similar to the practice of signing high school or college yearbooks in the United States. My German classmates usually chose a stanza from one of Germany's many great poets such as Friedrich Schiller, Johann Wolfgang von Goethe, or Heinrich Heine. Heine was by far my favorite. He wrote in a lucid, readable style I could identify with, while Goethe and Schiller seemed more remote, old fashioned. When summer school ended, I asked my teachers at Opportunity School to sign my autograph book. They didn't quote poets, but simply expressed their heartfelt wishes for my future. Ms. Whitney, my social studies teacher, wrote, "It has been so very pleasant knowing you. Your interest and cooperation in this 'new' world to you has been inspiring to the teachers as well as to the pupils." My algebra teacher, Ms. Elsie Gross, wrote, "A very serious lad is my Wolfgang today.

Hope he never changes." Winona Norton advised, "Give your best effort to all you do and life will reward you—and America will be glad you came to us." And my principal, Ms. Redford, wrote poetically, "God bless you, giving you time for the task, peace for the pathway, wisdom for the work, friends for the fireside, love to the last." Tears came to my eyes as I read their words.

Leila Yamamoto took my autograph book home with her, and when she returned it, she lowered her eyes as she handed it back to me. "I will miss you, Wolfgang Samuel," Leila said, two big tears running down her cheeks. She turned around and walked away quickly. Leila quoted a passage from Rudyard Kipling, writing, "If you can keep your head when all about you are losing theirs and blaming it on you; if you can trust yourself when all men doubt you, and make allowance for their doubting too; if you can wait and not be tired by waiting, or being lied about don't deal in lies; or being hated don't give way to hating, and yet don't look too good nor talk too wise." In her parting words Leila mirrored her own personal pain inflicted by a doubting nation, as well as her struggle to regain her identity as a patriotic American. I loved Leila in the way friends love each other. I knew I would miss her greatly.

Impish Dolores revealed herself as well, writing "I choose a friend not from the books. I choose a friend not for the looks; but, Hi ya Joe, I'd like to say, and hear him answer the same way. To a friend so true." She ended her comments in Spanish, "*Para Wolfgang un muy buen amigo felicidad te deseo siempre. Best wishes from me to you. Dolores Lopez.*" I loved my friend Dolores as well. That autumn Leila and Dolores followed their dream and went to college. Our paths never crossed again.

In September 1951, I enrolled at East High School, seven months after setting foot on American soil. I passed by East every day on my way to and from Opportunity School, so the school was not unfamiliar to me. It was an impressive building, looking more like one of the many-windowed palaces I had seen from a distance in Germany than a high school. Soaring Doric columns supporting statues of Colorado settlers and an immense fountain defined the entrance to the school grounds. The school, with its immense clock tower, was flanked by tennis courts, carefully tended lawns, playing fields, and student parking lots backing onto Denver's City Park. A broad boulevard, the Esplanade, ran past the school. East High School obviously was a school for the children of the rich and well-to-do. My own parents couldn't afford a car, and we carried our groceries home on the city bus, but at East High School many students were wealthy enough to drive to school in their own cars. I did not envy them. It was just an observation.

Classes ran from eight thirty in the morning until three thirty in the afternoon. For seniors classes ended an hour earlier. On sunny spring and autumn days the beautiful senior girls sat out front on the manicured lawns chatting, their fluffy skirts spread out around them like umbrellas at a garden party, while privileged senior boys cruised up and down the Esplanade showing off their new cars, trying to attract the girls' attention. In 1951, Denver had five neighborhood public high schools—North, South, East, West, and Manual. As in many major cities at the time, each public school reflected the economic, ethnic, and racial composition of the community it served. Race and money defined where and how people lived. West High School was predominantly Mexican; North was blue-collar white—many Germans, Italians, and Poles lived in north Denver; South was aspiring white middle and upper-middle class; and Manual was as black as East was white. Out of my class of 712 students, 12 were black, a number so small, they were practically invisible. The Mexican American component at East, although larger, was nevertheless small and kept a low profile.

I was apprehensive on my first day, but my fears were soon allayed. During assembly in the large school auditorium, a boy sitting next to me asked, "Where are you from?"

"Germany," I replied.

"How did you come over?" he asked, after a lengthy pause.

"By ship," I replied.

"The *Queen Mary*?"

I had never heard of a ship called *Queen Mary*. "The *George W. Goethals*," I replied, "an army ship." He immediately lost interest in me.

After assembly I found myself sitting in the presence of a counselor, Ms. Blanche Pigott, who tried to determine what grade I should be in and what courses I should take. She was a German teacher and before the war had studied at the Universities of Berlin, Hamburg, and Munich. Ms. Pigott briefly spoke to me in German. Then we discussed my educational background. I handed her my Opportunity School transcript and my German grade book from Fassberg, an 8″ × 10″ booklet with a brown cover, the Nazi color, which bore the black Nazi eagle with its talons resting on a swastika. I handed over the booklet with some trepidation, fearing she would say something negative, maybe call me a Nazi. She didn't. Instead, she focused on the courses I had taken and the grades I received. After she finished her review, she turned to me with a smile and said, "What am I going to do with you, Wolfgang?" I didn't understand the meaning of her question, but I knew she didn't expect an answer. "How old are you, Wolfgang?" Miss Pigott seemed to like my name and used it at every opportunity.

"I turned sixteen in February."

"Then you should be entering the eleventh grade, shouldn't you? Now, let me see what you need to qualify as a sophomore. You took European history, of course," she said without waiting for a reply. "At least you were right in the middle of it, weren't you?" I nodded my head. "I'll give you two units for that," she said. She continued to give me credit for being proficient in a foreign language, German, and for a number of other subjects. When she finished her assessment, she said, "Well, Wolfgang, you are a full-fledged junior now. Here is your class schedule. I'll take care of the rest of the paperwork. You better hurry, or you'll be late for your first class." She rose from behind her desk and reached across and shook my hand, "Welcome to America, Wolfgang."

I was stunned by her friendliness and generosity. I didn't know if I should laugh or cry. So far everyone had been so helpful. There seemed to be no animosity toward a German boy in this land of mountains and blue sky. I had feared that here or there I would run into some virulent hatred, but it did not happen. I was highly attuned to even the slightest indication of hostility, rejection, or disguised hate. I found none. Over the two years I attended East High School, no one ever mentioned that I had an accent or hinted that maybe my language skills were lacking. No one inquired where I came from—other than the boy sitting next to me in assembly on the first day of school. In my head, the war still raged—it hadn't really ended for me—yet in this city at the foot of the Rocky Mountains, no teacher or student ever mentioned the word "war." War was a subject for American history, as was the ongoing war in Korea. East High School and its student body seemed to drift in a world divorced from the trauma that had and still was enveloping much of the rest of the world. The focus was on boy meet girl, movies, football, basketball, proms and fancy dresses, penny loafers, white bucks, blue suede shoes, saddle oxfords, argyle socks, good grades, and, of course, going to college.

Clubs of all types catered to student interests at East High School, nicknamed "Angels." There were no clubs at Opportunity School, no basketball or football teams, no school colors or other trappings of an ordinary public high school. Opportunity School was about learning how to read, write, and acquire practical skills, such as typing; Opportunity School was about coping with real life today. In contrast, East High School was about preparing fortunate young people for higher levels of education at America's prestigious colleges and universities, to become the leaders of tomorrow. No topic seemed too insignificant not to merit the interest of some group of students and the formation of a club. There was an International Relations Club which I chose to participate in. I couldn't afford the time and money it took to join the Ski Club, although I really wanted to ski the Colorado mountains. The Euclidian Club was far above my mathematical skill level, and although I was a good chess player, I didn't have time for it. A Girls Rifle Club was sponsored by the Army Reserve Officers Training Corps. I didn't understand why girls would want to shoot rifles meant to kill, but there it was. There was a Pre-Law Club, Language Club, Naturalist Club, Archeology Club, Astronomy Club, and Bowling Club. Music, modern dance, drama, all had their devotees and their unique organizations. It was obvious that few of my fellow students worked after school, or on weekends, their time totally taken up by school and its various corollary activities.

There were more exclusive clubs as well, for which members were chosen. The White Jackets, a precursor of today's cheerleading squads, encouraged school spirit at athletic events. To belong, a girl had to have a high grade point average, outstanding citizenship, however that was defined, and poise. Every Thursday the White Jackets proudly wore their uniforms—white jackets and red skirts, East High's colors. The Seraph Sisters, whose name referred to the highest order of angel, served as aides to faculty; they were a small group of girls in the upper fifth of their class. The Pre-Medic Club required its members to have a strong interest in science, a B grade point average, and recommendations from two faculty members. And, of course, the jocks had their club as well—the D Club. East offered many athletic options, from golf to skiing, but the major focus was on football and basketball, sports still mostly unfamiliar to me. I felt fortunate to be at East, a school with excellent teachers and a student body which, in spite of the many distractions, largely focused on academic achievement.

I soon learned that most of my teachers at East were just as interested in my academic progress as the teachers I had at Opportunity School. But my classes here were larger, and as a result I did not receive the personal attention I had become accustomed to. My initial classroom experience was bumpy, at times jolting. In chemistry we studied the periodic table. I thought it fascinating and listened intently to my teacher and his explanations. The first test required me to fill in a blank table with the abbreviations for each element and its atomic number. I had no idea I was expected to memorize the table. As a result, I didn't do very well. I had to acquire test-taking skills, and no one had taught me that at Opportunity School. Chemistry and algebra tests were factual regurgitations and calculations, but in history, literature, and similar subjects I was expected to exercise my own judgment as well. I recall a "pop quiz" in history when I made an 82—a B-minus. Until then, all my grades had been in the 70s, Cs, or even lower. It was a warm day and I went outside and ate lunch on the lawn with a classmate. I said to her excitedly, "I got an 82 on the quiz. I am so happy." She continued to munch her sandwich and after clearing her throat said, "That's only a B-minus. Why do you think that's good?" I was crushed and never mentioned grades to anyone again, even when I received very good grades as I became more familiar with what was expected of me. There was so much to learn in my new American world.

One defining aspect at East ran through the student body like a chasm—money and privilege. There were those who had it, and those who didn't. The aspirations of the two groups were as different as the cost of prom dresses—which for the privileged could run into hundreds of dollars at a time when a new 1951 Ford, without radio and heater, cost a mere $999. While one group aspired to go to college, the other aimed for the ever-growing automobile factories of Detroit, or similar occupations. Later in the year, as I stood at the bus stop on East Colfax Avenue across from East High, a boy I knew casually from one of my classes joined me and said without prompting, "I am quitting school."

"You can't do that," I responded instinctively. I corrected myself, "You shouldn't do that. That's not good for you."

He laughed and said, "I am going to Detroit next week. They are paying big money there in the automobile factories. You should come too. We don't need all this school." The following week I looked for him in class, but he never showed up again. Even at age sixteen I was bothered that the boy threw away an education for some dollars which may in time prove meaningless. I had to fight so hard to get any education at all, both in Germany and in my new country, and this boy just threw it away as if it was of no value. I knew that it was school and learning that would allow me to fashion my future and provide opportunity I yet could not identify.

At East I had much more homework than I ever had at Opportunity School. Where and when to do my homework became an immediate issue. I was always on the move, going to or coming from school and work—rarely did I have time to sit down at home to do my assignments. By the time I arrived home, it was nearly midnight. Fortunately, the late evening bus was nearly always empty. So I did my assigned reading on the bus, wrote my papers on the bus, memorized Shakespeare's soliloquies on the bus. The city bus became my study.

By December 1951 I left Gus's Bakery. The incident with the coins bothered me. The more I thought about it, the more I was convinced that he planted the coins to entrap me, not anyone else. I was the only one to show up for work that early in the afternoon. The next shift didn't come in until seven o'clock that evening. I had no idea what his motives were. I didn't care. I trusted my instincts and thought it best to leave. Finding another job proved difficult. The newspapers were no help. One Saturday I simply walked down Broadway and went into one store after another asking if they needed help. I was turned down over and over again, until at an auto parts store the manager said, "When can you start?"

"On Monday. I have to quit my other job first." I filled out some papers, and he took me to a basement filled with exhaust pipes of all makes and sizes, shelves and more shelves stocked with auto parts. The manager, an older man wearing a blue suit and tie, introduced me to the men I would be working with.

"Joe is an epileptic," he said. "You will be working with Joe. He'll show you what to do. Do you know what an epileptic is?"

"No."

"Joe has occasional seizures. And when Joe has a seizure, you must make sure he doesn't swallow his tongue."

I thought, why me? Why couldn't he have told me earlier that watching out for Joe was part of my job. But I had signed on, and a promise was a promise. He was paying me eighty-five cents an hour, a dime more than I received at Gus's Bakery. Joe was friendly and helpful, as was everyone else. Within a week Joe had a seizure. I was working beside him, packing old automobile bearings for shipment to a manufacturer who would rework them for eventual resale. Joe suddenly bent over moaning, foam forming on his lips, his eyes rolled back in his head. He collapsed onto the concrete floor, gasping and thrashing around with his arms. I did as Joe and the manager had shown me that first day: straddled his body and pinned down his arms with my knees, using one hand to open his jaw, the other to pull back his tongue. I yelled for the manager, who came running down the worn and oil-stained wooden stairs. He watched me and said, "You are doing just fine. No need for me to take over." The seizure passed and soon Joe was back on his feet. It never happened again when I was present, but if it had, Joe knew he had someone by his side ready to help. He thanked me for what I did and shook my hand in gratitude. I worked in the auto parts store until the following summer.

While still attending Opportunity School, I had noticed that on Thursdays some boys boarded the bus wearing army uniforms. I knew the boys were too young to be in the army, but there they were, wearing real uniforms. It puzzled me. For me the uniform worn by American soldiers represented something positive. The men who ended the awful war I grew up in wore that uniform; and it was the same uniform worn by the airmen of the Berlin airlift who saved the city of Berlin from the Soviets in 1948. When the Berlin blockade began in April 1948, I feared the Russians would soon take over the rest of Germany as well. I was terrified at the prospect of having to live under the Communists again, and when I saw my first American uniform in Fassberg, I was relieved, believing an American presence meant the Russians wouldn't be coming to Fassberg soon. When winter came in 1948 and the nights grew longer and colder, I was comforted by the sound of low flying American transport planes turning overhead on their way to Berlin. One night one of the C-54 aircraft turned over my barracks, its load of coal shifted in the turn, and the plane plummeted to the ground only a short distance from the refugee camp I called home. I went to the crash site several days later. The site was black from coal, oil, and fuel that seeped into the soft, marshy ground. One engine lay half buried, others were underground, too deep to be seen. Three American flyers had died that night. Only three years earlier the same men were probably dropping bombs on my family when we still lived in Berlin. Now they were flying food and coal to the same city so its people wouldn't starve, go without light, or have to live under the hated Communists. I didn't understand these Americans who were willing to die for people who were their enemies only three years earlier. I wondered what made Americans do the things they did. In a childish way I thought then that I wanted to be just like them and would gladly wear their uniform if they only let me fly with them. The Berlin airlift was the beginning of my love affair with flying. I decided to find out what I had to do to wear that uniform.

As part of my orientation at East High School I learned about the Junior Reserve Officer Training Corps. The ROTC offices and classrooms were in the basement of the school, hidden away from most school activities and the student body. When I inquired, I was told that I could take ROTC in lieu of physical education, which was mandatory. So I signed up for ROTC, not to avoid physical education, but to be able to wear that army uniform which meant so much to me. On the first day of class we were issued our uniforms. Wednesday night I had trouble going to sleep. I was too excited about the next day when, for the first time, I would wear that precious uniform to school.

CHAPTER 10

A Distant Goal

The air was soft and gentle, the days mostly comfortably warm, even though it was already October. Late at night though when I got off the bus coming home from work, I felt a chill in the air, reminding me that close to a year had passed since I arrived in Colorado, and winter was not far off. Winter, the season I dreaded most in Germany, was just another season in Colorado. I had no idea if Colorado had winter storms like I experienced in the Lüneburg Heath, but if it did I had no reason to fear the icy winds and drifting snow. Although our home on Jones Street was tiny, its roof didn't leak like our barracks had in Germany. We had running hot and cold water inside the house and did not have to rely on a single community pump out in the open. The walls and windows of our house were sturdy and tight, and when the wind blew, it found no way to enter and cover me with a fine dusting of snow as it had frequently in the barracks. I was hoping for a mighty storm to blow up so I could experience the comfort and safety of our home while the elements raged outside. That Colorado winter storm never came. Snow, yes. But no howling winds.

One December morning, a Sunday, I decided to take the bus into town. Denver was my hometown now, and I had seen very little of it so far. I wanted to wander around, following no schedule, no predetermined route. I thought I might visit the bookstore on the corner of Colfax and Broadway, then go up to the capitol building with its gold-leaf-covered dome, walk up the granite steps, and face west to see what the town and mountains looked like from up there. I wanted to touch the magnificent bronze statues scattered about the capitol grounds. Maybe I would visit the city library if it was open and there was still time to do so. I carefully counted my change to make sure that I had enough bus fare, and put the twenty-six cents into one trousers pocket to make certain I didn't accidentally spend it. The rest of my coins I put in my other pocket. I didn't have any dollar bills to call my own. Hedy and Leo were still asleep. I moved quietly around the house, not wanting to disturb them, and made sure the screen door didn't slam as I stepped outside.

I felt good walking down Jones street. The neighborhood was quiet, the sky a sparkling blue, the morning sun surprisingly warm. For some reason the crisp morning air reminded me of how young I was, sixteen, and that I had most of my life ahead of me. My grandfather Samuel came to mind, and I wondered how one got to be as old as he was, live that many years, survive two wars. I couldn't picture myself ever being that old. I liked being young, liked the feeling of strength and the belief that whatever lay ahead I could shape and fashion. When I reached East Colfax, I headed for the bus stop next to the Safeway store, a former streetcar stop with a small shelter. The tracks were still there. The streetcars had been taken out of service the year before I arrived, in 1950, and been replaced with trolley buses. The city sold the streetcar bodies to anyone who could cart them away, Hank Sonnleitner told me, their yellow bodies scattered throughout the mountains as makeshift cabins.

I sat on a bench in the shelter. Buses only ran once an hour on Sundays. I was early. It wasn't nine o'clock yet. Looking west on Colfax I could clearly see the snow capped mountains in the distance, their peaks glistening in the early morning sun. I took off my jacket; it was going to be a warm day. There was hardly any traffic at this hour of morning, and I saw no one walking. Few people walked anywhere in America, I had noted, only kids rode bicycles, and their bikes looked cumbersome with big fat tires. Most Americans drove wherever they went, even if it was only a short distance. So many things were different in America. Others began to arrive and sat on the bench next to me, or just paced back and forth, eyes toward the ground. No one talked or looked into anyone's eyes. The bus arrived punctually at nine. When I dropped my thirteen cents into the coin box, the driver pushed down a lever and let the coins drop through a slot, then turned a crank to count the coins. I found the process interesting. Occasionally a collector came aboard, opened the coin box, and removed the coins. The driver never handled any money. I took a window seat, not difficult to find on a Sunday morning.

The bus began its slow journey down East Colfax Avenue, lined at this, its eastern end, by motels, gas stations, bars, and a diverse collection of small shops. A large neon sign above one bar proclaimed, "It's Later Than You Think." I didn't get the meaning. Later than what? Every time I passed the bar and saw the sign, I found myself mouthing those words. It annoyed me, as if I was a parrot reciting on cue. Once the bus passed Monaco Parkway with its beautiful homes, the stores and houses fronting Colfax improved in appearance. We passed East High School on my right. When I got off the bus on Broadway, I headed straight for the bookstore, but it was still closed. So I went across the street to take a look at the life-size bronze statues on the capitol grounds. One, an Indian standing triumphantly over the buffalo he had just killed, intrigued me the most. Further east, across from the Civic Center, stood another beautiful statue—a cowboy on a bucking bronco, the moment of struggle between horse and rider captured by its creator. I thought of the statue as representing the essence of the Old West, of the people who conquered and settled this part of Colorado, the farmers, ranchers, miners, and fortune seekers. Maybe I was just another fortune seeker, I thought. It was why I was here, wasn't it? To seek a better life than the one I left behind in Germany.

I crossed Broadway, wandering around aimlessly. Most stores were still closed. Many wouldn't open at all on Sunday. Looking down Sixteenth Street, I could see the slim tower of the Daniels and Fisher Building, the tallest building in Denver. I noticed what looked like a pawn shop, its glass doors standing wide open, letting in the fresh morning air. I went into the shop to take a look around, its interior brightly lit by the sun shining through the large display windows. I slowly walked around locked glass cases filled with jewelry, watches, expensive looking crystal, and china. In a large case in one corner many different types of guns were on display. Guns didn't interest me. An older man with a jeweler's magnifying glass clamped over his left eye glanced at me occasionally, then went back to whatever he was doing. He didn't say a word. I came to a shelf filled with cheap trinkets, earrings, arm bands, necklaces, medals, any number of other little things to hang, stick, or strap onto or into a human being—and one glistening set of gold army second lieutenant bars. When I saw them, I knew I had to have them. I looked closely and tried to read the small price tag hidden under one of the gold bars, but I couldn't make out the price. I walked over to the man behind the glass counter who was examining a ring through his magnifying glass. I waited patiently for him to finish. He acted as if I wasn't there. I finally said, "Sir, how much are the gold lieutenant bars in that glass case over there?"

Without looking up he said, "Three dollars and fifty cents." I walked back over to the display case and again looked at the gold bars. I dug all my coins out of my right trouser pocket and counted two dollars and twelve cents. Adding the thirteen cents from my other pocket, my return bus fare, gave me a total of two dollars and twenty-five cents, far short of what I needed. I walked back to the man and said, "All I have is two dollars and twenty-five cents." The man behind the counter dropped the magnifying glass from his left eye, startling me. The glass fell harmlessly to his chest, suspended from a gold chain. "OK," he said, "you can have them."

He walked over to the glass case, unlocked it, took out the bars, and handed them to me. I spread my coins on the counter. Without counting he scooped them into his right hand and put them in his trouser pocket. The sun was high in the sky when I began my long walk home, and as I had thought earlier that morning, it turned into a very warm, almost summer-like day. I clutched the gold bars tightly in my right hand as if they were the most precious things I'd ever owned in my life. It turned out that they were just that.

By the time I crossed Broadway, walking up the hill on Colfax Avenue, past the capitol building, on the shady side of the street, I was putting one foot in front of the other without thinking how far I had to walk to get home. Walking was not a chore, nor something new to me. It was all I had ever done when I still lived in Germany. I wasn't fortunate enough to own a bicycle, so I walked to school in summer, winter, spring, and fall, in all kinds of weather. I walked through snowstorms so fierce that when I arrived at school I found it closed, then walked back again—nothing ever stopped me from going to school. At age eleven I walked across the border from the Russian zone to the English zone in a raging blizzard. I just kept putting one foot in front of the other, again and again, and eventually I got to where I was going. Walking was second nature to me, not a chore nor a punishment.

My mind settled on my new acquisition, everything around me just sort of dropped out of focus—people passing, traffic, all became irrelevant background. In my mind I felt good about my purchase, but didn't really know why. Why did I buy those second lieutenant bars? It was an impulsive act, I admitted to myself, which at the least changed my plans for the entire day. Still, I knew that I rarely ever did anything without a reason—even if the reason wasn't apparent to me at the time. Feet turned into yards, yards into miles. When I looked up, I was passing East High School, nearly halfway home. I thought that I needed to find out what it took to earn those gold bars. Maybe if I earned them, then I would be able to fly airplanes like those of the Berlin airlift. Many of the Berlin airlift flyers wore gold or silver bars, just like the ones I had just purchased. I was hot and thirsty when I got back to Jones street, poured myself a big glass of Kool Aid, then sat out back in our wooden lawn chair, looking at the Lowry runway. It was quiet. Only rarely did planes take off or land on Sundays. I looked at my acquisition. I looked at the runway shimmering in the afternoon sun and imagined myself taxiing my jet to the end of the runway, as I had seen it done many times before, putting the power to the engine slowly and beginning the long take-off roll. Maybe someday I would be able to do that. I wrapped the gold bars in Kleenex tissue and put them in a place where I thought my mother wouldn't find them.

My classmates at East High School were the friendliest students I had ever been around. Nothing like those I encountered when I first came to Fassberg in January 1947. There I quickly got into fights when I wanted to play schoolyard soccer with other students during recess. I remember being told that if I even thought of coming into the schoolyard they would beat me up. One of the girls in my class, Irene Schweitzer, took pity on me and invited me to play with them on the girls side of the yard. That did it. I walked over to the boys side to face whatever awaited me there. The class bully promptly took up the challenge. The fight was a draw. We both had bloody noses. The teacher said nothing. On the following day I went outside again and stood my ground. In time, and after several more fights, I was allowed to play schoolyard soccer with the rest of them. East High School wasn't anything like that. Of course, it was a much larger school than the little school in Fassberg, and we were all a bit older as well. I was accepted at East, if not noticed. I made two good friends while there, boys who, like me, were different from the others. Jim I met by chance; Dave sought me out. Dave was over six feet tall, walked stiffly like a robot or a creation of Dr. Frankenstein's, and looked like he should have been a linebacker on the East High football team. He wasn't, but that was the image he tried to project.

Dave approached me soon after I entered East High School, speaking to me in perfect German, which took me by surprise. Dave taught himself to speak German and had only a slight American accent. He invited me to his house, a brick ranch on Fairfax Street. His parents had allowed him to convert a basement room into his own little domain. He showed me the dictionaries and language books he used to teach himself to read, write, and speak German. I was impressed with his fluency and his achievement at only age sixteen. Not only did Dave speak German, but according to him, he spoke Czech as well, which he said he taught himself by the same method. While I couldn't test his Czech proficiency, I could only assume that he was as proficient in Czech as he was in German. He did admit, however, that he found Czech a bit more challenging. Remembering my own difficulties with the English language, I asked him how he did it.

"It's not difficult," Dave said. "I followed instructions. You know, the little marks they use to indicate where to put the emphasis on a word. Stuff like that." I knew it took more than just following instructions in a dictionary; at a minimum it took a tremendous amount of self-discipline, concentration, and intellectual ability. I wasn't sure if I could have done what Dave accomplished at such a young age. Dave was well read as well, much more so than any other boy I had ever known, and could discuss with me any subject I chose to bring up. I might have experienced the furor and chaos of war and lived through its aftermath, but Dave had read about that war far more extensively than I had and could discuss the strengths and weaknesses of German and Allied generals, their strategies and tactics leading to victory or defeat. I wasn't big on reading war books or talking about the war. It was a visceral experience for me, an intellectual exercise for Dave.

Whenever I had time, I gravitated to Dave's house to talk, play chess, or arm wrestle, which at times degenerated into a raucous free for all between the two of us. I remember pinning "big Dave" on his couch by twisting his arm behind his back so he couldn't move without experiencing excruciating pain, which I applied judiciously, aiming for him to say, "I give up." That's what I said when he had me pinned. Dave simply couldn't say those three words, even though I had done so frequently without ever feeling that it diminished my ego. We were just wrestling, that's all. When I finally released Dave from my grip, I learned that he had difficulty dealing with failure. I already had failed in so many things, or at least I thought I had, and at age sixteen learned that failure was part of life, and often as good a teacher as success. I guessed Dave probably never failed at anything, or perhaps he avoided situations he thought he could not master. I didn't know which it was, maybe both. Clearly, having me, the 145-pound, five-foot-nine skinny kid, triumphing over the six-foot, 190-pound giant was something Dave couldn't deal with. He usually drove me home in the family car when it was time for me to go, but this time he just asked me to leave. I took my books, walked a mile to the bus stop, and made my way home. I decided not to put Dave in a compromising situation again. He seemed to have a great need to be in control of things, and being in control meant controlling me, his friend, as well. That I would never permit; still I didn't want to lose him as a friend, so I avoided situations where I perceived he might think of himself as losing face. Dave, like other students at East, never asked about the world I experienced and survived. As a result he never got to know me. I got to know him.

My friend Jim was temperamentally the opposite of Dave. He too was tall, nearly six feet, with an infectious restlessness about him, as if he couldn't wait to get on with life, get out into the real world and turn it upside down. Jim always looked spring-loaded, like he was going to go off any moment like a hand grenade with its pin pulled. Jim, like Dave, never asked about my background, didn't show the slightest interest or curiosity in my past. Even if he had asked, I don't believe I would have given him more than a perfunctory answer, as I did for years afterward whenever anyone inquired about my past. But neither Dave nor Jim ever asked one question about who I was or where I came from or what I experienced. I knew that for Dave and Jim to seek me out as a friend I had to bring something into their own worlds they thought they wanted or needed. For Dave, I thought, it was the opportunity to practice his German and to impress me with his intellect and knowledge. I used to sit with him in his room for hours and listen to him expound on World War II strategy and political ideology. For Jim, it may just have been that he had no one else. For both I was an audience, a listener.

Jim nearly always wore blue jeans, rolled up twice at the cuffs, and a long-sleeved white dress shirt with the sleeves rolled up to just below his elbows. His uniform. Jim's father, a World War II veteran who fought with the army in the Pacific and landed on Iwo Jima in the face of enemy fire, still jumped when a door slammed too loudly. I looked in his eyes when I first met him, deep, expressionless eyes of a man who'd seen more than he wanted to, still trying to cope. Jim loved to take his father's new blue Mercury, pick up Dave and me, and drive around for hours. We would drive east, nearly as far as the Kansas state line, west into the foothills, north toward Cheyenne, or south to Colorado Springs. His restlessness was like an electric charge that had to be bled down constantly. Whatever it was Jim was chasing, it always had to do with making money, lots of money, and it had to be made fast. The moment Jim convinced himself he had a winning idea he was ready to go into action.

Jim decided that there was big money to be made in selling eggs door to door. He promptly bought himself a '37 Ford coupe and went into the egg business. He projected huge cash flows and in his mind built an egg empire. One day I noticed that the word egg had disappeared from his vocabulary. I didn't ask what happened. Jim was already into his next vision, designing constant speed drives for jet engines. "And what do you know about jet engines?" I asked.

"I know lots about jet engines," was his instant reply. Before I knew it he was talking to executives at Sunstrand, redesigning their constant speed drives which had taken them years and millions of dollars to design and develop. From constant speed drives Jim graduated to wetsuits for the U.S. Navy, suits frogmen wore for underwater exploration. His suits were going to be better and cheaper than those the navy was using. Jim was forever on the move, chasing a rainbow and looking for that bucket of gold that was, according to Grimm's fairytales, buried at one end of the rainbow. It seemed to me that Jim was always digging at the other end. I learned to listen to Jim's many plans and ideas and not to ask too many questions.

Surging hormones in my maturing body assured that girls began to assume ever greater importance in my life, not a situation I was very comfortable with. I found girls easy to meet, but I had difficulty establishing relationships which went beyond a casual meeting in the corridor or the friendly exchange of words in the classroom while waiting for the teacher. My experiences in postwar Germany had a powerful restraining effect on me when it came to girls. As a ten-year-old, I had to cope with the cries of women pleading for mercy as they were raped by drunken Russian soldiers. In the summer of 1945, Hedy, Ingrid, and I were in a camp near Lübeck. The American soldiers had withdrawn days earlier. One afternoon, a group of Russian officers walked up to our barracks, tipsy, laughing, unsteady on their feet. They came in the back door smoking cigarettes hand-rolled in newspaper, with bottles of vodka and schnapps in their hands. "Frau," they shouted, laughing loudly. They were very different from the American and English soldiers we had met. The Americans had been kind and shared things with us; the English were disciplined and stayed away all together. Neither threatened harm. The Russians forced themselves into our lives. I remember my mother sitting behind our only table when they entered uninvited. Ingrid and I stood by her side, her face a mask of fear turned gray with terror, a grotesque smile disfiguring her beautiful features. The Russians remained friendly, pointing to a travel chess set. They spoke to my mother in Russian, gesturing—they wanted to play chess. My mother arranged the chessmen and played. She was a skilled player. She lost. Maybe she was afraid to win. Several of the Russians played with her—she lost each time. While she was playing chess, the others looked around the barracks occupied by other refugees from the east. The Russians finally left, only to return that night. They went directly to the room next to ours, where two young women from Berlin lived. The women screamed while the Russians laughed and danced Russian dances, one playing an accordion. Throughout the night I heard the women moan in pain, giving off occasional cries, their deep fear for their lives mirrored in every sound they made. The women pleaded for mercy, for their tormentors to stop—the Russian soldiers only laughed. My mother told me to hold my ears and go to sleep. We slept under the table, my mother's arms wrapped around Ingrid and me. By morning, the Russians were gone. They came back every night for a week.

At age sixteen I was a mess when it came to girls. I didn't know exactly what it was I feared, but the thought of intimacy, something I craved, quickly brought back memories from my past. As a result, the more desirable a girl, the more untouchable she became. As soon as a relationship matured to a point where a girl began to show a more than casual interest in me, I literally ran away. It wasn't only my violent past which skewed my relationship with girls, it was also my total ignorance about sex. In the eighth grade, my last year of school in Germany, we studied the human body. I remember how all of us, boys and girls alike, looked forward to our teacher enlightening us on what made a woman a woman, a man a man; but we were disappointed, he never talked about that. The human being we spoke of in class had a heart, kidneys, and lungs, could taste, smell, feel, see, and hear—but had no gender. I had no access to magazines or books of any kind which might have enlightened me on the subject. No one ever talked to me about sex. All I had to go on were the horrible impressions from my past—the dark side of sex. Although Hedy and I were close, I didn't feel I could talk to her about this subject and reveal my ignorance and physical needs, nor did she try to talk to me. East High School had nothing to say on the subject of sex either. Sex was a subject no one seemed to want to talk about. I kept getting older, my body matured, but I remained just as ignorant on this vital subject as I had ever been. I knew nothing about contraceptives and believed that if I had intercourse with a girl it would instantly lead to her becoming pregnant. The one thing I was determined not to become was a father at an age when I felt that I still needed a father of my own.

I met Beverly in American Literature. She took an interest in me the first day of class, helped me with my assignments, made sure I understood what the teacher wanted, pointed me to sources in the library, assisted me in things of that nature. Soon we met every noon during our lunch break. Both of us brought a sandwich to school so we wouldn't have to go to the cafeteria. On sunny days we sat outside on the lawn; on inclement days we stood together in a remote hallway, talking, looking each other in the eyes. Occasionally we saw each other in the evenings at her house, doing homework together, or we went to a movie. She always looked like she just stepped out of a fashion magazine, her blonde hair carefully coiffed, wearing only the slightest hint of make-up. I loved to look at her, wanted to kiss her on the lips, put my hand where it had never been before. I became scared of my own impulses. One day I told her I couldn't go out with her anymore, but gave no reason. I remember the way she looked at me, her beautiful eyes bigger than usual, as if she was crying, but there were no tears. She didn't ask why. I felt terrible. Beverly was my first girl-friend, and I didn't have a clue how to be her boyfriend.

CHAPTER 11

Ingrid's Return

Both Hedy and Leo worked long hours, Hedy more so than Leo, volunteering for overtime at the Lowry BX to bring home as much money as she possibly could. They arranged their lives to fit the goals Hedy set—first, a house, then a car. No more visits to the bar for Leo. Leo was not a man able to hold his liquor. One beer was enough to make him happy and willing to buy a round of drinks for everyone. That generosity quickly became a thing of the past. Instead, they joined the Edelweiss Club, to which many of the German and Austrian wives of American service men belonged. At the Edelweiss Club they could have a good time among friends, eat familiar foods, and dance to music that brought back memories of yesteryear. Hedy was an excellent dancer. Leo never felt the rhythm of music in his bones, but he didn't mind Hedy dancing with others, and watched patiently from their table, nursing the one beer Hedy allowed him to have for the evening, maybe two.

Unfailingly Hedy and Leo made the required monthly child support payments for the boy Leo adopted. It was an expense they had to cope with until the boy turned eighteen. Outside of the money spent on essential needs and a few small pleasures, all other income went into a savings account for the new house. Laughter and levity was one of the casualties of Hedy's unwavering focus on achieving her goals. There was a reason why Hedy was so adamant about getting a house of her own and making it her first priority among many. Our government quarters at 52 Jones Street reminded her too much of the German military barracks she and I once occupied—a time of suffering and personal degradation for her. The longer we lived in our Jones Street duplex, the more intense her desire became to get out of there, to get away from the borrowed furniture and reminders of her ugly past. On weekends, when Hedy wasn't working, she asked friends to drive her and Leo around the area to look at houses—not used houses, with other people's smells and ghosts, but new houses, to give her a clean, fresh start.

The winter of 1947 in the Trauen barracks had brought Hedy close to her breaking point. We had little to eat and wear, no soap to keep clean, no heat to keep the cold out of our beds at night. Nearly everyone lost his or her job at Fassberg airfield, including Hedy. Losing her NAAFI job meant she lost the hot lunch which was part of her pay and the scraps of food she was able to bring home for her children. The money she made had little value. The black market was king, and its principal currency was cigarettes and sex. That winter, Ingrid contracted rheumatic fever. Hedy took her to a former German military hospital, an assemblage of rotting barracks like the one we lived in. The team of military doctors and nurses who had remained behind still cared for the torn and ailing bodies of wounded soldiers and youngsters like Ingrid. Ingrid recuperated slowly. Then Hedy came down with hepatitis, her skin turning a brownish yellow. She walked the ten kilometers to the hospital where Ingrid was being cared for and remained there for treatment. I got very lonely for my mother. One day I set off to see her. Hedy was overjoyed at my unexpected visit. The nurses were kind and shared with me the little food they had. That afternoon Hedy asked me if I wanted to stay the night. Although the hospital was filled to capacity, after some whispers among Hedy and the nurses, a bed was found. "The room doesn't have any lights," Hedy informed me, "but you don't really need a light. The nurses will make up the bed and wake you at first light in the morning."

I remember being shaken awake by a nurse very early the next morning. "It's time for breakfast," the nurse announced cheerfully. "Go down the hall and wash up. Here is a towel and a face cloth. When you finish, please join your mother in her room." I did as I was told. Many months later I learned why the shades were drawn in the room I slept in and why there supposedly were no lights. It was the hospital mortuary. I slept next to two corpses. It was the only bed the nurses could come up with. In time, both Hedy and Ingrid returned home, not well, but better.

A ramshackle store run by a lecherous, short-statured, skinny man stood down the road from our barracks near the village of Trauen. The man was ugly not only in face, but in his heart as well. He and his rotund wife had numerous children, and I had heard he tried to coerce every woman who came to his store into having sex with him. Many did. People were hungry and mothers would do whatever was necessary to put food into the mouths of their children. Hedy was no exception. I could survive on a crust of dry bread and water, on salt and a few potatoes. Ingrid couldn't. She had to have a better diet to recover and make it through the winter. One bleak December evening Hedy came home from shopping in that little village store. She carried a basket filled with bags of sugar, flour, and hard candies, two pounds of butter, a pound of margarine, lard, baking powder, and jars of jelly and jam. "Look, Wolfgang," she said, "now I can bake Ingrid a cake." Her voice was tremulous. I looked for tears in her eyes; instead, I saw those large pupils again, the same way she looked when the Russian officers first came into our lives in 1945 with rape on their minds. Her forced cheerfulness couldn't hide her despair over what she had to do to obtain the food Ingrid needed to survive. I ran out into the cold and wandered across the frozen fields aimlessly, crying for my mother. Sobbing. Wishing she hadn't done that. I knew she had no choice. It hurt knowing Ingrid and I were her burdens. I did all I could to help—tended a small garden, looked for mushrooms in the forest, picked wild berries, went fishing, begged. It was not enough. None of us would forget the winter of 1947, a time Hedy wanted to forget, and one reason why she was adamant about moving out of Jones Street into a new house of her own.

Hedy and Leo found a development going up on the easternmost edge of Aurora, near Fitzsimons Army Hospital and the Rocky Mountain Arsenal. The new development was still being surveyed, although the first bulldozers had already arrived to scrape out streets and trenches for sewer and water lines. Before I knew it, Hedy and Leo signed a contract for a little frame house built on a concrete slab—three bedrooms, a small bathroom off a narrow hallway, and an L-shaped living and dining room adjacent to the kitchen. The little house had a big picture window looking out onto the street, the mountains barely visible in the distance, and a small backyard with a concrete incinerator to burn the trash. All that came for ten thousand dollars—a princely sum for Hedy and Leo.

Hedy was the first in her family to own her own home, a grand accomplishment for the daughter of a lowly farm laborer who grew up in a little row house with no running water nor indoor toilet. Over the next several months she went to the construction site on Wheeling Street whenever a friend was willing to drive her there. We watched the bulldozers scrape out the street, watched the sidewalks being poured, gazed in astonishment at the concrete slab that was to support our new home, water and sewer pipes sticking through the concrete floor waiting for something to connect to. We watched as the little house was assembled two-by-four by two-by-four. In March 1952 we moved in, fourteen months after stepping on American soil. I knew this wouldn't be the last house for Hedy, but it was a beginning. With the new house came new furniture and more bills. A car had to wait yet another year.

Our move to Aurora meant I was in the Aurora school district and no longer entitled to attend Denver's East High School. I had not foreseen that complication and was distressed when I learned of it. I had just gotten to know my teachers at East, begun to understand what was expected of me in class, and made a few friends. Suddenly I was supposed to give all that up. I went to see Miss Pigott, my counselor, the wonderful woman who had "made me a sophomore" when I first came to East. I was close to tears when I presented my problem. Miss Pigott listened patiently, then asked, "Wolfgang, do you really want to finish school at East High School? It will be a much longer bus ride for you. Aurora has a good high school, and I am certain you would adjust and do just fine."

I pleaded with her to please let me stay at East. "I don't want to leave," I told her passionately. "I've been in this country for just over a year, and I have already attended two different schools. Can't you do something to help, please?"

She lowered her head as I spoke. Then she rose from her chair and asked me to wait while she stepped out of the room, returning fifteen minutes later, several forms in her hand. "Fill these out, Wolfgang," she instructed me, "and have them signed by your parents. I will submit your request to the superintendent of schools for his consideration. I will write a petition in support of your request and urge them to allow you to finish your senior year at East High School. I cannot guarantee that your request will be approved. Now run along. Everything will be all right." She smiled and waved me on my way. Everything did turn out all right. Leo and I went to the downtown offices and met face to face with the superintendent of the Denver public schools. After talking to both of us individually, he signed the request allowing me to remain at East High School.

In late 1950 my mother had asked me if I would accompany her to the United States if she married Leo. She told me at the time that she also asked Ingrid, but that Ingrid had turned her down. She preferred to stay in Germany with our father, Willie. I believe Ingrid's choice was unexpected and painful for Hedy to deal with, but she didn't deny Ingrid her wish. Whatever made "Innimaus" happy was what Hedy wanted for her. When Hedy came to America, I knew she carried her daughter in her heart with her. Hedy always spoke of both of her children, of Wolfgang and Ingrid, never just of me. Ingrid was included in every conversation that warranted it. Hedy was sure the time would come when Ingrid would want to come back to her. That time came much sooner than she and Leo expected.

One of the first letters to reach us from Ingrid told of her being back in the barracks, living with Oma and Opa Samuel, our grandparents. We thought she was living with her new stepmother in Bad Oldesloe near Hamburg, in a household not ravished by war, with real furniture and a real bathroom, kitchen, and all the things that came with a normal home. Obviously, that wasn't the case. "Can I come to Denver?" wrote Ingrid. "You are my mother, my dearest, dearest mother. You brought me into this world and I want to be with you. Your loving daughter, Ingrid." Of course, Hedy's answer was "yes."

Hedy could hardly contain her excitement as she, Leo, and I spoke about Ingrid around the dinner table. How to pay for Ingrid's trip while they were in the process of buying a house was a problem. In the Ferguson household money loomed larger and larger as an issue. Ingrid had turned twelve in April. When Leo inquired about bringing his stepdaughter to the United States, the U.S. immigration authorities agreed. Since Ingrid was a minor child under sixteen years of age, her entry was authorized on the basis of Hedy's original visa. The American Consulate in Hamburg quickly issued Ingrid the required documentation. In June 1951 Ingrid wrote, "Dearest mother, you can't imagine how happy I am that soon I will have your arms around me. I am taking English in school. I will end my letter to you with a few words in English to show you how well I am doing: My name is Ingrid Samuel. I learn German and English. I go in the garden and shake the plum tree. You teach me English. I am a girl. My brother is a boy. I am the daughter of Mr. and Mrs. Ferguson. I have a satchel, a pen holder and a car. Love and kisses, your daughter Ingrid."

All of us were impressed with Ingrid's English, and we got a good laugh out of her letter. Ingrid couldn't know that we didn't have a car. She didn't know either that her coming to Colorado required money Hedy and Leo didn't have. After several banks turned Leo down for a loan to finance Ingrid's trip, he tried the Air Force Aid Society on Lowry Air Force Base—an organization established to assist airmen in need. Leo was indeed an airman in need, but the Air Force Aid Society didn't see it his way and turned him down. Leo became bitter about the lack of heart and understanding of an organization established for the very purpose of assisting people in need, like him. Leo's commanding officer called the Air Force Aid Society, but even he couldn't change their rigid stance on a small loan to finance Ingrid's trip to the United States.

In the meantime, Ingrid's excitement grew. In September 1951 she wrote, "I am so excited that soon I will be with you again. Opa said there is a ship leaving in November. I can't wait to be on it." November came and went and there was no ship with Ingrid on it. Ingrid had no idea of the financial difficulties Hedy and Leo encountered to finance her trip. The answer came unexpectedly. In a last, desperate attempt, Leo had applied for a loan from the American Red Cross. His application lingered, and Hedy and Leo had given up on ever hearing from the Red Cross when one February afternoon Leo received a call in his office from a Mr. Mills, the assistant field director of the Red Cross office at Lowry AFB. "I have good news for you, Sergeant Ferguson," said Mr. Mills. "Your application for a loan to finance the reunification of mother and daughter has been approved by our office on humanitarian grounds. We'll worry later about how you are going to repay us." Not only was the American Red Cross willing to take a chance on Hedy and Leo and lend them the money to defray Ingrid's travel expenses, they also offered to make all the travel arrangements. Hedy and Leo repaid the Red Cross loan within a year—it was a debt of honor. Leo never again gave a penny to the Air Force Aid Society during annual fund drives. After several weeks Ingrid's travel arrangements were complete, and by April 1952 everything was ready for her departure from Germany.

In the interim Hedy sent Ingrid several packages with dresses, skirts, blouses, and warm sweaters, wanting her to be dressed properly for a winter journey across the North Atlantic. Ingrid wrote back, "You must think I am still a little girl, mother. You are mistaken. I am already taller than my father. The suit you sent fits perfectly, but some other things are a little tight." In early April, accompanied by her father, Ingrid stepped on a bus in Fassberg and headed for the port city of Hamburg. Everyone who knew Ingrid was at the bus stop to send her on her way to America, including Oma and Opa's little white Spitz, Teddy. Teddy had brought much joy into our lives with his antics in our darkest days in the barracks. He ate everything he was given and slept on a pile of rags behind Oma Samuel's stove. He was a true member of the family, loved by everyone. One day after Ingrid's departure, Teddy didn't return home. No one ever learned what happened to the little dog.

In Hamburg, Ingrid boarded the *Italia*, an aging ocean liner which ran on a regular schedule between the ports of Hamburg and New York. Two days out of New York, on April 7, 1952, Ingrid turned thirteen. That evening the captain of the *Italia* arranged for a small birthday cake to grace Ingrid's dinner table. At the port in New York Ingrid was met by Red Cross representatives, who tucked her safely onto the *Coloradoan* at Grand Central Station, the train ride we had been denied by a strike in January 1951 when we first arrived in New York. The *Denver Post* wrote of Ingrid's arrival, "A tearful but happy reunion between a mother and her 13-year-old daughter she had to leave behind in Germany took place Saturday morning at Union Station when Ingrid Ferguson [Samuel] disembarked from the Burlington's Coloradoan, ending her long journey from Germany. While stationed in Germany more than a year ago, Sgt. Leo B. Ferguson married and shortly after was transferred to the United States. Mrs. Ferguson, who has two children, brought her son, Wolfgang, with them, but Ingrid was left with her grandparents. When it became possible for her to join them in Denver, Ferguson was assisted by the Red Cross, which advanced the funds for her passage and made arrangements for her travel. . . . I certainly take my hat off to the Red Cross for the way they helped us out, the sergeant said Saturday. They gave us the utmost assistance from start to finish. . . . Ingrid, whose thirteenth birthday arrived while she was two days at sea, didn't have much to say at the station. She was too busy choking back tears and hugging her mother and brother."

Not only were Hedy, Leo, and I at the station to meet Ingrid, so were Mr. Mills from the American Red Cross and a representative from the travel agency which had done such a wonderful job arranging Ingrid's journey from Hamburg to Denver. To everyone's surprise, Mr. Mills had arranged for a band of nearly twenty men and women to greet Ingrid upon her arrival at Union Station. The band played happy tunes appropriate to the occasion. For once, none of us gave a thought to money or any of our many problems. All that mattered was that Ingrid was reunited with her mother. Ingrid had indeed grown considerably and was taller than her mother.

We all settled into our new home on Wheeling Street, still without a lawn or backyard fence, things yet to come and to be paid for. Ingrid's arrival gave me a new perspective on America. I found it both amazing and touching that a German girl could be received with such genuine warmth less than seven years after a bitter war had been fought between the two countries. A band to welcome my sister. A reporter to cover her story. Photographs in the newspaper. Who had ever heard of such a thing? It was all so different here. There we were refugees from the east; here, we were real people.

Ingrid fit right into her new world. Soon she was babysitting in our new neighborhood, making friends and earning a little spending money for the little things a young girl her age needed. That autumn Ingrid entered the ninth grade at Aurora Junior High School. She had none of the language problems I encountered. It wasn't just that she had been exposed to some English instruction in Germany before coming to the United States; she obviously inherited from her mother whatever it was that made learning a new language so easy for Hedy.

CHAPTER 12

High School Graduation

My junior year at East High School drew to a close. My grades were mostly Cs with an occasional A or D. I continued to take typing. Although I typed sixty-five words a minute, I received a C in the course. At Opportunity School I received an A for typing forty-five words a minute. My teacher, who never once spoke to me during the academic year, didn't really seem to know who I was, except that I was a boy in a class of all girls. I accepted my grades without comment; I just wanted to pass my courses and graduate. A time or two I wondered if my teachers had any idea how difficult it was for an immigrant boy to master in a year what my American-born classmates had absorbed over a lifetime. I didn't feel sorry for myself. To the contrary, I was immensely grateful for the opportunity to be back in school again. Yet, an occasional kind word of encouragement would have gone a long way to make my high school experience less of a chore. At East High School I remained mostly a nonentity, passing unnoticed down corridors and through classrooms, like a boy without a face.

My friend Dave's family owned an ironworks on the north side of Denver where the Germans, Italians, and Poles lived. Dave asked me if I would be interested in a summer job. I jumped at the chance to do something other than stocking shelves in the auto parts store where I still worked after school and occasionally on weekends. The pay was $1.75 an hour—big money. I had never been paid more than eighty-five cents before. Dave also found a summer job for Jack, another friend of his who attended East, that is, when he wasn't skipping class. Dave and Jack were at opposite ends of the intellectual spectrum, and I never quite figured out how the two got together, much less what motivated Dave to sustain their friendship. Jack adored Dave, looking up to him as if he was a demigod. Not particularly motivated, Jack's chances of graduating from East seemed slim to me. Jack inherited ten thousand dollars from an aunt who died unexpectedly. His parents let him spend the money any way he wished. Ten thousand dollars was the cost of Hedy and Leo's new house. If I had that much money, I would have paid off their mortgage. But I didn't have ten thousand dollars; Jack did. He bought a Willy's Overland Jeep, then spent the remainder of his money frivolously. By the time I graduated from East a year later, in 1953, Jack had gone through much of his inheritance and quit school. I viewed my world through the prism of my own needs and values, so I believed Jack had wasted a great opportunity.

The three of us, Dave, Jack, and I, met every morning that summer near East High School and rode to work in Jack's new Willy's Overland. Dave, who worked in the plant office somewhere, dressed in a white shirt, tie, and slacks, and walked around the plant in his ponderous, Frankenstein-like way each morning and afternoon trying to look important. I had no idea what Dave was looking at or inspecting. He would stop here and there. After watching for a few minutes, he would nod his head approvingly and move on. Jack worked on the assembly line, moving mining car bodies from one work station to another, a dirty job. I worked on the bull gang, an even dirtier job than Jack's.

The bull gang did whatever was required. We mostly unloaded steel plates from railroad flatcars, using an overhead crane. A dangerous job, it was easy to lose a limb, even your life. The foreman was a muscular man in his late twenties, who without fail rolled up his sleeves to reveal his bulging biceps, making certain that all of us took note. His major topic of conversation was his many female conquests. Apparently no woman could resist his charms. At times he would stop work, a steel plate dangling dangerously from the crane, and make us listen to the intimate details of his amorous exploits. In that environment I was exposed to a compendium of American expletives. At first, taking the foreman's expletives too literally, I thought his language shocking. Then I began to talk just like him. Hedy and Leo put a quick stop to that when I began to use my newly learned vocabulary at home. When I wasn't unloading steel plates, I was assigned to chip away the porous black skin that formed over welds on finished mining cars. Using a pointed hammer I chipped away at the hard crusts, splinters constantly flying into my eyes. I was issued a hammer, but no safety goggles. When I finished, someone inspected the welds to see if they were flawed and had to be redone. Chipping welds and unloading steel plates was my daily routine.

One morning I stepped into the foundry where pig iron was smelted on fires so hot the men worked clad in leather pants and full-body leather aprons, their hands covered in leather gloves reaching above their elbows, heads shielded by leather skull caps. Big, muscular men swung ladles and buckets of glowing molten iron, pouring the dangerous liquid into clay forms to make wheels and couplings for mining cars. Everything in the foundry was either black or shimmering in tones of gold. The heat was like a wall when I entered, suddenly taking me from a ninety-degree summer day into a world where the temperature never dipped below one hundred degrees Fahrenheit. I couldn't figure out how the men who worked in that Hades-like environment could stand it. But there they were every day, sweating profusely, drinking enormous amounts of water, and whiskey, their bodies marked with elliptical white scars from hot iron spray that splattered and, in spite of all precautions, landed on exposed skin.

It was difficult to hear anything intelligible above the roaring foundry fires, the scraping sounds of coke being shoveled into hungry ovens, the clatter of machines, the hiss of iron pouring from glowing buckets, the sucking sounds of huge cooling fans, men shouting and yelling. Yet somehow these men who worked in this world of heat, noise, and constant physical danger managed to communicate with one another and formed a smoothly functioning team. Everyone seemed to know his role in the dangerous ballet being played out before my eyes. No one gave me a look as I entered the foundry, their full concentration on the task at hand. I went back that afternoon. Everything was quiet. The fires were banked. The huge fans silent. The men were tossing dice, wads of money in one hand, dice in the other, properly spit upon, shaken up against the ear, tossed hard or soft, depending on the thrower's inclination, always accompanied by a fervent prayer and a rich mixture of curses—curses so graphic, they made me cringe. Even on the bull gang I never heard such language. Every toss of the dice elicited shouts of joy and equally intense curses, hallelujahs, expressions of disgust, even despair. Money changed hands. Then the ritual began all over again. I had discovered and entered yet another new world.

In the assembly hall where the mining cars took shape, a different type of man was at work. They were of German, Polish and Italian heritage, operating huge machines that cut to proper size the iron plates I helped unload from railroad flatcars. After cutting, the plates were bent into the proper shape, which after still further processing would eventually emerge as finished mining cars, ready to be painted. Everything at the plant was iron and steel. During my lunch break I often went into the assembly hall to watch the men. They didn't throw dice; they played a simple game of flipping quarters. One or the other would call heads or tails, and at the end of the day they settled up. I got to know one of the machine operators. One day he asked me if I wanted to flip. By day's end he owed me over three hundred dollars. "I don't have that much money on me," he said. "Can I pay you off a few dollars at a time?" I knew that wasn't the way things were done. The men always settled their gambling debts at the end of a shift. No carry over. Something wasn't right. I just wanted to get out of the situation; I tried to lose, but couldn't. Nearly every time I called heads or tails it came up my way. I suggested we "go double or nothing." I won again. He owed me nearly six hundred dollars. When I lost on the next toss, I walked away. He knew what I had done. I didn't need enemies here. I just wanted to make a few honest dollars.

I needed to find another place to eat my lunch, away from the coin flippers. So I decided to watch the painter who worked on the opposite side of the assembly building painting finished mining cars a bright yellow. He was a thin, jovial man and liked his booze. He always had a bottle near him, wrapped in a brown paper bag. The painter worked alone, wearing a mask, and those parts of his body not covered by his coveralls, gloves, and hat, he smeared with petroleum jelly from a five-gallon tub. The fine paint spray got into everything. At the end of the day he wiped himself clean, the paint and the Vaseline coming off easily. He asked me if I would mind doing the job for a couple of weeks while he went on vacation. I said OK, as long as it was all right with management. He got permission to train me, which took all of one day. I already had learned most of the job by watching him work while I ate my sandwich. The following day I was on my own. Doing something different and satisfying as well was fun at first. At the end of my shift I could see the product of my labors—two, sometimes three, bright yellow mining cars ready for delivery to a customer. The downside was that working in a mask for most of the day was very uncomfortable, and washing dried paint off my skin and out of my hair was a challenge.

Several days later Dave stopped by during my lunch break, wearing his white shirt and tie, projecting a boss-man image. He greeted me like a subordinate. I asked him if I should get paid a painter's wage rather than my wage as a roustabout. He promised to look into it. On the way to work the next morning I asked him if he raised the pay question with management. He said he did, but didn't look me in the eye when he said it. I knew he didn't. It didn't matter. Working at the plant was the best paying job I'd had since coming to Colorado. But I sure was glad when the painter returned from his vacation and I could return to chipping welds and unloading steel plates. Hedy appreciated the money I brought home.

Leo was promoted to master sergeant, the highest enlisted rank in the air force at the time. It still wasn't enough income to buy a good used car. Surprisingly, driving a car was one of the first things I learned when I came to Colorado. In the spring of 1951, when we still lived with Tom and Marie in their small house in Derby, a friend of Leo's brother Raymond took a liking to me and came by occasionally to give me a ride in his car—a prewar, two-seater Ford. I watched him go through the motions—push in the clutch, shift into gear, let out the clutch, push in the clutch again, shift into a higher gear, let out the clutch. After I watched him do that several times, I was convinced that I could drive if given the opportunity. He noticed my interest, and one day motioned for me to get into the driver's seat and drive. I laughed and shook my head. He wouldn't take no for an answer and instead said, "Yes. Please. You drive. I know you can do it."

He took me out on the highway, which wasn't traveled all that much, put me behind the wheel, and said, "Drive." He sat beside me, casually lit a cigarette, appearing totally unconcerned. I knew only an American would do something like that, turn over his car to a kid. A German never would. I shifted without once grinding the gears—first, second, third. A piece of cake. I was looking right in front of the car, and the pavement was zipping by so fast I didn't know how to keep up. "Look up," he said between puffs on his cigarette, not a smidgen of concern reflected in his voice. "Look straight ahead and everything will slow down for you," he said in a mixture of German and English. It did. I was driving—thirty, forty, fifty miles per hour. It felt good. It was so easy, I thought, such an empowering experience. He kept puffing away on his cigarette, appearing not the least concerned that I might wreck his car. We came up behind a slow-moving tractor pulling a load of hay. He calmly turned toward me and without raising his voice said, "You are closing too fast. Slow down." I zoomed around the tractor a bit too fast, and in the process learned an important lesson about closure rates and traffic moving at different speeds on the same highway. I wouldn't make that mistake again. We drove around a bit more, and at the end of our drive he taught me how to back up and park. What a fun day that was. When he saw Leo, he asked if he could get me a driver's license.

"The boy is a natural," he bragged to Leo. "I taught him to drive in one session. Didn't grind the gears once." Leo laughed.

"Sure, go ahead. He'll need a license one day." So my friend-turned-driving-instructor took me to the Derby driver's license office, staffed by two kind-looking middle-aged ladies in flowery dresses with reading glasses low on their noses. My friend did the talking. He cautioned me beforehand that maybe I would have to go out for a test drive with someone. The lady in the flowery dress, looking over her reading glasses, asked me, "Where did you learn to drive?" I knew very few words of English, so my friend, a former GI who'd been stationed in Germany and picked up some *Gasthaus* German, translated. It wasn't pretty, but I understood.

"In the fields," I replied in German, "not on a street." My friend translated. I thought if I told her how I really learned to drive I would get him into trouble.

"In the fields," she repeated, laughing and shaking her head. Then she issued me my driver's license. I didn't drive a car again for another year. The next time I drove was when my friend Jim drove his father's new Mercury, picked up his girlfriend after dark, and asked me to drive while they made out in the backseat. I said fine. The Mercury was much newer than the prewar Ford on which I learned to drive. It even had directional signals—I didn't have to stick my hand out the window to indicate a turn.

Jim didn't know it was only the second time in my life that I had driven a car, and this time it was through the darkened streets of Denver.

Summer vacation ended and it was time to go back to school. My job at the ironworks ended as well. They only needed full-time workers. I found a job in a creamery near East High School, not far from where Dave lived. I sold milk products and ice cream for seventy-five cents an hour. Besides dipping ice cream, I mopped floors, cleaned the toilet, and did all the many tasks no one else wanted to do. When I asked for a five-cent raise, the owner said no. So I left and went to work as a stock clerk at a Woolworth store, much nearer to where I lived and on my bus route to school. There I worked until late spring of 1953 when Leo, through a friend of his, got me a job at the Lowry AFB Non-Commissioned Officers Club. The NCO Club paid $1.25 an hour and threw in a free meal as well. The best thing about the job was that the club was near the Lowry runway and I could on occasion go outside and watch airplanes take off and land. Once I saw an F-80 jet fighter land with its wheels up. The plane slid on its belly off the runway, then turned 180 degrees facing in the opposite direction. I wondered how the pilot could possibly forget to put his gear down. I still wanted to fly more than ever.

During my final semester of school I dropped out of ROTC. It was boring and no one seemed to take an interest in me. I was never picked for a leadership position, nor was my name ever called for anything. I was just a body filling a chair. Although I wore my uniform proudly, and always made sure it was clean and pressed, it was as if I didn't exist for any of the ROTC instructors, all World War II veterans. They looked right through me. Neither the captain nor the two sergeants ever greeted me or showed an interest in anything I did. They couldn't turn me away since I was a legitimate student, but they didn't have to like having a German boy in their classes. I decided to take physical education instead, or health, as it was called in the fifties. The situation was no better there. The coach focused solely on his athletes. As for the rest of us, he didn't care what we did as long as we showed up. Everyone got an A in health. That part I liked.

I did learn one thing in ROTC—to be able to wear the gold lieutenant bars I bought at the pawnshop in Denver I would have to go to college and participate in army or air force ROTC to earn what the instructors referred to as a commission. High school ROTC didn't lead to anything. Not only was I new to America with only the vaguest understanding of its practices and institutions; I had no money to speak of to finance a college education. There was no government-backed student loan program then, nor any other source of funds to help finance the education of the poor and indigent. Only one person in my family had ever studied at a university, a cousin of my father Willie's, the daughter of one of my grandmother Samuel's many sisters who lived in Berlin. No one on my mother's side, or in Leo's family, had given university education a thought. Finishing high school was about as much as any of them aspired to. I knew I would have to do this on my own, and I had no concept of the nature and scope of the obstacles I would face in my quest to earn the gold bars of a second lieutenant in the United States Air Force. But my ignorance probably was a blessing. Had I known the difficulties that lay ahead I would surely have been intimidated. I wanted more than anything to fly with the men of the Berlin airlift. I wanted to be just like them, be one of them. My future course was set for me, and nothing would change that in the years ahead.

College became the overriding topic of conversation for most senior students at East. They talked about college incessantly, were called out of class to meet with visiting university counselors, made applications, broadcast their acceptances, and basked in the glow of their successes. For many of my classmates it seemed that life was one big round of clubs, dances, football and basketball games, good grades, accolades, and the crowning achievement—the college of their choice. I heard the words Ivy League, Northwestern, and Berkeley bandied about. The students called out of class to meet with admissions counselors from those prestigious institutions rose from their seats fully aware of the looks they garnered from their classmates. They were the chosen ones. I didn't really understand much of what was going on. The process was not only new, but totally confusing to me. I talked to Dave and Jim about it, and they both said they intended to enroll at the University of Colorado, a state institution less expensive than private colleges and universities and, according to them, just as good.

With Dave's help I applied for admission to the University of Colorado and was accepted as a Colorado resident. At that time the university had to accept everyone who was a state resident, wanted to attend, and was in the upper half of his or her high school class. I was soon to find out how efficient the University of Colorado was at weeding out the slackers, incompetents, and party boys and girls in their freshman year.

I had no idea what a university campus might look like and was anxious to go up to Boulder to take a look. Dave borrowed the family car one Saturday morning, and we took the Denver-Boulder Turnpike to the small college town. A lovely enclave of reddish, native sandstone buildings clustered around tree-shaded quadrangles, flush-up against one of the most beautiful sections of the Rocky Mountains. I stood in front of Old Main, the oldest building on campus, looking southwest toward the Flat Irons, an upturned sandstone formation which formed the backdrop for this idyllic campus setting. What was I doing here? I wondered. Was I worthy to come to a place of such beauty? After all, I was a refugee boy more familiar with the sounds of exploding bombs and shattering bullets, the sights and smells of overcrowded camps, black marketeers, and women selling their bodies to feed their children. The university campus seemed like something out of a fairytale, a place of extravagant beauty and solitude, untouched by the ills of the rest of the world. Would I fit in? I finally began to understand the excitement of my high school classmates to leave for places such as the University of Colorado.

As graduation loomed I was called into my counselor's office and informed by Miss Pigott that after a review of my records she found I would be short one course, one-half credit hour, to graduate in June. I would have to go to summer school. I intended to work during the summer to make the money I needed to go to college. I protested that I had taken all the courses she recommended, so why couldn't I graduate? "I made a mistake, Wolfgang," she said honestly. "I am so sorry. It's just another five weeks."

"Can't you fix it?"

"No," she said, "I can't." I saw she was truly sorry for her oversight.

"Can I participate in the graduation exercises," I asked her, "or is there another ceremony at the end of the summer?"

"No, there is no ceremony at the end of the summer. Yes, you can participate in the commencement exercises, but you will have to sit with others like you in a special section at the rear of the auditorium. You will not be allowed to go on stage to receive a diploma. Your diploma will be mailed to you when you complete summer school. You'll learn all the details in the next assembly."

I was thrilled to graduate from high school in America and amazed to learn I ranked 325 out of 750 students, but I also felt diminished by my counselor's revelations. Once more I was put into a category of people with a blemish, like being a refugee, a displaced person, or any number of categories I'd been a part of in my past which branded me a lesser person. I had to sit in the back of the room to watch my classmates go up on stage, be congratulated, and receive their diplomas. I would not be allowed to do the same, and the occasion would never present itself again. Hedy, Ingrid, and Leo would not see me graduate in a proper ceremony. Why couldn't the school administration have come up with a blank sheet of paper to hand to students like me? Why couldn't our hands be shaken, congratulations extended, and our families allowed to see us walk across the stage?

The Angelus, the much-awaited yearbook for the class of 1953, was finally delivered. We asked classmates to sign next to their pictures, write a few witty or inane words, and wish each other lots of luck, success, and happiness for the future. My yearbook had some odd comments, such as "Sam, I didn't know your name until today. Lotsa luck! Jane"; or "I don't know you very well, but you are a swell guy. Sandy." There were some thoughtful comments as well, which made me think that maybe I was a part of the school after all. "I can't forget your name," wrote Sharon Wood. "I never before had the privilege of knowing a German boy. I am glad I did." Al Waxman observed, "I admired your ability to adapt." Then he forecast, "This trait will surely prove invaluable in the future." And Marty Fass thought me "a fellow with classic features, classic voice (not accent), and unusually distinctive personality. Shakespeare and English Lit were heightened by your presence." Of course, I had my favorite teachers sign as well—Miss Virginia Stearns, history; Miss Blanche Pigott, my counselor;

Mr. Howard Williamson, chemistry; and Miss Florence Harper, who, for me at least, made more than one of Shakespeare's characters come to life.

Most seniors didn't take a full course load their last semester, arranging their schedules accordingly from the very beginning. The social season at East was, for many of the more affluent students, a never ending parade of parties, dances, dinners, photo opportunities, and dressy occasions. There were kings and queens a plenty, and many equally richly dressed attendants for the senior prom, homecoming, and the May and sweetheart dances. The senior prom was held on May 16 in the posh Shirley Savoy Hotel with Chuck Bennett and his orchestra providing the evening's entertainment. The prom's theme was "City Lights," and benches and fancy lampposts with blue lights were scattered throughout the ballroom to provide the desired effect. It was a very formal event, a kind of coming out party, where a boy presented his girl with a corsage of orchids matching the color of her gown. Many of the corsages cost considerable sums of money, depending on the number and variety of orchids chosen by the boy to impress his date. On May 29 a senior class luncheon was held in the Silver Glade Room of the Cosmopolitan Hotel. As the *East High School Spotlight*, the class paper, put it, "The luncheon is one of the last get-togethers of the senior class, and many memories of the years at East will be recalled." If that wasn't enough, concluded the *Spotlight*, "One of the highlights of the graduates will be the senior class picnic on June 1 at Elitch's Gardens." I didn't have time or money to participate in any of these events, although I would have liked to.

Graduation was an elaborately staged affair. On the evening of June 3, 1953, 712 graduating seniors and the faculty of East High School were escorted to their seats in the Denver City Auditorium by ninety junior escorts and ushers. We were the largest graduating class in the city of Denver. Boys were clad in black caps and gowns, girls in white. The graduation theme was Freedom, Liberty, and Democracy, and to give expression to the theme graduates formed the letters F, L, and D by mixing white-gowned girls with black-gowned boys. My group of thirty-eight "incompletes" sat quietly in a remote corner in the rear of the auditorium. We too wore black and white, yet we were not part of the ceremony, only spectators.

The invocation was followed by eleven student speakers who spoke of the meaning of freedom and democracy. I could have told them a couple of things on the subject of freedom, or the lack of it, but no one asked. After the speeches, there was plenty of music by Bach, Mendelssohn, and Tchaikovsky, topped-off by everyone singing Francis Scott Keys' "Star-Spangled Banner."

The graduation program listed the names of all graduates, including those of us who would finish in summer school, an asterisk next to our names to identify us as incompletes. The recipients of prestigious awards and scholarships were listed prominently in the front of the program. Scholarships from Amherst, Brandeis, Brown, Columbia, Cornell, Dartmouth, MIT, Mills, Monmouth, Mount Holyoke, Northwestern, Oberlin, Princeton, Radcliffe, Ripon, Wellesley, and Yale were listed, along with scholarships and awards granted by Navy ROTC, Sears Roebuck, the B.P.O.E. Elks, Knights of Pythias, Westinghouse Science, and the American Can Company. Spanish, French, and German awards were also recognized. Prominent names in the class of 1953 were Norman R. Augustine—one of two students with a scholarship to Princeton, the recipient of the Bud Earnest Award in Journalism, and a recipient of a Certificate of Accomplishment in Mathematics; and Nancy Van Derbur, whose younger sister Marilyn, a junior at East, would eventually become a Miss America. The Class of 1953 was to make its mark in life with accomplishments great and small. For some of the boys the graduation themes of "Freedom, Liberty, and Democracy" were to become all too real only ten years later in the rice paddies of South Vietnam, and in the flak- and missile-tainted skies over North Vietnam. By then my high school years no longer mattered, and graduation day was long forgotten.

I finished summer school in July, and the school administration, as promised, sent me my diploma in the mail. That summer I worked as many hours as possible at the NCO Club to earn money for college. I had no idea of the actual costs I would face as a freshman. I knew Leo and Hedy wouldn't be able to help, especially since Leo decided to retire from the air force. Leo had been transferred from Lowry AFB to Frances E. Warren Air Force Base near Cheyenne, Wyoming, a former cavalry post three hours driving time north of Denver. Hedy didn't want any part of Wyoming. She wasn't about to move. "I have my house in Denver," she told Leo. "I have my friends here. I don't want to go anywhere else. I won't leave. Maybe it's time for you to look for another job, Leo." Leo put in his papers. His military retirement, at age forty-one, after twenty-four years of military service, was approved for September 30, 1953. Leo applied for a civil service position at Lowry AFB as a supply specialist, his field of expertise, and was lucky to be offered a position within a year. While he waited for a position to open up, Leo had to make a living. It was to be a difficult year for both Hedy and Leo, and they had no money left over to support me in college.

Leo Benjamin Ferguson, my wonderful stepfather, had enlisted in the field artillery in 1928 at age sixteen to escape a world of poverty and lack of opportunity. He spent much of his time at Fort Sill, Oklahoma, as an artillery gunner, then transferred to Scofield Barracks in Hawaii, to the same unit made famous in the movie *From Here to Eternity*. Leo and I went to see that movie when it first came out in 1953, the only movie we ever went to see together. For Leo it was like reliving his past. He kept on nodding his head during the movie, as if wanting to let me know that that's the way it was. "I too had to put on boxing gloves," Leo said after the movie without elaborating. There was no smile on his face. In 1939 he transferred to the Army Air Corps and found himself at Lowry Field when war erupted in December 1941. He remained at Lowry for the duration of the war and in 1948 shipped out to Germany in support of the Berlin airlift.

During the summer of 1953 I had a little time to myself, time to think about things new and unusual. One thing that bothered me ever since arriving in Colorado was that I didn't have to register anywhere, didn't need a government passport, was not required to have any form of personal identification. In Germany I had to register with the police and couldn't move anywhere without first getting permission from someone in authority. I actually had two passports in Germany—a refugee pass and an ordinary pass. In Colorado, I had nothing to prove who I was, and it continued to make me uncomfortable.

I recalled a conversation I had with Leo in 1949 when I still lived in the Trauen refugee camp on the fringe of the Fassberg airfield. I asked Leo through my mother, "Do you have identification cards in America, and what do they look like?"

"No," Leo replied, "we don't have identification cards. Only in the military," and he showed me his military ID card. Hedy didn't have to translate. I understood.

"Everyone has to have a pass," I insisted. "If you don't have a pass nobody will know who you are. You don't really exist without a passport. Maybe you don't remember, Leo."

Leo laughed, his blue eyes sparkling, and replied, "Wolfgang, I remember very well. We don't have identification cards in America. We are a free people. We don't need passes to tell us who we are or where we live." I was confused. I thought I knew what freedom meant—no police knocking on my door at night and taking me away; no schoolmaster forcing me to take courses I didn't want to take, or beating me up if I resisted. Freedom was being able to speak my mind without worrying about someone turning me in to the police and being arrested for subversive activities against the state because of what I had supposedly said. I still thought I had to have a pass, an official identification card of some kind. Without an identification I didn't really exist, did I?

By the summer of 1953 I still hadn't resolved my dilemma, didn't have an answer to my questions. I had a driver's license and a social security card which cautioned in bold letters NOT FOR IDENTIFICATION. That's all. Some people in America didn't even have that much. I remained uncomfortable, knowing that no bureaucrat, no policeman, no one in the country required me to have a pass of any kind. It was a new and strange concept for me to absorb and get used to.

CHAPTER 13

A Taste of Failure

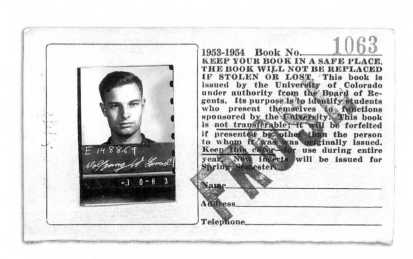

Early in September 1953 I moved to Boulder. Only freshman women were required to live on campus, since there wasn't enough housing to accommodate everyone who might have wanted to live in dormitories. Numerous fraternity and sorority houses provided accommodations for their members, while the rest of the student body had to make do with what was available "on the hill," that part of Boulder adjacent to the university campus. Housing there was scarce. Accommodations which under normal circumstances would have found few or no takers, were quickly snapped up by students. Dave and Jim came up before me and found a boarding house for the three of us, suitable only because it was cheap. The windowless rooms once served as root and coal cellars. I couldn't believe my eyes when I saw what they had come up with. A few low-wattage light bulbs barely illuminated our study tables. The place was damp, smelled of its past, and reminded me of a dungeon. I had little money, so it had to do. I thought our landlady should be ashamed of herself to demand money for a root cellar, but as we soon learned in Economics 101, it was simply a matter of supply and demand. The following semester Jim moved into a place of his own, and Dave and I moved into a fraternity house.

My first days at the university were both confusing and fun. I had all of one hundred and some odd dollars to my name. I knew that wasn't going to take me far. The first thing I needed to do was find a job. The woman who rented us her root cellar agreed to take me on as a hasher for the lunch period. In return I got to eat supper, as she called it, for free. I figured one good meal a day was all I needed. I considered modeling naked for the art department, which paid twenty-five dollars a session, but after thinking about it some more, I decided to pass. Instead, I took a job in the university cafeteria as a dishwasher. Two of us worked the late afternoon and evening shifts. Either I loaded the dishwasher, a huge contraption similar in layout to a carwash, and my partner unloaded at the other end, or we traded positions to keep from getting bored. Loading the washer included removing trays filled with dirty dishes and trash from a constantly moving elevator which moved the trays to our level from the main dining area below and took them back down again if we weren't quick enough. At times when we got so busy we couldn't keep up, the trays went up and down, up and down, again and again, until we finally got to them. All too frequently students inserted their trays incorrectly, jamming the elevator. Jerry was a sophomore who had worked there the previous year. When the elevator got stuck, he punched the OFF button, ran downstairs as fast as he could, located the offending tray, yanked it out, and got the elevator moving again. At times he had to climb into the elevator to free a stuck tray. Even two jobs, hashing and dishwashing, weren't enough to pay for my books, room, board, tuition, and still leave a few pennies for incidentals. I was always looking for more work or a better paying job.

Before freshmen could register for classes we were required to take comprehensive examinations to determine our level of proficiency in mathematics, English, and the sciences. Dave and I went into the football stadium, registered, picked up our test booklets, and sat down in the controlled test area. The test took several hours, and a day or two later we learned how we had done and what courses we were allowed to sign up for. As freshmen, we had few options. Most courses were prescribed, depending on one's academic major, including a minimum and maximum number of credit hours. I hadn't thought about a major. I viewed college in classical European terms and assumed I'd be taking courses in English, ancient and world history, the classics, Greek and Latin, and so on. Dave laughed at my naivete. "Where do you think you are?" He slapped his thigh, as he did when he laughed at someone else's expense. "Plain and simple, this is a trade school, Wolfgang. Here you learn your future job. It has nothing to do with learning about Plato or Aristotle, Greek or Latin. I want to be an engineer, OK!? So I am taking engineering. When I graduate, I will work as an engineer. How much more practical can you get? This is not Germany, it's America. So, what do you want to be when you grow up?"

"I want to fly airplanes," I replied dejectedly. "I haven't really given much thought to any of this. Someone told me I have to have a college education to fly. So what do you think I should take?"

"You have to decide that for yourself," Dave advised off-handedly. He was right, of course. I thought, if engineering was good enough for

Dave, why not for me? When our test results came back, both Dave and I had incredibly high scores in mathematics. Our actual courses were pretty much laid out for us based on the academic major and test results. Engineering Problems was a course that taught us to use the slide rule, if we didn't already know how to use one, and we did various mathematical calculations to become comfortable with the most important tool of the engineering profession at the time. The slide rule was our computer; without it, you couldn't function as an engineer. Our English composition class was English for engineers. Just the basics. Our small red textbook was written so an engineer could understand its contents and not get confused by extraneous rules and exceptions. The title, Structural Grammar for Building Sentences, made it obvious that English was something to be endured. Sentence building was as far as the engineering faculty was going to take us. In later years when I had engineers working for me, I understood why so many of them couldn't put their thoughts coherently onto a piece of paper. Freshman Chemistry was a free-for-all course where hundreds of students sat together in an auditorium and listened to a disinterested graduate student talk about arcane aspects of chemistry. Courses such as this served dual purposes, one of which was to weed out those students not suited for a college education. The system worked admirably.

In Engineering Drawing, another mandatory course, we drew fancy letters and shapes and learned to become comfortable behind a drafting table. I soon found the entire exercise utterly boring and wondered what I was doing here. The coup de grace for me became Freshman Mathematics. Since I placed so high on my achievement test, the engineering curriculum guide placed me in an advanced mathematics class, a five-credit-hour course rather than the standard, three-credit-hour engineering freshmen mathematics course. There I sat with the best and the brightest—fellows like Norman Augustine from East who received certificates of accomplishment in mathematics at graduation from their high schools. In spite of my test scores, I was totally out of my league. I didn't understand the implications of my placement until it was too late. I ended up taking eighteen academic hours that first semester; most freshmen took no more than fifteen. There was no counseling, other than course assignments made by disinterested graduate students. Here I was, two jobs, looking for another, signed up for eighteen credit hours in the school of engineering, taking advanced mathematics. I bought my textbooks, used of course, slide rule, T-square, paper, pen, and pencils.

Dave and Jim, having come up to Boulder a week or so earlier, were by now experts on the best watering holes on the hill. We headed for The Sunken Garden, "The Sink," where you sat with a multitude of other students in well-worn wooden booths drinking pitchers of 3.2 beer. The Sink stank of beer and cigarette smoke. Even by student standards, The Sink was a hole, not a place where many girls wanted to be seen, especially in the evenings. In the same Thirteenth Street block near the campus was Tulagi's, definitely upscale when compared to The Sink. Tulagi's had subdued lighting, great for making out, clean tables and booths, and a crowded dance floor where young bodies could press close to one another while moving an inch or so at a time. The dance floor was usually packed on Friday and Saturday nights. Tulagi's was an old-fashioned "body shop," a place where boy met girl. Tulagi's, like The Sink, served 3.2 beer. Drink enough 3.2, and it could quite nicely help make a fool of you. Cee-You, as the University of Colorado was referred to by its students, was a well-known party school in the fifties, with a plentitude of sumptuous fraternity and sorority houses, nearby ski slopes, a football team to cheer on, if not about, and lots of good-looking girls from Winnetka, Illinois; Dallas, Texas; Westchester County, New York; and similar places—rich girls looking for a good time before being swallowed up by matrimony.

I soon learned that many of the CU students didn't fit the standard eighteen- to twenty-two-year-old mold. The student body included a fair number of older males, easily identified by the assorted pieces of military uniforms they wore like badges of honor. Their college tab was picked up by the U.S. Government under the provisions of the GI Bill, paying the former servicemen's tuition, books, and fees, and providing a generous monthly living allowance, a bit less for the Korean War veterans. Several of the older students ate at the boarding house where I hashed. The veterans came early for lunch and got together on the front porch to roll dice, "craps," as they called it. Cigarettes dangling from the corners of their mouths, holding their money in one hand and throwing dice with the other, they shouted and screamed with delight if they won, cursed if they lost. In many ways, they were not much different from the foundry workers I watched throwing the dice the previous summer. More money changed hands in those brief noontime crap shoots than I had ever seen in my life. The same men also liked wine, beer, whiskey, and women.

The veterans were usually the ones who initiated panty raids on the women's dormitories on a Friday or Saturday night, after they had a few beers at The Sink or Tulagi's, or stronger stuff from their private stocks. They quickly drummed up a crowd, and before long hundreds of male students would march on one of the women's dormitories, shouting for the girls to come out and show their panties. Some of the more daring and inebriated climbed the walls of the dormitory, a feat facilitated by the rough surface and uneven setting of the natural stone used in the buildings' construction. The women responded enthusiastically by throwing panties from their windows, getting the mob even more fired up. I remained on the fringe, looking on. I didn't like mobs. I thought they were dangerous and easily led to irresponsible action. Before long the campus police showed up, augmented by the Boulder sheriff's office, to contain the mob and get the girls to stop tossing panties and keep their windows shut. The mob would dissipate slowly under the watchful eyes of the deputies and return to less destructive pursuits. Panty raids usually happened around midterms and finals when the academic pressure demanded a venue for letting off steam. The older military veterans, many with combat experience, introduced a sense of controlled violence into an otherwise benign university world. I doubt if many recognized that, but I saw it for what it was. Given a little more latitude, I knew that some of the men would readily take from the women more than just their panties. I'd seen it all too often in the world I came from.

I signed up for army ROTC. After all, that was really why I was here, to earn a commission so I could be a flyer. The army issued us officers' uniforms. I especially liked the thick winter jacket, like a navy peacoat, double breasted and very warm. The Colorado winter of 1953–1954 was cold, and I got lots of good wear out of that army jacket. ROTC was not academically challenging. As freshmen we were taught standard World War II fare by World War II or Korean War combat veterans, mostly army captains and sergeants. Half the time they showed us movies, not movies made for college students, but the stuff the army used to show GIs in 1944 before they shipped overseas into combat. Included in the movie fare were movies on venereal disease: what it was, how you contracted it, how you recognized you had been infected, and what you had to do to prevent getting gonorrhea, syphilis, and any number of other things which kept young men from being good combat soldiers. The dialogue was presented in plain GI terminology by actors who demonstrated how to properly use a "prokit," the preferred option to thick army issue condoms which supposedly kept you from contracting one of the pesky diseases. Our eyes popped at times, and we walked out of the movie sessions quietly. All of us freshman boys thought about sex, but many of us had not yet experienced intercourse.

A sergeant from a Boulder army reserve unit showed up one day looking for recruits. He assured us there was no chance of being called up for the Korean "police action" as things were winding down. We would get paid regular army wages for the hours we spent in meetings. Never one to pass up a chance to make an extra dollar, I promptly signed up with the 365th Combat Engineer Battalion, United States Army (Reserve). I attended my first meeting in early October, signed papers, was issued yet another uniform and given the rank of private E-2. That spontaneous decision to join the army reserve benefitted me greatly in later years. At the time though, I was only interested in the immediate money it paid to help defray my mounting college expenses.

My academic performance took an ominous downward trend. I was doing terribly in my most important courses—engineering mathematics and chemistry. Near the five-week point I visited my mathematics professor and humbly requested that he allow me to drop the course and revert back to the slower-paced three-hour course. The professor gave me a cold stare and said gruffly, "Samuel, I saw your test score. Give it the old college try. By the way, you can no longer drop courses. You know that, don't you? You should have made your request last week. It's too late now," and with that encouraging note I was excused. It was depressing. I knew I was totally unprepared to keep up in the class I was in.

I fared no better in chemistry. At the end of the semester I had accumulated nine credit hours of Fs. Not really knowing what to do, I switched to Arts and Sciences for the spring semester, never mind a major. I reduced my course load from eighteen to fifteen semester hours as well. By the time my freshman year ended in late May 1954, I had a C-minus grade-point average and many unpaid bills needing attention. I obtained a two-hundred-dollar loan from the university at a moderate interest rate, to be paid off in installments over the next year. A temporary band-aid. I knew I must find a well-paying summer job if I wanted to come back to CU in the fall.

I attended my reserve meetings, hashed at a fraternity house, and continued to wash dishes in the university cafeteria. Jerry, my cafeteria co-worker, was also an Army ROTC cadet. One Thursday, uniform day, in the spring, we both took off our blouses and ties and donned white, full-body aprons. It was one of those crazy days when students constantly inserted their trays wrongly into the elevator, and Jerry would race down the stairs to get the thing moving again. He removed one stuck tray and came running up and hit the ON button. Nothing happened. He hit ON, OFF, ON, ON—nothing happened. "Don't touch anything," he said to me, "there's got to be another tray stuck somewhere." He ran back downstairs. He was gone for much longer than usual, and I wondered what was keeping him. I looked down the elevator shaft but couldn't see him. Then the elevator jerked. I thought he was working on it. Suddenly there was a loud commotion, and I heard students screaming for an ambulance and asking if there was a doctor in the house. I ran downstairs to see the lifeless body of my friend dangling out of the elevator shaft. The elevator had crushed his chest. Nobody should die washing dishes, nobody. An inquest was held. I testified and relived the terrible affair one more time for experts guessing what could possibly have gone wrong with the elevator. The presiding judge finally declared it an unfortunate accident.

I turned nineteen in February 1954. Girls were constantly on my mind—morning, noon, and night. I still hadn't progressed beyond my high school hang-ups in my attitude toward women. I could always find a date for a dance, an evening at Tulagi's, or some other social affair, but beyond holding hands and an occasional kiss, I was as inept and fearful around women as ever. True sex, the experience so ardently longed for, remained elusive. I became almost paralyzed when I was alone with a girl, particularly when it became obvious that she probably wanted to do more than just clinch and kiss. Whenever a girl made herself vulnerable to me, I didn't know how to handle the situation.

A big dance was scheduled in the new Glenn Miller ballroom in the student union. Jim mentioned that he could fix us up with some really good-looking student nurses from Denver—the catch being, we had to get them back to their dormitory by eleven o'clock. We picked up the nurses in Denver; they were as nice-looking as Jim had promised. They were quite giggly, and liked to hold hands, hug, even exchange a kiss or two. By ten fifteen it was time to leave. It was Jim's car. He drove on the way up to Boulder and asked me to drive on the way back. We were running late, and the girls exhorted me to drive faster. They had a curfew and didn't want to be late and get penalized. I said to Dave and Jim, "OK, I am going to speed, but if we get stopped we split the cost of the ticket." We did get stopped by a friendly deputy sheriff just after getting off the Denver-Boulder Turnpike. A week later I stood in front of a justice of the peace who fined me forty dollars—forty dollars I didn't have. Jim paid his share, but Dave wouldn't. "I didn't agree to that," Dave told me to my face. I couldn't believe it. To me it was a debt of honor, a matter of integrity. That episode ended our friendship. Since Leo didn't have any money to help out, I went to his brother Raymond, who somehow came up with the dollars I needed to keep from spending two weeks in jail.

At the end of my first year of college I had a C-minus grade average, was in debt to the University and Raymond, and didn't have a summer job. To make matters worse, before I could start a job I had to participate in a three-week active duty summer encampment with my combat engineer reserve unit at Fort Carson, south of Colorado Springs. At Fort Carson I had lots of time to think and I realized that it wasn't the big decisions that got me where I was; it was many little decisions, often made on the spur of the moment, like joining the 365th Combat Engineer Battalion. Fort Carson was larger than the smallest state in the Union. Artillery with a range of twenty miles could free-fire without interfering with twenty thousand soldiers living and training on post. Entire army divisions could vanish from sight in the vastness of Fort Carson. Ours was just a company-size unit, joining up with other units of our battalion located throughout the state of Colorado. The sergeant who enticed me to sign up as a reservist assigned me to the communications section. It was my task to crank a generator to provide power for our field radios. Hard work! I was hungry all the time. I ate my meals, begged for seconds, and was still hungry. Cranking that generator gave me muscles and a huge appetite. Fortunately, the field exercise didn't last for ever, and I was glad to return to the barracks. I soon found myself qualifying with the M1 rifle and a submachine gun, which the guys referred to as a "grease gun." The grease gun was the same kind of weapon that armed the American soldiers when they captured us in early 1945, just west of the town of Wismar near the Baltic Sea. We were running from the Russians with a retreating German army unit that had the heart to take us along on their flight to the American lines—Hedy, Ingrid, my grandmother Grapentin, and me.

The Americans forced us into a refugee camp, a camp without water or food, with sanitary conditions, so awful that soon many of my young friends were dying of cholera. It was in that camp where I met my first American soldier. He carried a grease gun, just like the one I fired at Fort Carson. The American approached with a smile on his broad, brown face, waving his hand for me to come closer. He wore a tanker's uniform with brown combat boots laced high, pants bloused over his boots, a brown army shirt open at the throat, and a beige windbreaker. He wore his helmet the way all the other soldiers wore theirs, with the straps dangling loosely under his chin. He carried his grease gun upside down, slung over his right shoulder. He stretched out his hand and offered me a piece of something wrapped in yellow paper. I didn't know what it was or what to do with it. He noticed my hesitation and took another piece for himself and unwrapped it. A flat, gray stick. He shoved it into his mouth and began to chew vigorously. I followed his example and stuck this thing in my mouth and began to chew. It tasted good, but soon lost its flavor and turned into a rubbery ball—so I spit it out. The soldier shook his head in disappointment. He took off his helmet, revealing a shock of raven black hair, and wiped the sweat off his forehead with the back of his left hand. Then he gave me another stick wrapped in yellow paper. "C-H-E-W-I-N-G G-U-M," he said, repeating the phrase two more times. Then he took the gum out of his mouth and stuck it behind his left ear. He looked at me, smiled, and took the gum from behind his left ear and put it back in his mouth, again chewing vigorously. I got the message. I put the stick of gum in my pocket and said, "*Danke schön.*" I never forgot the American soldier with the grease gun who took the time to meet a German boy at the end of a long and ugly war.

I learned to fire a bazooka at a junked Sherman tank, or at least a sergeant tried to teach us to fire the bazooka. I thought he positioned us much too far away from the tank to have any chance of hitting it. The sergeant didn't think much of my suggestion and told me to keep my mouth shut and do what I was told. He didn't wear any ribbons on his chest, so I couldn't tell if he was a combat veteran or just a desk soldier. From his behavior, I assumed it was the latter. None of us hit the tank with the bazooka that afternoon. Then a bunch of us were put into driving school to learn to drive everything from jeeps to weapons carriers to ten-wheel army trucks. In the large trucks we were taken out on a hilly, dusty driving range, and while one of us jerked the truck around, the rest of us sat in back holding onto a bench for dear life. After a day of that I felt turned inside-out, totally exhausted. Whenever we stopped, I put my helmet on the bench, using it as a pillow, and went to sleep. At Fort Carson I gained an appreciation for what it meant to be an infantry soldier.

Summer camp wasn't all work. On Saturday noon, after passing an open-ranks inspection and marching in a parade, which ended precisely at noon, we were given the rest of the day off. We were ready to head for town and raise hell. About eight of us went to the mess hall to eat, then, without changing into civilian clothes, we headed for town. People in Colorado Springs liked and respected uniforms. One fellow knew the area well and took us to a place in Manitou Springs. "You'll like this place," he prom- ised. "Girls," he said, winking at us. Manitou Springs was up a canyon on Highway 24 near a bunch of tourist attractions—Garden of the Gods, Cave of the Winds, Indian Cliff Dwellings, the Balanced Rock. The main street was lined with souvenir shops and hamburger joints looking for a quick buck from passing tourists. We were feeling our oats after a week of eating dust, ordered a round of beers, and weren't exactly the most quiet bunch of young men. No one seemed to mind. A group of young women sitting in a large booth kept looking at us, smiling. They seemed to be in their twenties, nice-looking girls. Before I knew it we were buying them drinks, talking, and laughing. I found myself sitting next to a brunette who kept looking in my eyes as if she had found her knight in shining armor. We danced really close to tunes from a juke box, me in my combat boots. By the time we left that evening all of us had had a great time. Some of our group vanished; the rest of us took a cab back to Carson.

That attractive brunette agreed to meet me late on Sunday afternoon. I couldn't wait to see her again. After eating a light Italian meal, we went for a walk, holding hands. I could tell she liked me as much as I liked her, at least I thought she did. It was twilight, the last rays of the sun disappear- ing behind the mountains. I noticed a secluded place up a slight incline behind some bushes. I looked at Marilyn. She looked at me. We both scrambled up the hillside. I took off my prized suede jacket and spread it out on the grass for us to sit on. She reached under her skirt, stepped out of her panties and lay down. "This is what you really want, don't you?" she said, a smile in her voice and on her face. My heart pounded in my throat. I couldn't say a thing; I was too excited. I remember how wonder- ful it was. I suddenly understood a lot of things about men and women. We made love three times. I asked her, "Again?" She smiled and said, "No. That's quite enough, soldier boy." It was totally dark as we walked back into Manitou Springs. Marilyn and I, holding hands, went into a coffee shop. She told me she had another engagement later that evening, one she couldn't get out of. "I hope you understand, Wolfgang?"

"When can I see you again?" I asked.

"Soon," she said. "You know where to find me."

I took her back to the hotel where she appeared to be staying and caught a bus to Fort Carson. The spell was finally broken, my inhibitions gone. I saw Marilyn once more, the following weekend. I went with a friend to the Antlers Hotel in Colorado Springs to have a drink. We'd heard about the Antlers as one of the best hotels in town. I saw Marilyn sitting in the lounge across from a well-dressed man. A convention was in town, and the place was filled with people talking, looking, and laughing. I saw Marilyn smile her open smile at the stranger; he talking persuasively. Then they both rose and walked hand-in-hand to the elevator. I knew what she was. I felt no jealousy, no animosity. I was grateful that she shared herself with me, given herself of her own free will, and allowed me to discover myself as a man.

CHAPTER 14

On a Colorado Morning

Army reserve training at Fort Carson ended the first week in July. I had to find a job fast, but I couldn't find one in Denver that paid a decent wage. I had met Al Johnson at the university clinic in Boulder. He was tall and lanky, blond and blue eyed, his Norwegian heritage unmistakable. Al's smile was something that any hospital patient would want to wake up to from a near-death encounter. His mission in life was to help others. He helped me. I had contracted a bad case of athlete's foot and gone to the clinic for help. There I was given a purple tincture to put into a basin of hot water, and told to soak my feet three times a day—for hours. On the way out Al took me aside and said, "That stuff won't work, but it'll give you pretty purple feet, if that's what you want?" and he laughed. "Go get yourself some of this salve at the drugstore." He handed me a slip of paper. "It'll fix your problem in three days." It did. It was Al I turned to when I ran out of job options. I found his number in the phonebook, but didn't really expect to find him in Boulder. He had probably headed home for the summer by now like most everyone else. But when I called his number, he answered. We talked, and I told him about my predicament. "I have to find a job fast, Al. You have any ideas? I'll do nearly anything as long as it pays a good wage."

"Why don't you come to California with me?" Al suggested. "We could drive a car to Los Angeles. It's the cheapest way. All we have to do is pay for the gas."

"Whose car would we be driving to California?"

"It's quite simple, Wolfgang," Al replied. "A used clunker. Used cars bring more money in California than in Colorado. There are outfits constantly looking for people to drive their cars from here to there. You can stay with my folks and look for a job. The chances of finding something that pays well are a lot better in California than in this prairie dog colony of Denver."

"Prairie dog colony?" I protested. "I happen to like this place! Watch what you're saying. I think Colorado is the greatest place on earth."

"So do I, Wolfgang. Listen. I said Denver, not Colorado. There is a difference. Anyway, to get back to what we were talking about—a job for you which pays real money. There are a number of aircraft factories not far from where I live. They are always hiring." Al's proposal made sense, and besides, I always wanted to see California.

Al found a used-car dealer who wanted a 1951 Chevrolet driven to Sacramento. "You pay for the gas," the dealer said. At Al's insistence, he agreed, in writing, that he would reimburse us for any oil we might use. "Save your receipts. No receipt, no reimbursement," the dealer emphasized as we jumped into the unpretentious, gray two-door sedan. Two days later, Al and I were heading west on U.S. 40, across Berthoud Pass, Rabbit Ears Pass, through the little cowboy town of Steamboat Springs, and on to Salt Lake City. It stayed light late in July, and heading west we gained time as well, so we just kept on driving across the Great Salt Lake and into what I thought of as real cowboy country. The road turned as straight as an arrow out to the far horizon. Then it vanished from view, only to reemerge as a seemingly endless ribbon of asphalt as we topped the next ridge. Ridge-line followed ridge-line, barren landscape in between. The only signs of civilization along our route were equally straight Union Pacific railroad tracks and telephone wires strung for hundreds of miles alongside the tracks. I found it mesmerizing to spy a black snake in the far distance slowly moving toward us, then turning into an enormously long train of over one hundred freight cars pulled by four diesel locomotives. As we passed one another going in opposite directions, I listened for the sound of the train, but heard nothing; the tumbleweed- and mesquite-covered landscape and our own road noises swallowed the train's sound. The snake slid past as a train, turning again into a black snake as we sped away from each other. Trains, like airplanes, had fascinated me since I was a little boy. American trains were different from German trains, the cars twice as large and the trains easily twice as long. Nearly everything about America seemed to be larger, bigger, at times gigantic, and seemingly endless.

Late in the afternoon the sun, like everything else in the American west, became equally extreme on the treeless plains stretching from the Rocky Mountains to the Sierra Nevada. The dry, searing air blowing through the car had us totally dehydrated by day's end. When we stopped at one of the infrequent little watering holes along U.S. 40, such as Wells,

Winnemucca, or Lovelock, we drank a lot of water, had a quick burger or hot dog, and continued on our way. Our '51 Chevy turned out to be a lemon. It needed a ring job and went through oil as if we had access to an infinite supply of the stuff. We figured that the dealer knew exactly what kind of car he had given us. I dutifully collected oil receipts at each gas station to be sure we would get reimbursed. We went past Reno, Nevada, without stopping, and barely made it across Donner Pass with our ailing Chevy, arriving in Sacramento late in the afternoon of the second day. The night before, we slept for a few hours in the car in a restaurant parking lot. We had no problem finding the used-car dealership in Sacramento.

It turned out that Al and I had a few things to learn about the used-car business. Obviously, we should have gotten our oil money before turning over the car. When I presented the receipts for the oil we bought along the way, the dealer's secretary brazenly told me, "That's your expense. You pay for the oil and gas."

Maybe I was naive, but I was neither stupid nor timid when it came to issues of survival. "The heck it's my expense," I told her, leaning across her desk, staring her in the eyes. I whipped out the little piece of paper the Denver dealer gave us and thrust it in her face. "It says right here on this signed piece of paper that you will reimburse us for our oil purchases as long as we provide dated receipts. I want my money. Now!" I was in no mood to bargain and knew I had to be assertive, or we wouldn't have a chance of getting our money back.

The secretary looked at the piece of paper. "The boss is out," she said. I knew she was lying. "He'll be back shortly. We'll have your check ready in a little while." I had no choice but to wait. I stepped outside the trailer waiting for the mythical boss to return. In the meantime, Al went to the Greyhound terminal to check on the bus schedule to Los Angeles. "Without the oil money we don't have enough to buy two one-way tickets," Al informed me when he got back. It was getting late. I went back into the trailer. The secretary's answer was unchanged, "The boss ain't in yet. I don't know where he is. No one else can write you a check, mister. I am so sorry about that," she said through her crooked, misshapen teeth, "I'm really sorry. Come back tomorrow."

I knew this was the moment of truth. I leaned over her desk, nose to nose, eye to eye, and told her as coldly as I could, "Now listen real good. I am only going to say this once. I am going to work for the FBI." I thought for a moment she was going to fall out of her chair. "You probably know who the FBI is? I'll bet you do. And if I am not in Los Angeles by tomorrow morning there are going to be some very upset people. You find the man who can write the check or I'll be back with help, and you'll wish you were somewhere else." My little act was a desperate attempt to recoup our investment, which in my mind I had already written off as uncollectible. I expected the secretary to laugh in my face. I knew we'd been had. We handled the situation all wrong. But as I was talking to her I noticed the pupils in her eyes getting larger. I had seen that telltale sign of fear before, and I knew I had her.

"Just a moment, sir," she said in a very different tone of voice, scrambling out of her chair from behind her desk. I noted that suddenly I was "sir" to her. "I think I may know where the boss is. I'll be right back." She scampered out of the trailer and disappeared among a jungle of used cars. Within five minutes the truant boss arrived, looking like a caricature of Al Capone—big cigar in mouth, panama hat, a flowery Hawaiian-style short-sleeved shirt draped over a bulging stomach, high-water pants revealing his sockless feet in scuffed brown dress shoes. He didn't say a word as he approached. He pulled a checkbook from his back pocket, made out a check for twenty-six dollars, and dropped it on the desk. The secretary quickly picked it up and handed it to me.

"How about cash," I asked brazenly.

He was on his way out the door already, but he turned slowly toward me and just as slowly said in a measured monotone, "I don't carry cash, kid." He gave me a hard look, then left the trailer. I was ecstatic. I never expected my desperate ploy to work. We found a bank still open, cashed the check, bought two one-way bus tickets to Los Angeles, a jar of apple butter at a nearby store, and we were down to pennies. For dinner and breakfast we scooped apple butter from the jar with our fingers. Al couldn't believe it when I told him how I got our money.

Los Angeles, in spite of its appealing name, seemed to me a city without a center, a city without a heart. Houses were spread all over the place without rhyme or reason, mile after mile of incoherence. I didn't much like the place and wanted to return to Colorado the minute I stepped off the bus. Al's father picked us up. I was tired and felt a bit depressed, homesick for Colorado already. I had to remind myself that I was here to find a job, to make some money, so I could return to school. It didn't matter if I liked the place. Al's parents' house was a modest brick rambler with three bedrooms. His mother was at work when we arrived. His father worked in the admissions office at UCLA and left for work after dropping us off at the house. I could tell within minutes of our arrival that Al's family was just making ends meet, not much better off than Hedy and Leo. I couldn't stay here long.

Over the next two days Al and I went to the employment offices of several aircraft manufacturers. They weren't hiring—they were firing. It was 1954, the Korean War was over and the military services had quit buying airplanes and were busy canceling contracts. We stopped by a large bakery as a last resort, a bread and cake factory even larger than the one in Denver. Even the bakery wasn't hiring. "Sorry. Right now we have no openings. Come back next week. Maybe we'll have something then," was a stock answer no matter where I went. I filled out applications with little hope of landing a job. I had to make a quick decision. What to do? Al had been wrong about the L.A. job situation, and I didn't feel that I could stay with his parents much longer. So, I decided to return to Colorado. I asked Al to lend me the bus fare back to Denver. He did. Al and I had bonded on our trip west, and he was sad to see me go. "Stay," he begged. "You'll find a job tomorrow or the day after." I knew I had to move on with my life. Within ten days I drove from Denver to Sacramento, took the bus from Sacramento to Los Angeles, another bus from Los Angeles back to Denver. Leo and Hedy couldn't believe their eyes when I showed up at their doorstep.

It was high time for me to examine my options. I didn't see any opportunities out there at all, just the usual low-paying jobs which wouldn't take me anywhere. I was very much aware of my age and that this was probably a crucial time in my life, a crossroads. I had to get back into school somehow. If I didn't, I would never get to fly airplanes. I lay in bed that night and couldn't go to sleep. I had come so far, I thought, and suddenly I was at a dead end. I remembered experiencing this feeling of hopelessness when I lived under the Communists in 1946 and in the desperate winter of 1947 in the Trauen barracks. My circumstances were different, yet I felt just as abandoned, drifting aimlessly, without hope of finding a job. No job, no future—and with that, my dream to fly would die.

When I awoke the next morning, not having slept much, I found Leo already sitting at the dining room table nursing a cup of coffee and enjoying his morning cigarette. He had always been an early riser. Hedy was still asleep. She had worked late the previous evening and didn't go to work at the Fitzsimons Army Hospital PX until two o'clock that afternoon. When Hedy and Leo moved from Jones to Wheeling Street in Aurora, Hedy managed to switch from the Lowry BX to the Fitzsimons Post Exchange, which was closer. I sat down at the table across from Leo. "What's the matter, Wolfgang?" he inquired. "You don't look so good."

"Leo," I said gloomily, "I don't like to burden you with my problems, but I don't know where else to turn. I need your advice. I have no money and I can't find a job. Do you have any ideas?" Leo looked at me with his pale blue eyes, took a sip of coffee, slowly dragged on his precious Camel cigarette, and tilting his head back, blew smoke rings up toward the ceiling, the way he was apt to do when he felt really good or before saying something of importance to him. I knew his mannerisms. I waited.

"Wolfgang," he said in a confident tone of voice, "I think I may have a solution for your problem." I perked up instantly. I hadn't expected anything beyond a few compassionate words from Leo. "Have you thought of enlisting in the air force? It would give you a chance to get your bearings. Give you time to figure out what you really want to do with your life. You've only been in this country a little over three years, and you've done so much already. Maybe it's been a little bit too fast. You need time to digest it all. And the air force could be just the thing for you. If you sign up, it's only for four years. After that, you can decide to stay in or get out, do whatever you want. I should mention that there is a Korean War GI Bill, just like the World War II GI Bill that I have. Put in your four years, then you can return to college if you like and Uncle Sam will pick up the tab. How does that sound to you?" I was thrilled to hear what he had to say.

"I didn't know the GI Bill was still in effect, Leo. The war is over?"

"I don't really know either, Wolfgang," he replied, "but we'll find out. I know the captain at the Denver recruiting station; he would have the answer. Why don't I give him a call. Is that OK?" I nodded. At eight o'clock sharp Leo picked up the phone and called Captain Richards at the main recruiting station in the Old Customs House on Sixteenth Street and Arapaho. Captain Richards answered the phone personally. He and Leo reminisced a bit about old times. Richards was a former enlisted man who had gone through Officers Candidate School, OCS, to get his commission. They talked about me. When Leo hung up he said, "Well, hop on the bus and go see Captain Charles Richards at the downtown recruiting station. You know how to get there, don't you? He is expecting you. I have to tell you that they are not taking too many people right now, but if you do well on the aptitude test, he'll find a place for you. He also assured me that you are still eligible for the GI Bill if you enlist this month."

I didn't know what to say. I was so excited, so grateful, so up-beat, so happy. I hugged Leo hard. Then he was on his third or fourth cigarette of the morning. I headed for the bathroom to shave. Last night everything had looked hopelessly gloomy; suddenly everything turned around. I stepped out of the house into a Colorado morning—fresh crisp air, blue sky, the sun's rays promising a warm day. I could see the mountains in the distance, still covered with a mantle of snow around the higher peaks. I loved Colorado. If I only could, I would never leave.

Captain Richards was cordial and all smiles. I told him I was in the army reserves and didn't know how that affected anything. He said, "Don't worry, I'll take care of that." I showed him my high school graduation certificate, and he assured me that if I enlisted in July I would still be eligible for the Korean War GI Bill. He took time to briefly explain its provisions. The longer I listened, the more excited I got.

"I am ready to enlist right now," I said to him.

"Well," he replied, "take the aptitude test first, and we'll go from there." I sat down and took the Armed Forces Aptitude Test. Captain Richards scored the test personally and informed me I was a "Category II," one of the highest. He was pleased with my score, and so was I.

"Are you ready to enlist today?" he inquired.

"Yes, sir," I replied. "I am ready any time."

"Why don't you come back at four o'clock this afternoon. I have several other people who will be sworn in today. I'll see you then." I found a phone and called home to share the good news with Leo and Hedy, but there was no answer. I walked over to the Civic Center and sat on a bench shaded by a tree filled with raucous birds. The more I thought about what I was about to do, the more excited I got. At four o'clock, on the fourteenth of July, 1954, I was sworn into the United States Air Force in the grade of airman basic, along with twelve other young Coloradans: Jose Archuleta, John Brooks, Robert Cozzie, Roberto Gonzales, Robert Grimes, Leslie Hawkins, Robert Pritchard, Armando Ruybal, Reyes Salazar, Lee Smith, Gerald Stewart, and Gerald Turner. We thirteen were, according to orders issued by Detachment 2, of the 5115th Military Personnel Procurement Group, enlisted in the United States Air Force for four years with a date of separation of July 1958. "The applicants are assigned to the 3700th Military Training Wing, Lackland Air Force Base, San Antonio, Texas, reporting upon arrival to the Commanding Officer for processing and further assignment," the orders stated. "Travel by air directed. Personnel are Caucasian unless otherwise indicated." Captain Richards instructed us to return the following day with a minimum of personal belongings. "Just a toothbrush and shaving kit," he cautioned. "Everything else you need will be provided. Travel light. Do you understand?"

"Yes, sir!" we understood. I had gone into Denver that morning a civilian and returned home an airman in the United States Air Force. When Hedy and Leo returned home from work, my mother added to our festive atmosphere by announcing that on July 26 she was going to be sworn in as an American citizen.

CHAPTER 15

Lackland Air Force Base, Texas

On July 15 I reported to the Old Customs Building in downtown Denver, was handed a commercial airline ticket, and put on a waiting bus to Stapleton airport. We flew from Denver to El Paso, then on to San Antonio. It was a bumpy flight across the Rocky Mountains, and several recruits got airsick. I didn't. I thought the view was magnificent. It was my first airplane flight. I was thrilled. I could see the world spread out below. The engines were noisy where I sat, but the food was good and the stewardesses were friendly. Ours was one of several groups of new air force volunteers to arrive at the San Antonio airport about the same time. It was early evening when we deplaned. Weeks later, when I recalled my arrival in San Antonio, I realized that it was all planned that way, part of the education and transformation process we were about to undergo. From then on, everything was aimed at taking a bunch of civilian kids apart, breaking them down, and building them up again into disciplined and order-receptive airmen.

We were escorted onto waiting buses, and by the time we arrived at Lackland Air Force Base, it was pitch black outside. A few stars twinkled above, but we wouldn't be looking at the sky for a while. We wouldn't be going to sleep for some time either, although none of us knew that as we milled about looking for direction. Direction came swiftly in the form of a horde of screaming tactical instructors, three and four stripers, lining us up according to height, getting us to stand at what they called "Attention"—meaning that until we learned the simple exercise of standing rigidly with our stomachs sucked in, shoulders squared back, chins at right angles to the ground, eyes straight ahead, arms at our sides with forefingers touching the seams of our trousers, until we got that right, we would be playing this little game "until hell froze over." We were to keep our mouths shut, speak only when spoken to, and end every response with the word SIR. Loud and clear—SIR.

"Do you understand that boy!? I am going to make a man out of you yet! What's your name?"

"Wolfgang Samuel."

"Maybe you didn't hear my question, Airman Basic Wolfgang Samuel," the tactical instructor said in an even tone of voice, not whispered, but not quite as loud as before. "When I ask for your name your response is . . . keep your fucking eyes straight ahead when I am speaking to you!" He looked at my orders briefly, then thundered, "Airman Basic Wolfgang Samuel, AF17394268, SIR. Do you understand *that*!!!!"

"Yes, SIR! Airman Basic Wolfgang Samuel, AF17394268, SIR."

And so it went, until the tactical instructors had us standing in three straight lines, no one daring to twitch a muscle, and able to say name, rank, and serial number in five seconds or less. We stood there, and stood there, until someone finally shouted, "PARADE REST."

A few of us moved, but most didn't, not knowing what to do. The airman who would turn out to be my flight's tactical instructor—a tall, beefy, airman first class with three big stripes on his shirt sleeves, a man who looked as if he could wrestle a steer to the ground, with his garrison cap pulled down just above his nose, his eyes glowing like hot coals, his double-soled shoes with steel taps jarring the ground with his every deliberate step—that airman explained to us what he meant by *parade rest.*

"When I say 'parade rest,' gentlemen," he looked up and down our ranks, and I knew he didn't think of us as gentlemen, "that doesn't mean for you to go to sleep. It means that you move your right foot—you know your right from your left I hope—two feet to the right, snap your hands smartly behind your back, hands interlocking, thumbs on top of each other, looking straight ahead. Like this," and he demonstrated the maneuver. "Did you all get that!!!" It wasn't a question. It was a command.

We yelled, almost as if one, "Yes, SIR!"

"Now let us practice a little parade rest, gentlemen," he said, yelling out the command several times. We nearly fell over each other the first time we tried to execute the command. Half an hour later he had taught us how to stand at attention and at parade rest. We still had to learn what the command *at ease* meant. By that time it was eleven o'clock, and we were led into our barracks, assigned a bed—mattress rolled up at the foot of each bunk, blankets, sheets, and pillow laid out in front of each mattress. By the time we learned how to make a proper bed, it was past midnight, lights out, and we were ordered to "go to sleep!" It didn't take much for any of us to follow that order.

At four thirty in the morning our wide-awake tormentor, who had a private room in our barracks and would be our "house mother" for the next eight weeks of basic training, walked up and down the hall, the taps on his double-soled shoes ringing loudly, shouting for us to "Rise and shine. Rise and shine." We had thirty minutes to wash up, shave, make our beds, and be standing out front of our barracks ready to march to the mess hall for breakfast. His shouting never stopped. He referred to us in less than flattering terms, the kindest of which was that we were a bunch of old humpbacked women trying to get ready for a dance. "Get your asses moving!" he shouted. The most threatening comments were made in a whisper-like voice. We moved fast. We were out there. Ragged, but we were out there within thirty minutes, lined up at attention, in three almost straight ranks.

Airman First Class Schwanke marched us to the mess hall, picking one of us to count cadence. What was cadence? "Hup, two, three, four. Hup, two, three . . . ." That's cadence. "Stay in step, you idiot!" Someone next to me was crying, trying vainly to stay in step, and the wrath of our all-seeing tactical instructor came down on him. We finally arrived at the mess hall, came to a stumbling halt, and were told to fall out. As we started to wander off, we were taught what *fall out* meant.

"You dumb bastards," Schwanke shouted, "who do you think you are? Running around like a bunch of old ladies going to a church social. Get your asses lined up again and let's practice fall out." After we were properly aligned again, one arm's length distance from each other, each squad as straight as an arrow, our tormentor continued, "Anybody knows *fall out* means that you do an about face, then you assume a relaxed posture, not slovenly, mind you, and you walk proudly into the mess hall to do what I told you to do—EAT! I assume you still know how to EAT without wetting your pants. I will now show you a proper fall out maneuver. I suggest you pay very close attention, because I will only do it once."

Schwanke pirouetted halfway around his axis by placing the tip of his right foot behind the heel of the left, facing in the opposite direction. Then he ordered, "FALL OUT." At least half the flight fell on their faces trying to emulate our godlike three striper. The rest of us did passably.

We would have plenty of time to practice, I knew that. I had learned all of the standard commands in high school and college ROTC and had no problem executing them. For most of the boys, though, it was the first time they had anyone shout orders at them the way Airman First Class Schwanke did. It was a debilitating learning experience for some—exactly what the air force intended, of course. Before you can build them up, you have to tear them down. If we didn't understand that at the time, we would in due course pick up on it. Our tactical instructor executed his duty with apparent relish, efficiency, and effectiveness.

Next it was off to the barber shop—the great equalizer of men. Within two minutes or less a good barber could deprive an airman of his hair and in the process relieve him of seventy-five cents of his hard-earned money. Not bad pay for a couple of minutes of work. Then we drew uniforms, ate again, marched some more, got yelled at, and got yelled at even more. After day one we didn't remember what we had been before we came to Lackland Air Force Base.

On day three Schwanke directed us to write a letter home "to your dear mothers. We want her to know that her sweet little son is well taken care of. Tell her that. That is an order. Do it, NOW." I wrote, "Dear mother, Leo, and Ingrid, I only have five minutes to write. All I can tell you is, it's mighty tough down here. Every one of us lost his hair. So long. Write soon. Your son and brother, Wolfgang." Two days later, on July 19, I found a few more minutes to write again: "Hi Mom, I hope everyone is well. Do you know that my head is shaved bald? We also have to wear sun helmets because it is so hot down here. They are really working us hard. I have no time to myself except to sleep—and not much of that. Love, Wolfgang."

After the first week of basic training we knew how to execute every command, how to wear our green, sacklike fatigues, and our summer and winter uniforms, and we had learned how to make a proper bed with the blanket stretched so tight you could bounce a quarter on it. We learned the finer details of housekeeping, such as how to roll our socks properly, how to fold our underwear, how to display the few things we owned in a drawer, how to hang our shirts and coats, and finally, how to wear a wheel hat, a garrison cap, and the much more comfortable flight cap, the latter given a much less flattering name by earlier generations of soldiers and airmen. After one week we knew all those things, as well as how to clean and wax the hardwood floors of our new home, how to clean the bathrooms and anything else that might need cleaning from the concrete front steps to the remotest corner of the broom closet. Our barracks were clean, clean, clean, and would have easily put an industrious 1950s housewife to shame.

Our two-story barracks had two wings and a common room in the center of each floor. We assembled every day in the first-floor common room for instructions from our tactical instructor. He would walk up and down in front of us, his six-foot frame straight and tall, shirt tucked tightly into his pants. All eyes followed his every move as if our lives depended on him, each of us trying to read every word off his lips as it was uttered. Airman Schwanke was in total control.

To make certain we wouldn't have even a moment's rest, the tactical instructors had flights compete against each other on Saturday inspections. I was in Flight 698 of the 3724th Basic Military Training Squadron. There were twenty flights in the squadron. The tactical instructors checked everything—bathrooms for the slightest spot or fingerprint on a fixture; floors for gloss (a dust bunny could be a real killer); drawers and cabinets for prescribed display. In the meantime we stood at parade rest, lined up in front of our double-decker bunks, snapping to attention when the group of tactical instructors entered our room. Finding even a wayward piece of lint on someone's properly displayed jacket was enough to disqualify an entire flight. The "lucky" winning flight was known as the "honor flight" of the week and, to proclaim its superiority over all others, could carry a little triangular blue flag when marching to class and to the mess hall. Along with the honor came a seventeen-inch black and white TV, which, with much ceremony, was set up for that week in the second-floor common area of the honor flight's barracks. Of course, we had no time to watch TV. All those little shenanigans did their part in making disciplined airmen out of a wacky bunch of kids.

Discipline, military bearing, and the ability to execute commands were the first order of business. Then came instructions on the appropriate way to wear uniforms, instructions on personal hygiene, and instructions on military rank and courtesy, which taught us how to speak to officers: don't speak to them, just answer their questions. Saluting was deemed extremely important by Airman Schwanke. He lined us up outside in the blazing sun in two ranks facing each other, and we practiced the salute until we were soaked in sweat. We dreaded the thought of ever having to meet an officer, mythical beings, more intimidating and godlike than even our tactical instructors. None of us had ever met an officer before in our new capacity as airmen. By week two we had become a sharp-looking bunch of guys and began to feel good about ourselves. By this time all of us felt that we had been together for years and couldn't even remember ever having had a different life. A few were let go. Bed-wetting meant an immediate discharge.

Our routine remained the same. We got up at four thirty, were out front by five, marched to the mess hall, ate breakfast, marched back to the barracks, had a few minutes to ourselves to brush teeth. By seven thirty we were marching to our first class at eight. Food was served on familiar metal trays. We went down the chow line in a quiet, disciplined manner. Cooks in gravy-stained whites plopped "shit on a shingle," creamed beef on toast, on our trays; butter, jam, fried potatoes, pancakes, scrambled eggs as hard as concrete, and bacon were all there for the taking. We ate it all, as much as we could grab. There never was enough time to go for seconds, so I loaded up the first time to overflowing and always managed to put all of it away. At least twice a week for lunch or dinner we were served liver and onions—not my favorite, but I ate it. For the first time in my life I ate scallops. I didn't have the faintest idea what scallops were or where they came from, but whatever their origin, on my tray they surfaced as something fried into hard, brown balls. With an ample amount of tartar sauce the brown balls didn't taste bad. Food was food. We were hungry all the time.

Once a week several of us were detailed to KP, kitchen police, to help with cleaning and other tasks the regular mess hall employees didn't want to do. KP was an assigned duty just like guard duty or marching. It was the one place, however, where we could move around normally. By nine o'clock in the evening it was lights out; talking was prohibited, and it didn't take any of us more than a minute to get to sleep. In basic training I only had two or three nightmares, waking up screaming in the middle of night, bathed in sweat. No one heard, or no one cared. Others had nightmares as well. There were a couple of sleepwalkers amongst us. We helped them get back to bed.

After two weeks I wrote my first long letter home. "Dear mother, thank you for your letter. I was very happy to receive mail from home. We live in new barracks, three men to a room. The food is like all army food—good, but monotonous. We do a lot of marching and have many classes and tests. It is very hot down here in Texas and many of our boys have passed out marching. They make us eat salt tablets each morning and afternoon because we sweat it all out of our bodies during the day. What I hate the most are the many shots we get every week. Excuse my writing, but the lights went out ten minutes ago and I am scribbling by the light of my flashlight. So much for tonight, I have to go to sleep now. Love, Wolfgang."

Shots held a special horror for me, going back to my early school days in Sagan. The teacher never told us in advance when we would get shots. She would just announce that it was shot time and march us up to the *Aula*, the large room where we went to listen to people in brown uniforms extolling the greatness of the Führer on his birthday, the twentieth of April. In the *Aula* we lined up alphabetically. Samuel was always near the end of the line. By the time it was my turn, having watched so many others crying and shaking, I was ready to faint. I put on an act of bravery, laughing and telling stories to others standing in line, and the shorter the line, the more I talked and the sweatier I got. When my turn came I got dizzy, but never fainted. The shot rarely hurt. It was watching the needle penetrate a girl's arm, smelling the alcohol the nurse rubbed over the bleeding puncture, standing in line and seeing and smelling it all, that made me anxious. It was no different at Lackland. We lined up alphabetically, and I relived my childhood trauma, shuffling along, sleeve rolled up tightly on my right arm, sweating profusely in my baggy green fatigues as I approached the medic with the needle and the alcohol swab.

High school and college ROTC paid some unexpected dividends for me. Airman First Class Schwanke observed that I didn't fall down when doing an about face, noted that I knew how to count cadence, and saw how I helped others learn to march and master other military maneuvers, making life a little easier for him. Schwanke appointed me Flight Leader, his deputy so to speak. He began to sleep in most mornings while I put the flight through its paces. He wouldn't show up until we were ready to march off to our first class at seven thirty. After week three I wrote home, "Dear Mom, There is nothing more wonderful than getting a letter from home. The most important thing in our lives is food. The rumor has it that they put saltpeter into our food. Ask Leo what that does to a young man. Love, Wolfgang."

CHAPTER 16

Flight 698

The intense pressure let up a bit. Here and there we got a few minutes to ourselves, time to write a letter or sit on our beds and bullshit, something all of us loved doing. We wanted to learn about each other—where we came from, why we joined the air force—and, of course, we talked about topic number one, girls. We came from as far as Oregon and Iowa, from as near as Texas, Colorado, Oklahoma, and Arizona. There was a smattering of southern boys amongst us from South Carolina, Alabama, and Mississippi, white and black. Their deep southern drawls were always good for a laugh, as was a Texas twang. No one took offense. All but six of us in Flight 698 of the 3724th Training Squadron were classified by the air force as Caucasian—a designation which appeared to include Germans, like me, as well as people of Mexican heritage. For the first time I became conscious of the largely unspoken discriminators of ethnicity, race, and skin color. The air force made certain to reflect race on my orders, but in our flight we were all the same—just airmen.

Two of our "colored" flight members, as they referred to themselves, chose to befriend me. Rucker was a tall, lean young man from Mississippi, with a slow, deliberate, gangly gait, as close to dancing as a man could come by just walking. Marching wasn't something Rucker ever became comfortable with. Our flight always lined up according to height whenever we marched anywhere, that put Rucker out front, to the consternation of Airman Schwanke. Nothing Schwanke shouted, whispered, threatened, or promised had any effect on the way Rucker marched. I believe ours was a snappy-looking flight, but whenever we marched past any group of people, Rucker's gliding marching steps elicited smiles.

At first Rucker and I just made small talk. Slowly he got around to the topic he really wanted to talk about, driving a big truck, "with lots of wheels on it," as he put it. Rucker was worried that when the time came and our assignments were handed out, he would be sent to "cook school," instead of a school where he could learn to drive a big rig. "Because I am colored," he said. "Can you put in a good word for me with Airman Schwanke? Because, when I get out," Rucker said emphatically, his eyes shining brightly, his long finger shaking in my face, "I want to buy my own truck and drive all over this here United States of America."

I felt flattered that Rucker would confide in me, trusted me, and asked a favor of me which I had no power to grant. On the other hand, I was surprised that he thought people would deny him an assignment because of his skin color. I was naive. I still had a lot to learn. Rucker's simple request and his mention of "color" gnawed on me. Was I right back to the injustice I fled from in December 1946? Under the Communists suspicious things happened to people, not because of their skin color, but because of what they believed, or what someone thought they believed. People vanished at night never to be seen again, like my grandfather Grapentin, who was beaten to death in his prison cell. Rucker didn't know when he brought up the subject of discrimination that it was like a knife twisting in my gut; he didn't know the fear he released within me. It just couldn't be that way in my new country. It just couldn't. While I told Rucker I would speak up for him, I also tried to persuade him that no one would do what he feared because of the color of his skin. He smiled at my ignorance. "Samuel, I sure hope you are right," he said laughing loudly, "because driving trucks is all I want to do with my life." He paused thoughtfully, then said, "If my dream comes true, you can ride with me anytime, anywhere I go."

We laughed, slapped each other on the back, and laughed some more. I liked Rucker a lot. He was honest, generous, and kind. He reminded me a lot of Leo, and I told him so. He really got excited when I told him I drove a ten-wheel army truck through the sand and hills at Fort Carson, Colorado. He wanted to know every little detail about my driving experience—what the truck looked like, how I shifted in the sand, how I went through the gears going up and down steep hills, how many gears the truck had, what kind of maintenance it required, and how much and what kind of fuel it used. On and on. Rucker loved trucks. Girls too, but trucks clearly came first with him.

Mason, my other "colored" buddy, had thoughtful eyes. Mason was tall and thin, with long, graceful piano-fingers. He was an artist who could shape anything with his hands into something exquisite and beautiful. One day Mason—we all went by our last names—came into my room carrying the model of a jet airplane. When I looked at that plane, it took my breath away. The carving was so meticulously accurate, so perfect in every respect, a true thing of beauty. It was a model of a sleek bomber with six jets beneath its swept-back wings. The replica almost looked like a fighter plane—a B-47 jet bomber.

"Can I hold it, Mason?"

"You sure can, Samuel," he said with a smile coloring his voice, "because I'm going to give it to you. I hear you want to be a pilot. Maybe you will fly a plane like this one day. I sure hope you will." I was stunned by Mason's thoughtfulness and his generosity. We were strangers, thrown together by chance. Most of us had nothing to our names, and yet Mason wanted to give me one of his exquisite creations. I rose from my bunk and thanked him, but told him I couldn't accept the B-47 model as a gift. "It is much too beautiful and valuable to give away, Mason." He lowered his eyes. I feared I hurt his feelings. "You don't even know me very well, and you want to give me this piece of art which took you many hours to create. I don't even have a place to put it, and as I said, it's too valuable just to give away. I can't take it." I ran my fingers over the canopy, along the tapered fuselage, back to where the two gun barrels stuck straight out of their mount. "You are a true artist, Mason, a creator of beauty. I want you to know that I feel honored by your generous gesture."

The B-47 was perfectly proportioned, about thirty inches in length, carved out of solid wood with a knife and perfectly smoothed with the finest of sandpaper, then lacquered and painted several times to a high gloss in the colors of a newly activated bomb wing. Mason told me all that and I could read the love of the artist for his creation in his expressive eyes. In years to come, I would spend over two thousand hours sitting in the confines of an ejection seat in the reconnaissance version of the B-47 bomber, but that experience was still years in my future. Mason and I talked about his airplane a little longer. He told me about the B-47's various features and how he had incorporated them into the model, from doors for the approach and brake chutes to the tail guns and the HF antenna—the only thing not made of wood—which ran from behind the cockpit to the vertical stabilizer. "Have you thought of selling it?" I asked Mason.

"Nah," he said, "I just do it for fun. Who would buy a thing like this anyway?"

"Why don't we have an auction and sell it to the highest bidder in our flight? Someone in our flight probably has more money than you and I put together and can afford to buy something like this. What do you say?"

"You really think someone would pay money for my airplane?"

"Of course."

"If you think so," Mason said, "we can give it a try. Maybe nobody will like it?"

"Come on, Mason," I said. "This is art. Even a dummy like me can tell that. It is so good it should go into an art gallery." His smile reached from ear to ear. Mason was a good-looking man, with fine features and the sensitivity of the artist.

"I sure like you, Samuel," he said, patting me on the head—he being over six feet to my five-nine. "I'm glad you are my friend."

I got the word out to the flight the next morning. Mason brought the model of the B-47 to our morning formation and we passed it up and down the ranks. Someone came up with twenty dollars for the B-47 model without us even having an auction. Mason sent the money home to his mother.

Our schedules varied between academic instruction and practical learning. In academics we learned about dress codes, air force customs, courtesies, and rank and its privileges. An equal amount of time was given over to air force history, including many hours of World War II movies depicting the ferocious air battles over Germany. For the first time I was afforded an airman's perspective of the war I once observed from the ground below as a child. I saw the fierce German fighter opposition hurling themselves against the thousands of guns of the huge Flying Fortress formations of 8th Air Force bombers. I gained a lot of respect for the courage of the German fighter pilots, undoubtedly something the curriculum didn't call for. To me, all men who flew airplanes in combat were special, no matter which side of the war they served on. Flying airplanes was inherently dangerous, and the men who nevertheless chose to face the odds arrayed against them surely were cut from a different cloth than the rest of us. I had seen too many crashed airplanes in my short life to have any illusions, yet I still wanted to fly. Airplane crashes were common in the fifties. As I watched the violence on the screen, heard the sounds of screaming engines, the rat-tat-tat of guns, I felt sadness for the bomber crews who perished, felt equal sadness for the fighter pilots who shot them down and were shot down in turn. I closed my eyes often. I didn't want to see all that slaughter, which brought back memories I tried hard to suppress.

I witnessed my first bombing raid near Sagan in the spring of 1944. Although many of my friends had lost their fathers, the war had not come close to my family until then. On a clear April day the air-raid sirens went off and helmeted wardens, all women, came running out of their apartment buildings to chase everyone into cellars which served as our bomb shelters. I quickly hid behind a bush. The warden didn't see me. I wanted to watch the Americans and knew I wouldn't be able to see anything from a basement window. I heard a strange sound, at first thinking it was a swarm of bees. The sound became louder and louder. I strained my eyes, and in the distance I saw what appeared to be a dark cloud with a faintly shimmering quality. The cloud grew larger and larger into hundreds of American B-17 bombers, the sun reflecting off their canopies and whirling propellers. The sound of the engines was something I would never forget. As the planes came closer, the windows in our apartment house began to rattle, and the ground beneath my feet began to vibrate. Just before that huge formation of bombers was to pass directly overhead, the planes made a ponderous turn to the north, over the nearby town of Sorau. What I saw next was a huge, black mushroom cloud forming in the cloudless sky. The cloud remained over Sorau for the rest of the day, slowly drifting off to the northeast before dissolving by nightfall. It was the first of many air raids I was to witness and experience, many raids much larger than that first of less than four hundred bombers.

In addition to the classroom instruction, we were taken to the firing range and taught how to fire the M1 carbine. We were in the military. The Korean war just ended. The least every airman should know was how to handle a gun. I enjoyed firing the carbine. When we went out on the range to collect our targets, I was pleased to see that I had fired well enough for an expert medal. The black center of my target was torn so badly it was difficult to see how many rounds I had actually put in it. The range master took one look at my target, then tore it up in front of me. "Our carbines are too old and worn for you to shoot that well," he said. "Your neighbor probably fired on your target by mistake."

"No," I protested, "he didn't. If that was the case his rounds would be all over my target, not centered in a neat cluster." I got my neighbor's target. "Here, look at it. Most of his rounds are in his target. Count them." My neighbor's rounds were widely spaced, but most were there. I had learned how to hold a rifle in army ROTC, learned to sight the target carefully, hold my breath, steady my aim, and squeeze off each round slowly, never knowing when the gun would actually fire. I knew I had done everything right, and the range sergeant arbitrarily took my achievement away from me. I talked to Airman Schwanke, who shrugged his shoulders, "Forget it, Samuel," he said. "It's not important." It was important to me.

In addition to basic training for new airmen, the first phase of aviation cadet training was conducted at Lackland Air Force Base as well. We occasionally marched past the aviation cadet barracks, old World War II barracks, not nearly as nice as ours. I learned from an airman in one of our sister flights that he had been accepted into the aviation cadet program. "I will be assigned to the first available class right after I graduate from basic," he told me.

"What do I have to do to apply?" I asked him, and he told me. I obtained permission from Airman Schwanke to go to our orderly room to start the application process. I soon found myself at the base hospital getting a flying physical. All went well until they checked my eyes. I had 20/20 distant vision, 20/15 close-up vision, and great depth perception and night vision. Then the corpsman got out a book of about twenty-five test charts, each chart containing variations of colored dots within a sea of similarly colored dots which made a number, like 7, or 28, or 57. Most numbers were easily seen unless one were color blind; some were purposely more difficult to see. I went through one chart after another.

Child's play, I thought. I was nearly finished when I came up against one chart where no matter how hard I tried I couldn't make out the correct number. I protested to the corpsman, "It's only one chart. How important can that be?" But it was all over for me. I had flunked my physical on that one chart. For some reason I was not upset. Disappointed, yes. But not upset. I would follow my original plan: serve four years in the air force, get out, go to college, take ROTC, get my commission as a second lieutenant, and then go to flight school. I certainly should have been worried, because I would have to take the same flight physical again, but I wasn't. I had overcome so many obstacles in life, I figured, I would overcome that one when the time was right.

Next to our flight's barracks was a WAF, Women in the Air Force, barracks. We looked at women much like starving men look at a richly set table. Every morning the women, wearing skirts which reached down to just inches above their ankles, or tight fitting dark blue slacks, lined up in front of their barracks the way we did. We couldn't take our eyes off them. Our classes were separate. There was no mixing of the genders in basic training. We managed to talk to each other on Sundays at church and at other similar after-duty-hours occasions. I met a nice-looking WAF, Leslie, and asked her if she would go into town with me on Sunday, my first twelve-hour pass. I was thrilled when she said, "Yes."

The WAF flight had begun its training the same day we did, so we were on the same schedule. To go into town we had to be in uniform. San Antonio was used to military uniforms. We were instructed not to hold hands on or off base while in uniform. Of course, since we always wore uniforms, hand-holding was, for all practical purposes, banned everywhere at all times. As soon as the military police at the gate checked our passes and the bus exited the base, I took Leslie's hand. We had a great time visiting the Alamo and eating at a steakhouse recommended to me by Airman Schwanke. Returning to Lackland that afternoon, we went to our separate mess halls to eat and then to the seven o'clock movie. It was dark when the movie let out. Leslie and I walked hand in hand past a large open area that displayed some of the old World War II airplanes—B-24 and B-17 bombers, smaller twin-engine B-25 and B-26 bombers, and P-38,

P-47 and P-51 fighters. We didn't want to look at airplanes; we wanted a place that offered a little privacy. We kissed, but there were many other couples doing the same. We left to look for some place more private, but so did others. At Lackland AFB there was no privacy anywhere near the basic training barracks. Those who ran the training program knew all about young men and women and their hormones. The shrubbery around classroom buildings was deliberately cut short. No two people could hide unseen and consummate a relationship. There was only enough privacy for a fleeting kiss and touch.

Basic training ended after ten weeks, and those of us who finished were promoted to the grade of airman third class—A/3C. Completing training meant we could sew our first stripe onto shirt sleeves and uniform coats, and we received a slight pay increase. Our pay, around seventy-five dollars a month, now increased to the lordly sum of one hundred and five dollars. A steady pay check was something few of us had ever experienced. I immediately began to pay off my two-hundred-dollar loan from the University of Colorado and Al's advance which allowed me to return from Los Angeles to Denver. I forgot about the money Raymond lent me to pay off my speeding ticket and didn't pay him back until years later, when I remembered.

In basic training we learned all that senior air force leaders wanted us to learn, from falling in to falling out, from firing a rifle to field-stripping a cigarette. We were, I thought, a fine-looking bunch of airmen the day we marched together for the last time to our brief graduation ceremony. We had bonded well as a group, lost only six out of a group of over eighty men, and were ready to enter the *real* air force. Most of us were a little saddened that our flight was disbanding. I know, I was. Flight 698 ceased to exist. I never again met a member of Flight 698, yet Rucker, Mason, and Schwanke became a permanent part of my life's mosaic.

CHAPTER 17

Carswell Air Force Base, Texas

Leo finally received that long awaited telephone call offering him a civil service position at Lowry. The new position provided steady employment commensurate with Leo's past experience and was physically much less demanding than his temporary job in a creamery. With Leo's employment assured, and Hedy working as well, my parents were finally in a position to think about buying a car.

Two weeks prior to graduation from basic training, all of us trainees had met with air force personnel specialists to determine our future assignments. Using aptitude test scores as guides, the specialists tried to match each one of us to available duty assignments or technical schools. No one cared about skin color, as my friend Rucker had feared. He got his wish and went off to learn how to drive big trucks. It was during this assignment phase when I learned that I enlisted just in time to qualify for the Korean War GI Bill, the emergency being declared over on July 31, 1954. I enlisted on July 14. Had Leo not mentioned the air force option when he did, had I delayed my return from California for any reason, I would have missed qualifying for the financial backing which in years to come would finance my college education.

During my interview with the assignment counselor I stated that I wanted to go study Russian in the foreign linguist program, so that I could become an intelligence intercept analyst. I had learned about the foreign linguist program through the grapevine, and the Russian language school was practically next door to Lackland at Kelly AFB. I thought it would be exciting to work in that capacity against the Communists who had done so much harm to my family. Since my aptitude scores were high enough and I already spoke another foreign language, my assignment counselor thought I was the right man for the program and put me in for it. After a lengthy wait my application came back—denied for cause. I needed my American citizenship before I could obtain a top secret clearance to qualify for intelligence work of any kind, particularly for something as secretive and sensitive as intercepting the communications of an adversary.

At the end of basic training I still didn't have an assignment and was put into what was referred to as a "holding status." I was given menial tasks to perform: mowing lawns, KP, picking up trash. I was moved into a transient barracks, an old World War II open-bay barracks occupied by airmen awaiting discharge for minor disciplinary infractions or misdemeanors deemed unacceptable by the air force. They were on their way out. I was on my way in. Not a very compatible situation. The contrast between my recent basic training experience and the transient population I was forced to live among was unnerving. The men boasted of their offenses and openly drank beer and stronger stuff in the barracks throughout the day without anyone in authority saying anything. Their uniforms were dirty and unpressed, their personal habits and language equally demeaning. Every day I hoped to hear that this would be my last day in this environment. After a week of living in the transient barracks I went to personnel and asked, "What are you doing about my assignment?" "Nothing," was the answer. "Too much work," they claimed. "Be patient," I was told.

"I can type sixty-five words a minute," I reminded my personnel counselor. "Can that qualify me for something?"

"I'll see what I can do," he replied.

Within a week I was handed a set of orders directing me to "report not later than November 10, 1954, to the 7th Bombardment Wing (Heavy), 8th Air Force (SAC), Carswell AFB, Fort Worth, Texas, to serve in the Air Force Specialty Code 70230, clerk typist." Typing, a skill I acquired at the Opportunity School when I first came to Colorado in 1951, provided the basis for my first air force assignment. I recalled my grandfather Samuel's advice, "Nothing you do in life is ever wasted."

In 1954, the Strategic Air Command, SAC, had an inventory of 2,640 combat aircraft, including 342 B-36 heavy bombers and 1,060 B-47 medium all-jet bombers, operating from forty-one airbases in the United States and overseas, mainly in Europe and North Africa. The command was rapidly growing in size and influence, and many more B-47s and even larger eight-jet B-52 bombers were to join its growing aircraft inventory in years to come. SAC was commanded by General Curtis E. LeMay, who had made his name in the early days of daylight bombing against Nazi Germany and later in the Pacific theater of operations, reducing the cities of Japan to ashes with low-level B-29 firebomb raids. LeMay became a legend among airmen in his own lifetime: tough, unyielding, ever intent on building the Strategic Air Command into the largest, most efficient combat command within the air force, a virtual air force within an air force. The 7th Bomb Wing at Carswell Air Force Base, with its heavy B-36 bombers, constituted a key element of SAC's combat posture. I was euphoric over my assignment.

I picked up my orders from the personnel office, was handed a bus ticket, and told to get myself to Fort Worth as quickly as possible. "They are shorthanded," my detailer emphasized. Wearing air force blues and carrying a blue duffel bag over my shoulder, I headed for the Greyhound bus station in San Antonio. While I wondered what Fort Worth was like, I didn't really care. The air force could have assigned me to the remotest radar site in Alaska, and I still would have looked forward to the assignment with great anticipation. I felt ready to go anywhere and experience whatever world the air force was inclined to open up for me. I arrived in Fort Worth late the same day and called the base operator to ask, "What I should do to get out to the base?"

"Don't do anything," the operator said. "Stay where you are. Someone will be out shortly to pick you up."

Once deposited by air force bus at Carswell, I signed in at personnel and again was assigned to transient quarters, across from the flight line, where I could see the huge tails of B-36 bombers sticking up from behind their hangars. These transient quarters were considerably different from the ones at Lackland. The men who stayed here were in fact real transients, coming or going on official air force business, not delinquents. The next day I processed in and was permanently assigned to Headquarters Squadron, 7th Bomb Wing.

Apparently a B-36 bomber had crashed not far from Carswell Air Force Base, and during the afternoon hours the enlisted crew from the ill-fated aircraft, gunners and crew chiefs, were put up in my barracks. The B-36 crew was a jovial bunch, joking about the experience of bailing out of the stricken bomber. "This is my second time. Wonder if there will be a third," one sergeant joked. Every one of his crew mates agreed a third time was a sure thing for him. They laughed loudly, their gallows humor obviously helping them to deal with the traumatic experience of the crash.

Soon after my arrival, orders were published putting me into an on-the-job training program as an administrative clerk typist. I actually worked as a payroll clerk. All of the wing's pay records were maintained by Headquarters Squadron, and I maintained the pay cards for all enlisted men on flying status—gunners, flight mechanics, and crew chiefs. Every month each enlisted man on flying status had to present documentation signed by his aircraft commander certifying that he had flown his minimum of four hours for that month. Enlisted flyers didn't have the option to transfer flying time from one month to the next, so it was always a matter of getting their time or losing their flight pay. Most of them lived from hand to mouth, and forty dollars flight pay was a big portion of their income.

A military organization without orders is, of course, inconceivable. Order-giving and order-taking is the foundation of military discipline as I had learned all too well in basic training. In the 7th Bomb Wing most orders were given on paper rather than verbally. Orders were published for nearly every activity anyone was expected to perform—for status changes, such as promotions and skill levels, for additional duties assigned, or any number of other things. While in the "old days" verbal orders or an entry in a log book was sufficient, in the new air force every order and instruction was reduced to paper. A problem that surfaced for me at Carswell for the first time and which would dog me for the better part of my air force career was my name. People insisted on switching my first and last names. Even if an order read, "LAST NAME: Samuel," they seemed compelled to go ahead and change my last name to Wolfgang. New orders then needed to be issued to amend the original orders, since there was no Airman Wolfgang in the system. For nearly every order issued to promote, transfer, assign, or otherwise change my status, I routinely received two sets—the first order referring to Airman Wolfgang, the second set amending the first from *Airman Wolfgang to Airman Samuel.* The name confusion reached its pinnacle years later, in 1962, when I reported for duty in the 55th Strategic Reconnaissance Wing at Forbes

AFB, Topeka, Kansas. Looking at the Aircrew Arriving/Departing Station board, I noticed that both Lieutenant Wolfgang and Lieutenant Samuel were shown as in-bound. I introduced myself as Lieutenant Samuel and asked the gruff-looking lieutenant colonel behind the desk if Lieutenant Wolfgang had signed in yet. The answer was, of course, "No." Laughing, I told the colonel that Samuel and Wolfgang were one and the same person. The lieutenant colonel didn't think I was funny and reprimanded me for being insubordinate.

Within the first week of my arrival at Carswell I was assigned permanent quarters, again in a World War II two-story barracks, this one assigned exclusively to house Headquarters Squadron personnel. Flimsy partitions separated individual living areas—a bed, a locker, a footlocker at the end of each bed, and a small bedside night stand with a table lamp comprised our sparse furnishings. Inspections were performed regularly. Beds had to be made in a military fashion each morning after reveille was played over the base loudspeaker system. I ate breakfast, lunch, and dinner in the mess hall. Other than providing heavy china plates instead of metal trays, it was the usual military mess, functional to the extreme.

It was a weekend when it happened. I still didn't really know anyone in the barracks. At lunch I sat with a small group of airmen whom I recognized as living on the lower level of my barracks. One of them ate like a pig, slurping his drink loudly, sticking his fork into his meat in an awkward manner, barely able to cut the meat with his knife, often just sticking a large chunk of meat into his mouth and swallowing it nearly whole. I offered to show him how to handle a knife and fork. "It's so easy," I said to him. "Here, why don't you try it this way," and I demonstrated. He was about my height, but heavier. He glowered at me and continued to slurp down his food. We all got up together from the table, dropped off our plates, and walked back to the barracks. I found myself in the middle, surrounded by my table mates. One of them said, "Come on over to my bunk. I want to show you something."

I was too naive to catch on. Because it was a weekend, the place was practically empty. Once we got to his bunk area, the airman invited me to sit on his bed. The others sat down as well. I knew then that I had gotten myself into a bad situation. The muscular fellow who didn't know how to eat with a knife and fork opened up with a foul-mouthed tirade against me. He was offended by me and, in his words, was going to beat the crap out of me. The others got up from the bed and circled around, egging him on. "Beat the bastard's brains out," one shouted. Another whispered loud enough for me to hear, "Kill him, Buddy. Kill him." I knew this was going to be bad, and there was no one there to help me. Buddy attacked with his fists, landing some brutal blows. I got hold of his right arm in midswing and twisted it behind his back, forcing him to the floor, the way I once beat my friend Dave in Denver when we had horsed around at his house after school. Dave couldn't move when I put the armlock on him. This man couldn't move either, and he dropped to his knees. Every time he tried to move I applied pressure, making him cry out in pain. He glowered at me.

"Why don't we just walk away from this," I suggested. "Give up. Promise to stop the fight, and I'll let go. No hard feelings."

"Never, you son of a bitch," he muttered. Suddenly, the others standing around us began to cheer for me. "Kill him, Wolfgang," one shouted. "Kill him," another chimed in. I gathered they didn't care who won the fight. They just wanted to be entertained, wanted the thrill of experiencing violence against another. One of them took off for his area and quickly returned holding a hammer. He pushed the hammer in my face and said, "Take it. Kill him." How did I get into this? I wondered. How do I get out of this alive? It was Sunday noon and I was fighting for my life in a military barracks on an air force base. I knew I couldn't stand here forever holding this guy on his knees. I decided to let go and run for my life. The instant I let go, he grabbed the hammer and came after me. I know he would have killed me on the spot had he caught up with me. I ran out of the barracks into the open where people were walking. He stopped pursuing and went back inside. I didn't return until later that day. I expected to be attacked in my sleep, so I stayed awake the first night. Nothing happened. He must have gotten transferred out on Monday because I never saw him again. The others I ignored.

My life at Carswell quickly fell into a routine. I reported for work at seven thirty in the morning and opened for business at eight. Usually several airmen were already waiting in line to straighten out their flight pay. I took an hour for lunch, always eating in the mess hall, and called it a day at four thirty in the afternoon. I changed into civilian clothes before heading for the mess hall for dinner. Since I didn't have a security clearance, I was never allowed on the heavily guarded flight line, never got to see a B-36 bomber up close. At eleven o'clock Taps played over a scratchy loudspeaker mounted on top of the water tower. For us guys living in the barracks it meant lights out.

On Saturday mornings, at 0900 sharp, everyone assigned to Headquarters Squadron stood at parade rest on the parade ground for review and inspection. The dress was class A uniform: blues in winter, khakis in summer. The inevitable parade followed the review. If Saturday coincided with payday, which happened twice a month, then after the parade we airmen lined up in front of a pay table next to the Headquarters Squadron orderly room. The executive officer, a captain, sat behind the table with a large till of money and a loaded 45-caliber pistol by his side. After the first sergeant, standing slightly behind and to the side of the executive officer, called out a name and the amount of money due, the captain then counted it out and placed it at the edge of the table. When it was my turn I approached, came to attention, and rendered a salute, saying loudly, "Airman Samuel reporting for pay, sir!" I then took a step forward, took my money off the table, came to attention again, saluted, did an about face and moved on. Everything at Carswell was very army-like, from reveille in the morning to the barracks inspections, parades, pay procedures, and the playing of Taps in the evening. The air force had only come into being as an independent military service in September 1947, barely seven years earlier. Many sergeants and officers still wore their army browns instead of air force blue. Change came slowly to the new air force. At Carswell Air Force Base I experienced the end of an era.

At Thanksgiving I wrote home, "Dear Mother and Leo, All morning we stood at attention and marched around the parade ground. My feet are still cold. I wished I could have spent Thanksgiving with you. They served a really wonderful meal in the mess hall with all the trimmings. I even ate some turkey." During the war years in Germany when we had little meat to eat, my grandfather Samuel frequently sent us packages filled with plump chickens. We ate lots of chicken, and my mother Hedy nearly always fixed the chicken the way she liked it best, as chicken fricassee. One day I just couldn't eat another bite of chicken fricassee, couldn't stand the smell of chicken fricassee. I was only eight, and Hedy, not wanting to waste any food, forced me to clean my plate. I threw up all over the table. Her punishment was terrible. She beat me unmercifully with a cane rug beater, insisting that I eat my chicken. I couldn't, and I didn't. After that I never again touched anything with wings—no chicken, no turkey, no duck, no goose. Hedy changed her ways after we fled Sagan in January 1945. She made many sacrifices for her children and never again laid a hand on me.

In that same letter, I told Hedy and Leo that "I like my bachelor life. I don't think I want to get married soon." Hedy wrote back that Ingrid was doing well in school; she attended junior high school in Aurora and apparently fit right in. Hedy and Leo had also bought a car, a used 1951 Chevrolet two-door sedan with radio and heater and turn signals. On leave in January 1955, Hedy and Leo proudly took me for a Sunday drive, an American tradition in the 1950s. We visited Leo's relatives, including Pop and Raymond. Pop as usual had a wad of chewing tobacco in his mouth, spitting a stream of black juice into the weeds before giving me his hand. I liked the old man who never had much to his name except a large family. Leo's mother died soon after our arrival in February 1951, and there was a thing called a viewing. I had no idea what a viewing was. I recall walking into the funeral home and being told to wait for a few minutes in an anteroom. Then we were escorted by the funeral director down a narrow hallway flanked by large windows with drawn curtains. The director pulled back the curtain to one of the windows and there, in a brightly lit cubicle, in a reclining pose, was the corpse of Pop's wife, dressed and made up like a mannequin, only I knew she was made of real flesh. I felt vomit coming up from my stomach and hurried outside. I couldn't take another death, couldn't look at the vulgar display. I later apologized to Pop and Leo. Pop took me aside, put an arm around my shoulders, and pulled me close. "You have a lot of living to do, my boy," he said softly. "Don't let this get to you."

In January 1955 higher headquarters tasked the 7th Bomb Wing to provide a number of airmen to air force units in Europe. I and several other airmen were marched to a test center and given a typing test. I was told whoever attained the highest score—typing speed being the principal determinant—would have the choice of a three-year tour of duty in England, a coveted assignment. Many volunteered. At sixty-five words a minute I was easily the best typist among my peers. Within two weeks, in February, the 19th Air Division, of which the 7th Bomb Wing was a part, issued orders releasing me from my current assignment and directing me to report to Camp Kilmer, New Brunswick, New Jersey, not later than April 25, 1955, for shipment to the United Kingdom. I was elated.

Soon after arriving at Carswell in November 1954 I had applied for my citizenship. In early March I was notified to appear before a magistrate of the United States Court of the Eastern District of Texas in the town of Texarkana to be sworn in as an American citizen. As soon as he heard about my notification, a sergeant in my office offered to drive me to Texarkana. Sergeant Preston's ex-wife and their two young children lived in a small village just outside Texarkana. "I can visit with them," he said, delighted at the prospect of getting a day off to spend with his children.

The magistrate turned out to be an elderly gentleman in a pinstriped blue suit which had seen better days. I took a seat across from him at a table in his office. He shuffled some papers, then looked at me over his wire-rimmed glasses and asked, "Mr. Samuel, are you ready to answer a few questions?" I nodded my head. "This won't take long," he said. "For the first question, can you tell me which is the capital city of the United States of America, New York City or Washington D.C.?"

"Washington D.C.," I replied.

"What state is Washington D.C. located in?" He looked at me encouragingly. I noted that his hair was thinning and thought he might be a grandfather. He looked kind. Nonthreatening.

"I believe it is a separate district, sir, not part of a state. The District of Columbia."

"We are moving right along, aren't we?" he said, a smile coloring his gentle voice, as if he already knew the outcome of the exercise. "A couple more questions should do it for us. What are the three principal branches of the federal government? Take your time. There is no hurry."

"The executive branch, the office of the president," I ventured. He smiled encouragingly. "The legislative branch, the Congress of the United States, consisting of two houses; and the judicial branch, the Supreme Court."

"Very good, Mr. Samuel. Which of the three branches you just mentioned is the most important? In other words, which branch has the greater authority? The President, the United States Congress, or the Supreme Court?"

His question confused me. "I thought they were separate and equal, sir. At least that's what I learned in high school," I replied.

"Well, you certainly know your government, Mr. Samuel." We continued to talk for a bit longer; then he said, "This is quite enough, I believe. Would you like to change your name?" His question startled me.

"Why would I want to change my name, sir? I have done nothing wrong." The magistrate laughed.

"People do, Mr. Samuel."

"Please raise your right hand," he instructed me, "and repeat after me: I, Wolfgang Willie Eberhard Samuel, swear to defend the constitution of the United States of America against all enemies, foreign and domestic . . . so help me God." The swearing in was brief and to the point. "Congratulations, Mr. Samuel," he said, pulling a certificate from a folder. "You are now an American citizen with all appurtenant rights and privileges." With that statement he handed me my Certificate of Naturalization which described me as being of ruddy complexion, with gray eyes, brown hair, weighing 150 pounds, with a scar on my right middle finger, single, and formerly of German nationality. I had never thought of myself as ruddily complected; in fact, my French Huguenot ancestry prevailed in me and had given me a rather dark complexion. My eyes were hazel, not gray. I did have a scar on my right middle finger, an injury I carelessly inflicted on myself with a dough-cutting tool in Krampe's bakery in Hannover. It didn't matter how the government chose to describe me, I was an American citizen—and very proud of that.

CHAPTER 18

A Different World

The usually drab mess hall had been spruced up by the cooks for Thanksgiving dinner with plastic white tablecloths and decorations appropriate to the season. The dining area really looked nice, I thought, and the food was equally well prepared. I had finished eating, but didn't feel like going back to the barracks just yet. I sat there quietly, watching my friend Tom Moran eat and listening to his persistent, if not persuasive, attempts to talk me into going to church with him on Sunday. "I don't like going by myself," he repeated himself for the third time. "Makes me feel self-conscious. Why don't you come along? Try it. Be a friend. You'll like it." I listened, nursing the last few swallows of my orange juice. "You have to be bored out of your skull staying in the barracks all the time," Tom persisted. "Come on. Go with me. What do you say?" To emphasize his point he gently dropped his left fist on the table. "Maybe we'll meet some girls! There are some good-looking babes in that church. I never found the courage to go near them, but they're real lookers. Come on, Sam. Go with me and see for yourself." Everyone at Carswell called me Sam.

"Good-looking girls, huh? Now that's a reason for me to go to church. Why didn't you say so in the first place?" Tom grinned from ear to ear.

"It's an Episcopalian church," he added. "Does that make a difference?"

"No. I am Lutheran. I don't have strong convictions about church rituals. That's all window dressing." We sat there quietly for a while. Then I asked Tom, "Do you believe in God? Is that why you go to church? Or do you just go out of habit?"

"I think I believe in God," Tom replied after a thoughtful pause. "I like going to church, if that's what you mean. Have done so ever since I was a little boy. It's a habit, I agree, and I feel uncomfortable when I don't go. Church has always been an important part of my life. Wherever I go I try to find a church that reminds me of home, of my family. Yes, I think I believe in God. To be honest, I haven't really given it serious thought. I just accepted everything I learned from my parents, from Sunday school teachers, and other adults in my life. How about you, do you believe in God?"

Our casual conversation had taken a serious turn. I didn't intend for it to go that way. I felt uncomfortable sharing my past with others, but I owed Tom an honest answer. He had been honest with me. "Let me tell you a little story, Tom, about God and me, and you decide if I believe. It was late April 1945, I had just turned ten, and we were fleeing Russian tanks with a German army unit. The soldiers took pity on us and took us along—my mother, me, my sister, and my grandmother. In a convoy of seventy or eighty horse-drawn wagons they headed west, trying to reach the American lines to surrender. One night we came under rocket and artillery attack. A village directly ahead of us burned fiercely, blocking our way. Artillery shells and rockets exploded all around. Suddenly our wagon lurched to one side and came to a halt. The rest of the column continued on its way and disappeared over a hill. There we sat, alone, with a broken wheel. The Russians were only a mile or so behind us. There was fire everywhere, pandemonium on the road below. Rockets and artillery shells screaming overhead, shell fragments whacking into our wagon. To our rear I could see Russians shooting off red and green flares, and more burning villages. The light from the many fires reflected off a low-lying cloud deck, coloring the clouds shades of red. It was a scene like out of Dante's *Inferno*. I was lying in the back of our wagon, watching, and thought that we had been abandoned. A surge of fear raced through my body, so strong I felt like I was choking to death. I crawled to where my mother sat alone on the driver's bench, tears streaming down my face. I always believed that as long as my mother was with me everything would be alright. This time I knew that not even she could make things right again. I said to her, 'Mutti'—that's what German children call their mothers—'I am so afraid.' I could barely get out the words. 'Is the dear God going to help us?' I remember her tired yet steady eyes. She stroked my hair back and said calmly, 'Wolfgang, the dear God is always with us. He will help us and show us the way. Have faith my son. Everything will be alright.'

"I don't know why, but I believed her. Her touch was calming, her voice and eyes steady. The intense fear I had felt drained out of me. You know what happened next? The artillery and rocket fire stopped. The driver of our wagon reappeared and transferred us to another wagon, and then we caught up with the rest of the convoy and eventually made it to the American lines. That wagon we transferred to was a supply wagon filled with food, and that food kept us alive in the difficult weeks ahead. Do I believe in God, or was it all just coincidence? I believe there are things we humans don't grasp easily, things we can't touch and see, but they are real nonetheless. Believing in God is one of those things you just have to take on faith."

"That's quite a story, Sam," Tom said softly. "You answered my question." He was my age, nineteen, from New Jersey. We were about the same height and weight and had gravitated toward each other because we sort of saw things the same way. "About those girls, Sam," he returned to our earlier conversation, "they are a bit out of our league. I want to be honest with you and not lead you on."

"What do you mean, they are out of our league?"

"They have money, Sam. Lots of money. Rich kids go to that church. Not guys like us who can barely afford a pitcher of 3.2 beer."

"So what. Let's find out what rich kids are like. All they can do is tell us to get lost." We laughed and got up to go. Tom and I were poor boys. Neither of us owned a car. We even saved on bus fare to Fort Worth by walking to the bus stop outside the main gate and waiting in the small shelter for someone to stop and give us a ride. Someone always stopped to give an airman a ride. It was just as easy to get a ride back to the base later in the evening, if you didn't mind the occasional hassle. If it was after ten o'clock, the return pick-ups frequently were men looking for male companionship. They were harmless and didn't bother us once they knew we weren't interested. It was still early in the day, so Tom and I hitched a ride into town and went to a bar where they knew our frugal habits. I had a Bloody Mary, a glass of beer with a small can of tomato juice on the side. As Tom and I sat staring at the Schlitz sign over the mirror on the wall behind the bartender, two cops entered and started checking IDs. They were nice about it, talking to the customers sitting in booths behind us, asking others for their identification. They looked at Tom and me, but never came over to check on us.

"Another?" the bartender asked wiping the counter with a wet rag. He was a young married sergeant from the base earning an extra buck tending bar. Tom and I nodded our heads in unison. "They are nice guys," he whispered. "Come in occasionally, but don't hassle airmen." We drank our beer slowly. We thought the bar a nice place to go, better than the barracks, but not a place to meet girls.

On Sunday Tom and I hitched a ride into town to attend the eleven o'clock service. "I checked out the earlier service," he whispered as we looked through the program. "No girls. They don't get up that early." After the service I started to leave. Tom took my elbow and said, "Let's not go just yet. Remember what we came for?" he smiled. "There's a small room adjacent to the sanctuary where they serve coffee and cookies. That's where the girls hang out. Maybe we'll be lucky today and get to meet some." We each got a cup of coffee and milled around, feeling a little uneasy not knowing anyone. Several parishioners came over to greet us, introduced themselves, and made polite conversation. Some had sons in the service, others had been in the service themselves during the war and wanted to talk about it. Tom nudged me in the side with his elbow. I noticed a group of girls standing in a circle in one corner of the room—talking, holding cups of coffee in their hands, throwing occasional glances at us. One striking blonde kept looking at me, or at least I thought she was. With hair flowing down her back to mid-waist, she wore a maroon silk suit, matching shoes and hat, pearl choker and bracelet, and cute little pearl earrings. Suddenly she walked directly toward me, coffee cup in hand, extending the other leather gloved hand toward me, saying, "I'm Harriet. Welcome to our church. You must be from Carswell?"

"I am," I replied. "Can you tell just by looking?"

"You soldiers have a certain look. Yes, I can," and she gave me a warm smile. I felt the blood rushing to my head, and perspiration forming on my forehead. Suddenly I felt overwhelmed by her presence. Her movements spoke of training and education that only the wealthy could afford to give their children. Could she see that my knees were wobbly? In her high heels she was a little taller than my five-foot nine. Her eyes were a deep blue, like my father Willie's. Steady eyes, self-assured. She was light complected, her skin smooth, without blemish. She asked my name. I collected myself sufficiently to stutter, "Wolfgang."

"Wolfgang," she said in a melodic voice, drawing my name out like it was a special treat, "what a lovely name." I noticed Tom approaching with another girl. I was relieved to have company.

"This is Mary, my best friend," Harriet introduced us. "She lives next door to me. Wolfgang is from Germany, Mary. Isn't that exciting?" Mary and I shook hands and exchanged a few polite words. Then Mary turned back toward Tom to continue their conversation. They seemed sort of glued together, I thought, standing quite close for a first meeting.

"You have such a cute accent, Wolfgang," Harriet continued, looking at me coyly. "I am certain your girlfriend loves it as much as I do. I just love to listen to you talk." I put down my coffee cup, afraid I would spill it. Why was my shirt collar so tight?

"I don't have a girlfriend," I heard myself saying. "Haven't been off base very much to meet any girls."

"You must be lonely then," Harriet said with a touch of irony in her voice. Was she being polite, or was she reaching out?

"I'm new here, Harriet," I said, using her name for the first time, "and being at Carswell it's difficult to meet girls, especially when you don't have a car. I spend most of my free time in the barracks. Besides, as you probably know, one-stripers like me barely make enough money to take a girl to a movie."

"I know nothing about the army," Harriet responded. "Have you had lunch yet?"

"No, not yet. Tom and I were going to skip lunch. It's not important."

"Nonsense. Why don't you and Tom join Mary and me for a sandwich at my house." Before I knew it, I was sitting next to Harriet in a new, yellow and white, two-tone Oldsmobile 88 hardtop. Tom and Mary sat in back, very close, and Harriet and I were up front. Neither Harriet's mother or father were home when we arrived. I expected her to drive up to some pretentious mansion, but that wasn't the case. Her house was an older, two-story brick home on a tree-shaded street with a large, inviting front porch. Harriet and Mary disappeared into the kitchen while Tom and I settled into comfortable rattan chairs. After ten minutes or so the girls emerged carrying trays laden with a plate of tuna sandwiches and glasses of iced tea with a sprig of mint on the rim of each glass. I was hungry after all, and the sandwich tasted delicious. We four sat on the porch for some time talking. It was a warm, sunny day. Then the girls drove Tom and me back to Carswell and dropped us off right in front of our barracks. There was no one about on a Sunday afternoon to see us arrive, or we would have been the envy of our barracks.

As Tom and I got out of the car, Harriet said, "Our second pastor has a youth group which both Mary and I belong to. He is young, just married, and lots of fun. We meet at his house every Wednesday evening. Would you like to come? We have about twenty young men and women our age in the group. We sing and talk about things. It's a fun group. You would like it."

"Yes, I would like that," I responded a bit too hastily. "But I don't have a way to get there."

"I'll pick you up at the gate." A tentative smile played around Harriet's lips. "Six thirty then?"

"Yes, I'll be there at six thirty." I waved at Harriet as she drove off.

I turned toward Tom, "Are you going on Wednesday?"

Tom looked sort of starry eyed. "Mary and I hit it off right away," he replied. "At least I think we did. I really like her."

I didn't want to get my hopes up about Harriet, but I found myself fantasizing about things I should probably not even be thinking of. The whole thing would soon blow over, I decided in the drab environs of my barracks. But it didn't blow over. Soon after our first tentative meetings we began to see each other every night, every weekend. Every minute I could spare I spent with Harriet. It was the beginning of a relationship that would profoundly change the direction of my life. In later years I wondered how things lined up in life: Was everything predetermined, as my father always said it was; or was it all a game of chance, an accident of the moment? Maybe it was a little of both.

On Friday, March 18, 1955, nearly four months after Harriet and I first met, I processed out of the 7th Bomb Wing at Carswell Air Force Base. Processing out meant that I picked up my records early that morning at the personnel office and followed a detailed checklist to clear the base. The most important stop was the finance office. If that didn't get done right, my pay would be screwed up for weeks to come. The finance clerk carefully sealed my pay records after annotating the amount of advance and travel pay he had counted out to me in crisp twenty-dollar bills. He would mail my pay records, along with my personnel file, to my new unit of assignment. My last stop was the Headquarters Squadron orderly room where I turned in my out-processing checklist, had it reviewed by a clerk for completeness, and only then was allowed to sign myself out on the sign in/sign out register. For the next thirty-seven days, thirty days leave plus seven days travel time, I was in sort of a float status between assignments.

About three o'clock in the afternoon Harriet drove up in a shiny new green and cream-colored Olds 98, her mother's car. I stood in front of my barracks waiting, wearing my class A uniform, duffel bag by my side. I tossed the bag into the large trunk of the Olds and jumped into the car beside Harriet. We drove over to the orderly room where I was going to sign out. She didn't pull into the parking space labeled VISITORS as I asked her to; instead, she parked directly in front of the steps leading into the orderly room. By then I knew Harriet rarely played by the rules. I intended to go in alone, but she insisted on accompanying me. She wore a tight-fitting, beige cashmere sweater set off by a single strand of pearls. A wide, black patent leather belt accented her figure, and the folds of her skirt were designed in such a way as to draw attention to everything feminine about her. She wore bobby socks and Italian penny loafers with a dime tucked into the tongue of each shoe. Her hair was pulled back tightly and held together by a pearl-studded clasp; an expensive Swiss watch, costing more than I earned in a year, adorned her left wrist, and a huge diamond ring graced her right ring finger. Harriet looked expensive. Harriet was expensive.

One of her pastimes was shopping for new clothes and accessories. I once accompanied her to Neiman Marcus in Dallas. There I sat in a large reception area, quite some distance from Harriet and her sales consultant, a woman my mother's age. No dresses were anywhere in sight. The two talked, then the consultant disappeared through a door and emerged with a roll-around rack hung with assorted dresses, suits, skirts, blouses, and whatever else girls wear. Harriet briefly examined each item, feeling its fabric as the woman held it up for her approval. She hung a few things aside, and then the consultant disappeared with the rack of clothes, and we left.

"Didn't you buy anything?" I asked her on the way out. She looked at me in honest surprise and said, "Of course. I bought nearly all she had set aside for me. She knows exactly what I like, has a good eye for style and color, and saves me the drudgery of picking out my own dresses. We have better things to do with our time, don't we darling?" and she gave me a suggestive smile. Harriet always referred to me as darling, unless something annoyed her, then I became Wolfgang. The dresses were delivered the following day. No money changed hands in my presence, nor did I see Harriet look at a price tag. Harriet's adoring father, Thomas, paid for his daughter's purchases. For someone like me, who once wore sandals made from the tires of abandoned German combat aircraft, her kind of shopping was a unique experience, like being in a totally different world.

Harriet's father was nearly always away, traveling the Texas and Oklahoma oil fields, selling pipe and oil-well accessories, such as drill bits. I learned from Harriet that over the years her father had picked up his share of oil leases, making him a wealthy man. Theirs was a world I knew nothing about, except that it was all about oil and stocks and money and shopping. Harriet's father was a balding, highly intelligent, self-made man—something he was proud of and quick to point out. He was equally proud of having served in the Great War. "I played poker with Harry Truman on the battlefields of France," he told me. "We were in the same artillery regiment. When it was all over, Harry and I were about even." That was about as much of his life as he cared to share with me. He measured his words carefully when speaking and always wore a dark suit with a vest—no matter the outside temperature—and a ten-gallon hat.

That afternoon, when I, accompanied by Harriet, entered the Head-quarters Squadron orderly room to sign out, Harriet's presence caused the typewriter clatter to cease abruptly, the babble of voices to stop. There was total silence for three or four long seconds. Then everyone tried to continue with what they were doing before Harriet had entered their world, but it was obvious to me that no one could concentrate as long as she was there. I saw the sideways glances, the assessments, the questions she raised in their minds, the looks that undressed a woman. I knew what they would be talking about that evening.

"Darling," Harriet said as she drove toward the main gate, "did you see their tongues hanging out?"

"I don't know what you mean, Harriet. Why do you say such things?" I was embarrassed by the reaction in the orderly room. I didn't like to draw attention to myself. Harriet liked exactly the opposite.

"As I told you, darling, men are so predictable," she continued, undeterred by my response. "When you men see a beautiful woman you immediately undress her with your eyes. You can't help it, darling, you are made that way. Then all you can think of is . . . , well, you know what I mean. Right?" She could at times be so frank and uninhibited. It made me uncomfortable when she talked like that. "I know you are wondering why I went in there with you, darling. Obviously not to look at their beautiful furniture. I wanted to make them jealous of you, envy you. That I did. They all have their own little fantasies, and that is alright. But to indulge them they have to pay a price."

"Pay what price?" She was annoying me a little, getting me caught up in her theories of men and love, which I didn't always share.

"You are so naive, darling. Do I have to explain everything? But then, that is one reason why I think I love you. The price those men paid for fantasizing is that they know darn well that they will never have a woman like me. It hurts, darling, when men are confronted with their limitations."

"Is that so? You know a lot more about men than I do about women, Harriet. I love you, but I don't always understand you. Did you learn all that stuff at Hockaday?"

"Don't worry, darling, you don't need to understand everything about me. It would worry me if you did. Besides, we women know things you men can't figure out in a lifetime." We passed through the main gate. The two young air police stared at Harriet and smiled. She smiled back. I was used to that.

I spent the next four weeks in a stranger's house, an unpretentious three-bedroom brick rambler on a cul-de-sac in a tree-shaded middle-class neighborhood of Fort Worth, totally quiet in the morning after the men had gone to work and the children left for school on their bouncy yellow buses. I enjoyed the tranquility of the place, liked to listen to a mockingbird go through its repertoire of imitations, watch a flock of sparrows fight over a small morsel of food on the sidewalk. I couldn't recall when in my past I had such an idyllic existence with no pressures on me of any kind. The house owner was supposedly off vacationing in Bermuda and was gracious enough to allow me to use his residence in his absence, at least that was the story Harriet told me. The owner, whoever he was, was "a friend of the family," she said. I thought it more likely he was a former lover of hers who surrendered his house keys when she asked for a small favor. It didn't matter. I knew I wasn't the first man in her life. Harriet's mother thought I still lived on base. "She doesn't need to know everything," Harriet persuaded me.

For Harriet our arrangement had its advantages. We could be together without being seen and without anyone asking probing questions which might get her name into the society pages of the *Dallas Morning News* or the *Fort Worth Star Telegram*. Not that she cared, but she didn't like to embarrass her doting parents, especially her father, to whom all her wishes, expressed or implied, were a command. She was an only child and indulged like one. Harriet was educated in an "upperclass way." At age nineteen she was a woman, not a girl, as comfortable in the presence of the senior senator from Texas as she was with her maid or others who made her life comfortable. She had a natural regal presence and was noticed wherever she went. Although a well-groomed society girl, first and foremost Harriet was a Texas girl. For her the sun rose and set on Texas. There was no other place on earth she would rather be.

It was my last day. Thirty days had passed all too quickly. Early the next morning I would be on my way to Camp Kilmer, New Jersey. Harriet arrived after the morning school buses had come and gone. It was very quiet outside except for the chirping birds, the cooing mourning doves, and the trill of a mockingbird. I heard her drive up, carefully open the unlocked front door, and tiptoe down the hall thinking I was still asleep. She smiled when she saw me looking up, said nothing, and walked over to the little table in the corner displaying a marble copy of a Michelangelo nude. With practiced motions she unbuttoned the back of her dress, let it slide to the floor, stepped out of her half-slip, removed her jewelry and carefully placed it on the little table next to the nude, kicked off her shoes, undid her stockings and rolled them down with practiced motions, removed the clasp holding her hair, letting it fall around her shoulders, shook her head, making sure her hair fell just right, then unhooked her brassiere and let it float to the floor, stepping out of her panties last. She slid into bed beside me. I loved to watch her undress and she loved to put on a show for me. We stayed there until noon.

"Are you glad I came?" she whispered.

"Of course, I'm glad. I don't even want to think about being without you, but I guess I better get used to it." I was feeling good, relaxed, totally at peace, the way a man feels whose immediate needs had all been met. "You know there were times when I was sixteen, seventeen, and eighteen when I thought I was going to die if I didn't have a girl soon." Harriet was out of bed getting ready to take a shower. She had a luncheon to go to at Colonial Country Club.

"Why are you telling me this, darling? Why didn't you have sex sooner? I don't understand. Girls like sex. All you have to do is ask politely," she laughed and stepped into the shower. I waited until she came out again.

"I was so afraid to give in to my body. I didn't understand what was happening to me. I was so incredibly ignorant. And I was very, very shy."

"Poor darling," Harriet whispered mockingly. "So, when did you finally get the courage to have a girl and find out what it was like? You didn't die, so you must have found salvation somewhere. Who saved you?"

"You have to promise not to laugh if I tell you, and it isn't what it sounds like. She was a woman of the night." Harriet stopped what she was doing and laughed loudly, looking at me in disbelief.

"You mean you bought a woman? That is disgusting!"

"No, no, I didn't buy her. We just met innocently and ended up making love. I didn't find out she was what she was until later. She was generous and kind to me. I only think of her as a compassionate woman."

"OK, I believe you only because it is you. You are so ignorant, darling, when it comes to sex. So I am really your first woman?"

"Almost."

"I suspected that. At times it is hard for me to believe that you are nearly twenty years old."

"I'd better hurry," she said with that peculiar firmness in her voice that made servants serve and men do her bidding. "I need to run. The girls will not understand if I am late." I watched her get dressed, finding it hard to believe she was my girl. Deep down I knew, Harriet would never belong to any man.

"I have no idea how you managed to hold it together for so long, darling," she said, as she was buttoning her dress. "I was twelve when I had my first man, against my will mind you, but it was my first man. Why this chastity for so long? I don't understand. Even though you told me all those reasons of your body changing and your past. You don't fight it the way you did."

"I think you've forgotten I'm an immigrant boy. Three years ago I came to America with nothing—no money, no education, couldn't even speak the language. All I knew was that some day I wanted to fly airplanes. I wasn't going to do anything that got in the way of my dream, least of all get a girl pregnant. Can't you understand that?"

"Oh, you are so silly, darling. There is no money to be made in the army. You have to get a real job someday. Go to Rice and become a petroleum engineer. Dad will get you in and pay for it. It's the only school for you."

"One thing I know for sure, Harriet, I'll never be an engineer. I tried it and I didn't like it. By the way, I'm not in the army; I'm in the air force. There is a difference."

"It's all the same to me," she said firmly, pulling her hair back, attaching her pearl clasp. She looked in the full-length mirror mounted on the bedroom door, approving of what she saw. "I am not going to marry a soldier boy, do you understand that, darling? We'll have to work that out. There just isn't any money in being in the army or the air force, or whatever you want to call it. How will you be able to afford a woman like me with those strange ideas in your head? You'll have to do better than that." She stood in the bedroom doorway, looking fresh and appealing. "Goodbye, darling. See you later this afternoon."

The front door clicked shut. I heard the powerful engine of the Olds 98 spring to life, then all that remained behind was silence and a lingering touch of her perfume. She liked Dior perfumes, Miss Dior and Diorama, fragrances which she applied liberally after a bath or shower. I took a deep breath of the air she and I had breathed together. I opened the drapes, and the sun poured into the room changing its character. I opened the windows to let the fresh spring air enter and mingle. It looked like another beautiful Texas day. I showered, dressed, and added the towels to the sheets I had stripped off the bed. I started the laundry. Tonight I would spend in the guest room of her parent's house.

The Greyhound bus laboriously climbed the long incline into the Oklahoma badlands, traversing a seemingly endless field of lava which looked like it was manmade, perfectly square pillars jutting to the surface at an angle. Since coming to the United States in 1951, I had never ceased to be amazed by the diversity of the land, the huge forests, the impressive prairies which reached from the Mississippi River all the way to the snow-covered peaks of the Rocky Mountains. The Oklahoma Badlands were different again. I watched the outside world as it slid by my window until I tired and began to nod off. The bus stopped in Tulsa where I changed to another which took me to St. Louis. After more changes I eventually wound up in New Brunswick, New Jersey, where I was to report to Camp Kilmer for eventual shipment to a new duty station somewhere in England.

To someone at some air force headquarters I was just a body in transit, one of many such bodies shuffled around until deposited at some faraway place for a year or two or three. Then the whole exercise began all over again, only in reverse. Those doing the shuffling never knew or saw the people they moved around their imaginary chessboards. To them, we were just numbers—serial numbers and air force specialty code numbers—to be plugged into an organizational scheme which in its entirety represented the United States Air Force and the defense and security of the nation. I looked like any one of the thousands of airmen, soldiers, sailors, and marines passing through America's bus terminals. We had that clean-cut, youthful look about us, something we weren't especially aware of, but many of the older passengers were, and they looked at us at times with the uncomplicated envy older people are capable off when recalling their own youth. We were all young faces, mostly going to our first duty assignments out of boot camp, basic training, or technical school. We crossed America in all directions on our way to strange new destinations. I had become one of the many young American soldiers crossing the land by Greyhound bus on my way to a foreign shore. I had become an American.

I chose a comfortable window seat in the middle of the bus. My grandfather Samuel told me once never to sit in the front or the rear of anything, so I chose the middle. Opa had given me lots of little sayings to live by. One I remembered particularly well now that I was in the military: "Never volunteer for anything if you ever become a soldier. If it were something good or easy they wouldn't need to ask for volunteers. Especially stay away from things for which they promise medals, promotions or anything else of value. It is sure to be a task from hell." My grandfather Samuel fought in many of the great battles in the Great War in the east and west. His counsel stayed with me through the years and probably saved my life in a still distant war called Vietnam.

The swaying of the bus, the sound of large tires ripping their way across asphalt and concrete, the wind, and the drone of the diesel engine made me drowsy. My head kept falling to one side, waking me when I hit the window. I tried not to, but my thoughts drifted to Harriet whenever I woke; in recent weeks she had eclipsed nearly all else that mattered in my life. The past four weeks we spent together as lovers would on an extended honeymoon. Our last night was at her parent's house. Theirs was a nice home, but not ostentatious. Her mother dreaded being identified as nouveau riche. She considered ostentation in bad taste when it came to how she lived, but that principle did not apply to her only child, and namesake, of a late marriage. Harriet had always received the best of everything in clothing, cars, school, or travel. From the first grade through graduation, she attended the exclusive Hockaday School in Dallas, a boarding school for the daughters of the rich and privileged. Harriet knew only girls like herself. Her contact with ordinary people of limited means was restricted to servants or providers of services. After high school graduation she went through the usual coming out rituals for Texas girls of her status—was the queen of this, the duchess of that, and took the obligatory escorted trip to Europe. She attended Texas Christian University for a year, but soon decided that college was a bore. That's when we had met. Whatever Harriet wanted was hers for the asking. She was the apple of her father's eye—his Yellow Rose of Texas.

CHAPTER 19

Camp Kilmer, New Jersey

Harriet had picked me up in mid-afternoon at the little house in the quiet leafy neighborhood where I had spent the better part of the past four weeks as the guest of someone I never met and never would meet. I tried to leave everything the way I had found it, neat and tidy. I did the laundry, folded the towels and sheets and put them away, cleaned the kitchen, which I hardly used, and made sure nothing remained behind in the refrigerator. I locked the front door for the first time since I arrived and gave the key to Harriet when she picked me up. Harriet's mother greeted me at the door in her usual polite fashion. She invited me to join her for a glass of iced tea, ringing a crystal bell for Amelia, her longtime maid. Amelia, a thin tall woman with a regal carriage, emerged from the kitchen, her ebony skin contrasting pleasantly with her white lace-bordered apron and dark blue dress. She brought us three glasses of iced tea on a silver platter, little sugar cubes peaking from a crystal bowl and a sprig of freshly cut mint decorating the rim of each glass.

I never quite knew what to talk about with Harriet's mother. She broke the silence by saying, "I enjoy hearing you talk, Wolfgang. I think your accent charming. I am sure Harriet has told you the same. I hope you don't mind me saying so?"

"Of course, I don't," I replied.

"And you are going so far away Harriet tells me. To England?"

"Yes, ma'am."

"Are you allowed to tell me where they are sending you?"

"I don't know exactly where I'm going until I get there. Right now all I know is that I have to report to a military base in New Jersey, where I'll be put on a boat that will take me to England. I am just a low-ranking airman; they don't tell us anything." I laughed; she smiled.

"My husband and I are expecting an invitation to present Harriet to the Queen." I was puzzled and must have looked it because she went on to say, "Yes, of course, my dear boy, there is such a thing. You may not have heard of it. It is much sought after by Texas debutantes. Part of their coming out, so to speak. Maybe you can be our guest for the weekend when we are in London? I am sure Harriet would like that."

"I would love to," I replied, still puzzled by what she told me. Didn't she know that her daughter was nearly twenty years old, not a girl anymore, but a woman? I didn't know what "coming out" meant for girls in Texas, but I thought it probably had something to do with puberty, such as confirmation in Germany, when boys and girls were pushed into the adult world. Harriet entered the room and said in the tone of voice of a daughter who always got her way, "Mother, I can't share him with you much longer. It's his last day. You understand, don't you?"

"Of course, dear," Harriet's mother replied. "I must excuse myself anyway, Wolfgang. I have some ladies coming over in a few minutes and I'd better get ready for them." I rose to my feet. Her salt-and-pepper hair made her look older than she really was. I presumed her to be in her late fifties, or early sixties. In contrast to the sophisticated make-up worn by Harriet, her mother wore none. She was a bit shorter than her husband, but beautiful still, in a fading sort of way. She must have had Harriet quite late in life. "Have fun, dears," she said, smiling at us as she left the room. I thought for just an instant I detected a wistful look in her eyes, as if perhaps we made her recall her own youth. Then she was gone through the swinging doors into a part of the house I had never entered.

"Does she know about us, Harriet?"

"She may have some idea, but she would never say anything. She is too much of a southern lady for that. She lives in another time, darling. I am sure in her heyday she didn't just hold hands with her beaus. I am not certain if she and father still do it. They are probably too old. He isn't home often enough to indulge. I once heard that if a couple put a penny in a jar for every time they made love in their first year of marriage it would take them a lifetime to empty it. If my parents have any pennies left in their jar, they'll probably never empty it." Harriet grabbed my hand and pulled me out onto the porch. We decided to go over to the Colonial Country Club for our final dinner. The grizzled old Maître d' expressed his appreciation when she agreed to dine in a private room. I didn't wear a tie and my casual attire conflicted with the rules of the club for the main dining room. Several times the old man expressed to Harriet how much he appreciated her understanding and that the food would make up for any inconvenience. Our steaks were indeed exquisite. I was no judge of steaks, having had little experience along those lines, but if size, appearance, taste, and tenderness were part of the criteria for judging a good steak, then these steaks were the very best Texas could produce. I recalled our first dinner date at the Petroleum Club, on the top floor of the Amon Carter Building in Fort Worth. I tried to order pork chops. Harriet nearly fell out of her chair in embarrassment and immediately corrected the situation by firmly taking charge of menu selections from then on. She ordered steak, "the way it's done in Texas," she counseled me.

After dinner we drove to Lake Worth and parked. The clouds were dissipating to the west, and the second rush of light from the evening's sunset passed. The stars, dim at first, quickly assumed a glittering brightness in the black Texas sky to the east, and a sickle moon appeared on the horizon. According to Harriet the stars shone brighter over Texas than anywhere else, just like Texas steak was the best in the world. I had heard from her how unique and superior Texas was in nearly every aspect when compared to any other state of the union, not to mention the rest of the world. I liked Harriet's enthusiastic acceptance of her own world. Even more, I liked being alone with her, sitting next to her, smelling her perfume, and feeling her nearness. Harriet was a woman who radiated strength and vulnerability at one and the same time, who attracted attention yet commanded restraint. I thought her a total contradiction at times and couldn't get enough of her.

Harriet knew where to park, where we wouldn't be bothered by others seeking equal solitude. We had first come to the lake when we met last November. Then I sat next to her, unable to touch her beyond holding hands. It was she who moved her hand within mine, turned her face toward me, and came close, breaking the spell. We stayed for an hour or so. "Mother will be asleep by the time we walk in," she said. "Don't worry about waking her. Father is out on the road selling pipe, of course. That's his thrill."

Harriet drove the familiar road back to her house. I sat quietly by her side, thinking about Tom and Mary who had developed a relationship equally close to Harriet's and mine. Both girls had cars, so there was no need for us to double date. We did, however, go to the Wednesday evening church youth group meetings together. We all sat on the floor in a semicircle around our pastor, who wasn't all that much older than we, still young enough for us to relate to him. We'd talk about marriage, relationships, and sex in an abstract way. The pastor never spoke of sex in a doctrinal sense, of having sex purely for the sake of procreation, but rather led us to discuss its various facets and implications, guiding us to seek our own answers within the context of Christian beliefs. Sex was, of course, one of the primary things dominating all of our eighteen- and nineteen-year-old bodies. The pastor's wife often joined our circle, and she would add a feminine dimension to our discussions, leading us to consider issues that might arise from intimate behavior, the responsibilities that may accrue to the partners, and liabilities that may evolve from irresponsible behavior. We never spoke of sex in the army way, that is, how to prevent getting venereal disease. The army, or the air force in my case, viewed sex strictly as a possible liability to mission accomplishment. Therefore, providing functional instruction on disease prevention, providing condoms or protective kits—all to prevent its soldiers and airmen from becoming casualties of their compulsive behavior—was an understandable approach. But it was not appropriate for a group of church-going youngsters. Our meetings were a learning and sharing experience, without anyone being explicit or personal. We shared our concerns, our ignorance, our expectations. I liked going to the meetings, being with others my own age, addressing issues I had difficulty dealing with and couldn't discuss with anyone else. Just knowing that others had difficulties of a similar nature was a helpful insight for me. I discovered that the transition from boy to man, from girl to woman, was an equally difficult one for us all.

One Wednesday evening Tom and Mary announced their engagement to our group. Before I left for England, they married in a simple wedding service conducted by our pastor, but not attended by Mary's parents. Her parents opposed Mary's choice. They had wanted her to marry a rich Texas boy, or so she said. I said to Harriet, "If we were getting married and your parents wouldn't give us their blessings, I'd just as well live as we do now and not get married."

Harriet looked thoughtful. Then she said, "You know, Mary's parents are real hypocrites."

"Why is that?"

"Well, they made their money during the Alaska gold rush. Do you know about the Alaska gold rush?" She didn't wait for my answer. "Around the turn of the century Mary's grandfather went up to the Klondike, Dawson and places like that. Later on he went to Nome when the gold played out at Dawson. He went wherever the money was. Ran a saloon where he sold bad whiskey for good gold. He made a boatload of money, and Mary's family is still living off of it. I don't know what they do besides cashing checks and spending the money as fast as they get it. They, of all people, have no right to deny their only daughter what is rightfully hers to decide." I had never heard Harriet speak that way before, so genuinely angered about something that didn't affect her personally. I guess I still had a lot to learn.

I awoke abruptly as the bus driver braked hard for a truck that suddenly pulled out in front of him. He cursed, then passed the slow-moving vehicle. After three days and two nights of cross-country travel, late on the third day, my Greyhound bus finally rumbled into New Brunswick, New Jersey. I felt stiff from all the sitting, exhausted from not getting any real sleep, and dirty from not being able to take a bath or a shower. I longed to take a shower, one like I took in Fassberg back in 1948, or was it 1949? The first hot shower in my life.

At the time I lived in a decrepit refugee camp and barely had any clothes to wear—no underwear, no socks. When Hedy met Leo, he gave me a pair of American uniform pants, several green army undershirts, and boxer shorts. One Saturday Leo asked me if I would like to accompany him to the airbase. We rode our bicycles on a dirt path leading through potato fields and pine forests, past the site where 20 mm antiaircraft guns once stood until they were cut up for scrap iron, then alongside the railroad tracks into the air base. There were no guards to stop us. We rode across the airfield to one of the large aircraft hangars, huge steel structures with flat roofs, a layer of dirt on their roofs planted with grass, heather, and trees to provide camouflage from the air. Parked inside the cavernous hangar were twin-engined C-47 transports, no longer used in the Berlin airlift now that the larger four-engine C-54s had arrived. We climbed an iron staircase that led to a balcony under the roof and to several rooms used as sleeping quarters by American airmen. Leo's room contained four neatly made cots, their blankets tightly stretched. At the foot of each bed sat a green footlocker. Two metal cabinets stood against one wall, each occupant sharing one half of a cabinet. There were no locks. Leo took off his jacket, undid his tie, and removed his shirt, and indicated for me to do the same. Then he took two green army towels, two bars of soap, and a bottle of shampoo from his cabinet and motioned for me to follow him. I, in my underwear, followed with some trepidation. Leo handed me one of the towels and a bar of soap, then pointed to a shower stall. He undressed and stepped into another. I watched him turn on the water, steam rising from the concrete floor as he began shampooing his hair. I didn't know what to do. At thirteen I had never taken a shower, hadn't even had a bath in a real bathtub for close to four years. Leo again pointed at a shower and waved his hand for me to get in. I took off my undershirt, but couldn't get myself to take off my shorts. Once I got the water temperature adjusted I really enjoyed the experience. It felt so wonderful to have hot water bounce off my body. What a luxury! I took the bar of reddish soap which smelled of iodine, lathered myself all over, then rinsed with more of the glorious hot water. I stood in the shower for a long time. I thought of taking off my shorts, but I just couldn't get myself to do it. Leo was already out of the shower, dried and dressed when I got out. He said nothing about my wet shorts. When we got to his room, he handed me a pair of dry shorts without comment, and I quickly put them on. My first shower was the best shower I ever took in my life. Maybe I would be able to take a shower like that tonight, then stretch out on a real bed and get a good night's sleep.

I was the last person to get off the bus. My duffel bag lay on the dirty concrete of the station where the driver had thrown it when he unloaded the bus. It was a station like all others, no cleaner and no dirtier. What all of them needed, I thought, were a couple of German *Putzfrauen*; they would keep the places sparkling. I grabbed my duffel bag and headed for the door. A military policeman approached.

"You headed for Kilmer?" he asked in a deep southern drawl, pointing his riot stick at me.

"Yes."

"Around the corner," he said, then turned away, continuing to patrol the station, looking for other new arrivals. I saw the rear of an army bus jutting out from behind the station, one of those nondescript military buses, functional but very uncomfortable to ride. The bus looked as if it were made from the same material as Quonset huts in World War II, painted a nondescript gray-green, sort of like a prison bus. I walked around to the front and saw the sign—CAMP KILMER. It was misting, making everything slick and slimy, and it was getting dark rapidly. I felt exhausted, a touch of familiar depression beginning to pull me down. The bus was half full when I boarded. I dropped my two bags in an empty seat and sat down beside them. More soldiers and airmen stumbled onto the bus. Then, without saying a word, the driver closed the doors and drove off. Another bus pulled into its place. The rain grew heavier.

When the bus arrived at Camp Kilmer, I was assigned to a two-story World War II barracks, just like the open-bay transient barrack I lived in at Lackland. A tired-looking orderly stamped my orders and annotated them. Time: 2100 hours. Date: April 25, 1955. Where sent: Bldg 403. I was assigned a bed on the second floor of the aging barracks. At least they weren't bunk beds. The orderly instructed me that the morning formation was in fatigues, at seven o'clock sharp in front of the barracks—rain or shine. After dropping my belongings on my bed, I remembered that I hadn't eaten much over the last three days, only a few hot dogs, dried out burgers, and chips, so I headed for the mess hall which was open twenty-four hours a day.

The mess was huge, like a food factory. I grabbed a compartmented stainless steel tray and went down the chow line. One cook slapped a generous helping of mashed potatoes on my tray, another poured brown gravy over my potatoes, and still another flipped a large crispy-brown chunk of liver in the center section of the tray, topping the liver with a generous helping of mushy fried onions. Further down the line a soldier filled the remaining space with a medley of vegetables—peas, carrots, and corn. I grabbed two clammy rolls and several butter patties and headed for an empty spot on a long table. I ate everything. Then I went back to the line and grabbed a couple of pieces of apple pie and decorated them with two huge balls of vanilla ice cream. Not exactly Colonial Country Club food, but I had already adjusted to what I really was—a soldier, or an airman to be precise. After eating, my sense of gloom dissipated. I knew from past experience that when I was really tired and found myself in new surroundings I frequently suffered one of my recurring nightmares. I took that long-awaited hot shower, then wrapped my towel around my waist, and trudged up the wooden stairs to the second floor. I stuffed my loose things into a foot locker and went to sleep. No dreams. No nightmares.

The seven o'clock formation was led by the senior man in the barracks, a staff sergeant. Rain came down steadily, soaking everyone to the skin. The red New Jersey mud clung to our boots like glue. An army lieutenant, who took the morning report, stood on an elevated wooden platform in proper rain gear. The reporting over, the lieutenant relinquished the stage to a master sergeant who read the orders of the day, encased in plastic so the rain couldn't dissolve them as the sergeant held them in his hands. One instruction required us to check the squadron bulletin board twice a day for duty assignments and shipping instructions. After the formation was dismissed, I did that immediately and learned to my disappointment that during the night someone had typed my name under Kitchen Duty. After breakfast, I reported to the kitchen and was assigned to the clean-up detail. Floors, pots, pans, mixers, mess trays, more floors, huge stainless steel mixing bowls—all came my way as the day wore on. After breakfast, after lunch, after dinner—the same all over again. By evening I felt like the proverbial dish rag and smelled as bad.

During the night the rain stopped. The seven o'clock formation over, I headed for the bulletin board and found my name listed again—this time to receive an overseas briefing in the base movie theater. I ate breakfast, changed uniforms, and at ten o'clock sat in the theater waiting for the show to begin. A parade of sergeants and junior officers told us what, where, how, and when to do or not to do. I blocked the drone of voices and incantations out of my consciousness, until I heard the words bombs, World War II, and German bombers. A sergeant stood on stage instructing us how to behave in England. "Now when you come to London," the sergeant emphasized, "some of the kids you'll run into will have had more wartime experience than you've had watching World War II movies. So, don't try to act the war hero in your fancy uniforms. Don't make fools of yourselves." The sergeant then changed the subject and started to lecture us on not flashing our money around. What money? At one hundred-five dollars a month I didn't have anything but coins to flash around. My thoughts went back to the sergeant's comments about war. I looked around the theater. All the faces were young. If they only knew how much war I'd seen. I remembered *real* war, remembered the insides of people blown about, their faces missing, their bodies burning like roasts over a fire. I never would forget the smell of burning flesh, a smell no one had ever been able to include in a war movie. I remembered the dead American pilot lying by the side of the road, his half-burned parachute still attached. War was very ugly; I hoped I would never have to experience it again. I looked at the boy sitting beside me, fresh from the Midwest, I thought. His eyes were bright and shiny, excited about the adventure he thought lay before him.

The movie started. It was about venereal disease, not war. What VD was and how to avoid it. "Don't go out with girls who have VD," the sergeant shouted into the darkened theater. "If you do, always use a precaution! A condom." I had seen those same movies in Army ROTC at the University of Colorado. The movies seemed dated even then, aimed at an audience of World War II soldiers. Ten years later, they were still showing the same movies shown in 1943 and 1944. Mostly, they tried to scare the timid into abstinence. I didn't really know what soldiers actually did, I hadn't been one all that long, but what I knew from my past experience watching them in Fassberg and other places, they pretty much did what came naturally—VD movies or no VD movies. When we were finally dismissed, I didn't feel much wiser than when I entered the theater. Surely one of the purposes of the lecture and movie was to keep us occupied. The army made sure there was little idle time for us to get into trouble.

After lunch I went to check the bulletin board once more. It was raining again, and the assembly area in front of my barracks was a six-inch-deep sea of mud, guaranteed to seep into even the best GI boots. A carpet of sticks, three feet wide, tied together with wire and laid down flat, made a fairly dry walkway between the mess hall and the barracks. When I got to the bulletin board, I noticed a new shipping list. I searched for my name, and when I found it, my heart pounded in my throat. "Personnel on attached passenger list," the notice read, "assigned or attached this squadron (pipeline) are assigned to organization indicated, APO New York, and will proceed to Brooklyn Navy Yard by railroad or bus on 30 April for further OCONUS (outside continental United States) movement via USNS *General S. Buckner* to Southampton. By order of the commander."

Orders to that effect were ready for me in the orderly room. The orders stated in both French and English that: "1. The personnel on this passenger list are authorized to proceed on or about 30 April 1955 to Southampton on a permanent change of assignment. 2. This trip is authorized in accordance with Agreement between the Parties to the North Atlantic Treaty regarding the Status of their forces, signed London on 19 June 1951." A list of names was attached to my orders. Only the page with my name on it was provided. I couldn't believe my eyes. There was my name at the bottom of one of the columns assigning me to the 28th Weather Squadron, whatever that was.

I was shipping out to England on the thirtieth, three days from now. I no longer saw the mud. My eyes were as starry as those of the young airmen who sat beside me in the movie theater. Before me rose the adventure of crossing the Atlantic once again, seeing yet another new land, meeting new people. Life could be so wonderful, even in the military.

Three days later, when our buses arrived dockside, there was a surprise waiting for me. Next to the USNS *General Simon B. Buckner* lay the much smaller USNS *George W. Goethals*, the very ship on which Hedy, Leo, and I had come to the United States four years earlier. Then I was a German boy; now I was an American airman. I took a last look at the *Goethals* as I walked up the gangplank before stepping into the belly of the *Buckner*. I could clearly see the ghosts of yesteryear standing at the *Goethals* railing.

CHAPTER 20

USNS *Simon B. Buckner*

The USNS *General Simon B. Buckner*, unlike the *George W. Goethals*, was not a Liberty Ship, but the first of a new class of troop transports built just prior to the end of World War II. Significantly larger and faster than its Liberty Ship predecessor, the *Buckner* was designed to deliver large numbers of troops to the far reaches of the Pacific Ocean area. Nearly 150 feet longer than the *Goethals*, the ship had two stacks, to the *Goethals'* one, and moved at a sustained speed of nineteen knots. Although only three knots faster than a Liberty Ship, at 17,000 tons, compared to 12,093 tons for the *Goethals*, the *Buckner* could carry twice as many troops, nearly five thousand, and go two thousand miles further without refueling. In 1955, both the *Buckner* and the *Goethals* were operated by the U.S. Navy as part of the Military Sea Transportation Service, MSTS, as troop and dependent transports on Atlantic and Pacific routes.

Hundreds of soldiers and airmen inched their way up two narrow gangplanks leading from the dock to the ship's deck only to vanish into the belly of the *Buckner*, which was to take us from the docks of New York City to the port of Southampton on the south coast of England. When it was my turn to step across the threshold from bright daylight into the ship's darkened interior, I became momentarily disoriented, my eyes adjusting slowly to a shadowy scene of functional efficiency—hammock bedsteads arrayed from bow to stern, stacked one above another only inches apart from floor to just below the deck planks. No one who has not traveled on a troop ship can imagine the sardine-like confinement of this mode of transportation. Even a simple breath of air seemed rationed in the ship's interior. We were given little time to settle in before I felt movement under my feet. I knew that when the last soldier vanished into the hull of the ship the gangplanks would promptly be removed and powerful little harbor tugs would muscle the *Buckner* away from its dock into deeper waters.

My bed, in the most forward section of the ship, was no more than a tightly stretched tarp, narrow and uncomfortable. Bad news. Every movement of the ship was reflected in the bow compartment with heightened intensity. The middle of the ship was the best place to be, as there the upward and downward movements were felt the least. Not only was I in the most forward part of the ship, I was also assigned the top bunk in my stack of four. Getting in and out required acrobatic skills. Not only that, but every time I turned over when sleeping, I hit my head on a pipe running directly above my head. It was a rather painful encounter at times. By the time I learned to cope with my environment, we arrived in Southampton.

My lower bunkmates soon curled up in fetal positions, didn't eat, got sick, still didn't eat, then became even sicker. Barrels were placed throughout the ship to allow the seasick to vomit into if they couldn't make it to the latrine on time. By the second day, the stench in the hold became unbearable for me, and I decided to spend most of my time on deck. Others didn't seem to be bothered by the rank odors, maybe because they never went outside to smell fresh air and got used to the stench. Many sat in small circles amidship, near the latrines, cigarettes dangling from their lips, playing poker from early morning to late into the night, often through the night to the next morning. The poker game never ended; only the players changed. Up on deck the breeze was stiff and cold, to me refreshing, in contrast to the stench below. I got a bit woozy the first day, but soon found my sea legs again and was fine for the remainder of the voyage. I ate my three meals every day just as I had when I came over on the *Goethals*.

I found a place amidship out of the direct path of the ocean breeze and huddled there for hours at a time—thinking about my past, about Colorado and the mountains I missed so much, and about where I was going. But mostly I thought about Harriet. Of course, I missed our physical intimacy. But being away from her allowed me for the first time to think of her in other than physical terms. I had to acknowledge that she had helped me to finally come to terms with the demons of my past. She had not only educated me, but healed me as well. I began to see her in a different light as the wind whipped through my hair and the sea spray settled on my baggy coveralls. Harriet had made me see that the natural was beautiful and ultimately fulfilling. Yet there was a dark side she shared with me on our last night together. Only hours before I was to take the bus from Fort Worth to New Brunswick, we smoked one last cigarette on the porch, then said good night to each other and went to bed. It was about eleven o'clock, maybe a bit later. Just before I fell asleep, I heard her tiptoe into the room and slide into bed beside me. We made love, then lay quietly. There was a question I wanted an answer to, and I decided to risk asking it. "When did you make love for the first time, Harriet? You said once something about being twelve years old. Were you joking?"

I felt her body jerk. After a moment's hesitation she said, "I wasn't joking, darling. Do you really want to know?"

"Yes, if you are willing to talk about it."

"I was twelve," she whispered. "I went to church every Sunday evening. We children met with the minister for lessons, sang songs, then had a snack. Cookies and milk. Robert was a friend of the family, twenty, a college student who volunteered to drive me to church. Father was always away, so my parents appreciated Robert's generosity. He wanted to enter the ministry, I once heard him tell my parents. One evening we were delayed for some reason. It was getting dark when we left. On the way home Robert pulled off the road and parked in a secluded spot under a large tree. He said, 'I have a secret to share with you, Harriet. Can you keep secrets?' I felt flattered that a grown man would want to share a secret with me, a little girl of twelve.

"'Will you promise not to tell anyone?' he whispered. 'Not even your best friend? Not even your parents?'

"I assured him that I would tell no one. I trusted him totally. He was a friend of the family. Some people even joked at times when both of us were around that maybe one day when I grew up Robert and I would be married. Everybody laughed when I ran out of the room in embarrassment. Robert told me to lie on my back, to relax, put my head in his lap. His words were gentle and persuasive. 'You have nothing to fear,' he said. I did as he told me to. I lay on the front seat of the car with my head in his lap. Then he put his hand on my stomach and moved it around in a circular fashion, telling me to relax and to think of nothing, 'Just relax and I will impart the spirit of the Lord in you,' he said solemnly, or something like that, as if he was performing a church ceremony. 'It will give you great joy and allow you to explore the universe and see it in all its beauty.' He kept on talking about God, about the universe, and about how he would help me gain insights into unimaginable pleasures."

"His hand kept moving ever downward as he spoke, then rested on my thigh. 'Do not be afraid,' he whispered, 'you will feel a warmth enter your body where my hand rests. That is as it should be.' His hand then came to rest on my very private me. He was right, I felt things I never felt before, became excited by the movement of his hand and my belly felt strangely rebellious. I didn't want to admit it, but what he did felt good, and I think I may have wanted him to go on, but at the same time I felt it was all wrong. Felt trapped and helpless. Robert was six feet, weighed close to two hundred pounds, and he intimidated me into silence. I felt his hand in my panties, making me feel good in a strange way. I could not move. Could not say anything, and let him do as he pleased.

"Then he removed his hand, put it back on my stomach and asked me to sit up. 'Did you feel the spirit of the Lord enter your body?' he asked. I nodded. I didn't want to admit to myself what I just experienced. I felt guilty and said nothing to anyone when I got home. I thought it was all my fault because I had those strange feelings when he touched me. The following Sunday he again pulled off the road and parked under the same tree. Please, lie down Harriet, he said. He said nothing about putting my head in his lap. Again he spoke of the spirit of the Lord entering my body and what a revelation the experience would be. Then he said, 'The time has come for me to reveal to you the secret we talked about last Sunday.' His hand was on my stomach and moved inside my panties, only he didn't stop there. I was terrified, totally under his control as he loomed above me. I felt it was all wrong, but I stayed quiet. I don't think I was capable of doing anything else, he was so big and strong, and I was terrified. When I felt him spreading my legs, I closed my eyes. I wanted to hide, but there was nowhere to hide. I felt his hand under my hips, then something huge entered my body. I tried to pull back. Cried out in pain. Tried to tell him to stop, that he was hurting me, but he put his large hand over my mouth, held me so tight I couldn't move or talk. 'Be quiet,' he said. His voice was harsh, not friendly. 'It will only hurt a little.' His words and what he was doing confused me. I wanted to be home in my bed. While he spoke, I could feel him moving within me. 'See, it doesn't hurt at all,' he gasped, 'you will soon begin to enjoy this, just the way you enjoyed me touching you last Sunday.' As he moved faster and faster, he said into my ear, 'Now you know our little secret. Remember! Don't tell anyone.' When he got off me, he told me to put on my panties and drove me home. I hurt, but I was too ashamed to say anything to my parents who were so taken by Robert, praising him profusely every time he came to our house. I felt ashamed, intimidated, and thought my parents would call me a liar if I said anything. That summer, every Sunday until he returned to college, Robert parked under that big tree. After that I never let him near me again. I was twelve years old."

I never heard Harriet cry before. She wept for a long time. When she regained her composure, she asked in a tearful voice, "Can you still love me now that you know my secret?" I didn't know what to say, never expected to hear anything like her story. Without another word she slipped out of bed and vanished into the darkness of the house. Her pillow was drenched with her tears. I felt devastated for her.

As I sat on the deck of the *Buckner*, the wind shifted, blowing into my face, drying my tears. I felt a deep sense of compassion for Harriet the person, so horribly violated as a child. I walked to the furthest point of the ship, where the bow sliced through the heaving waves. The ocean spray stung my face, and the wind blew hard and cold. I needed to be alone, and the violent forces of nature provided a stabilizing effect on the turmoil I felt within. I didn't know how Harriet coped with her pain, how she covered it all up for so many years without speaking of it to anyone. I wondered how she would cope in the future? Could she put it all behind her like my mother had? Or maybe none of them, no matter the age, ever put rape behind them. They just lived with it. I didn't know.

On the seventh day of our at times stormy voyage we arrived in Southampton. After we tied up at a remote dock, gangways were installed, providing passage from the ship to the dock. We were prohibited from going ashore. Most of us were utterly sick of ship life and wanted nothing more than to feel mother earth beneath our feet again. Local urchins stormed the ship selling fish and chips to soldiers and airmen tired of eating fried liver, hamburgers in gravy, mashed potatoes, scrambled eggs cooked so hard they were served in slices, crispy-black bacon, pancakes with imitation maple syrup, and scallops rolled in cornmeal and deep-fat fried into the hardness of rifle bullets. Military food, even if prepared well, and at times it actually was, soldiers would always reject in favor of something less palatable but prepared by civilians. For ten shillings the little English boys brought us piping hot french fries in a cone made from newspaper and a generous portion of deep-fat fried cod doused with vinegar.

Early the next morning, duffel bags slung over shoulders, hundreds of us exited the ship in orderly military fashion down a steep ramp and boarded waiting buses. I had no desire to ever again cross the Atlantic in a troop ship. It was a sunny spring day. The earth beneath our feet felt firm, and color soon returned to the faces of those who had suffered from prolonged seasickness. The buses drove inland to Shaftsbury, to an old World War II pre-invasion camp used in 1955 as a processing center for incoming and outgoing military personnel. We stayed for one night in barracks which at one time housed some of the soldiers who landed on the beaches of Normandy. It was a very efficiently run operation, and by noon of the second day in England we were put on trains and buses to our final destinations. Those of us with assignments to the 28th Weather Squadron boarded a bus to Bushy Park, a leafy London suburb which once housed the World War II headquarters of General Eisenhower. Aging, one-story barracks accommodated the headquarters elements of the 28th Weather Squadron, providing administrative and logistical support to its many detachments at American military airfields throughout the United Kingdom. The detachments gathered local weather data and provided forecasting services to flying units.

After signing into the squadron I was ushered into a barren interview room furnished with a table and two chairs, with no pictures on the walls. The room struck me as comparable to an interrogation room in a prisoner-of-war camp. The door flung open suddenly, and in strode a tall, supremely confident-looking lieutenant colonel, his tunic not quite hiding the fact that he was developing some girth around the middle. He looked as if he was in a hurry. He took off his garrison cap and wiped a few pearls of sweat from his forehead with a handkerchief before sitting down. Looking at me from across the table, his face friendly, eyes searching, he said, "I am Lieutenant Colonel Arnold Hull, commander of Detachment 2, 28th Weather Squadron at RAF Sculthorpe. That's northeast from here, Airman Samuel, near King's Lynn." He studied my face, then said, "What's your background?"

"I am a high school graduate," I said. "Ran out of money in college and joined the air force. I can type sixty-five words a minute."

He talked with me for a few more minutes, then called over his shoulder to an assignment clerk in the next room, "This is my man. I am taking him with me. Go ahead and cut his orders." Lieutenant Colonel Arnold R. Hull rose from his chair, and we shook hands, which I thought was a good sign. "I am your new commander, Airman Samuel," he said. "I am sure we will work well together. I have to run now. The folks in the other room will explain to you how to get to your new duty station. Cheerio." Colonel Hull donned his hat and left the room. A clerk handed me a set of orders. I read the orders and noted that they sent me to Detachment 40 at High Wycombe, on the outskirts of London. I looked at the clerk quizzically. He grinned.

"We already had you assigned to Det 40 at High Wycombe, but Colonel Hull came in today and interviewed all of you new guys, and just now picked you as his admin clerk. He outranks the Det 40 commander, so he gets what he wants." The clerk busied himself cutting a new stencil. Once finished, he smoothed out the waxy paper and carefully placed it on the drum of a stencil machine, then made about twenty copies of my new orders sending me to RAF Station Sculthorpe. "I hate this part of my job," he said. "The ink always bleeds through if you are not careful and gets all over your hands and uniform. That stuff is hell to get out. Watch out when you do this. Here, look at my sleeve." He showed me a black streak on the left sleeve of his shirt, "I'll never get that ink out. I have to buy a new shirt. You'd think we could invent something better." He handed me my new orders and returned to his desk. "Enjoy the rest of the day," he said. "There is a BX on base if you need anything." Then he added, "Let me show you how to get to the train station." He pulled out a map and showed me which station to go to and how to get there. I appreciated his assistance.

The next day I found myself on an English train chugging through the Norfolk countryside toward King's Lynn, a small port city near RAF Sculthorpe. Norfolk was agricultural, as poor as the Lüneburg Heath region of Germany, and dissected by narrow, meandering roads lined with hedgerows. There Norman conquerors built their castles, now in ruins, some of which I hoped to visit. They looked quite different from the castles of Germany, square and warlike. The countryside was a deep green, a detail that warned me to expect lots of rain. The King's Lynn railroad station was unpretentious. I got off the train and remained standing on the platform until everyone else had left. What next? At headquarters in Bushy Park they hadn't told me how to get from here to RAF Sculthorpe. Dressed in air force blues, duffel bag by my side, blue handbag at my feet, I felt very conspicuous.

"Hey, Yank," I heard someone yell. I looked around and saw the proprietor of a public house standing in his doorway, waving at me. "Come on in and have a beer."

I was startled and quickly replied, "Thank you very much, sir, but I am on duty. I can't drink."

"Going to Sculthorpe, mate?" he said in a deep, British country accent.

"Yes. I don't know how to get there. Can you help?"

"Not to worry, Yank," he said. "Come on in and make yourself comfortable. We'll get you there." I trudged into the pub carrying my duffel bag over my shoulder. The smoke-filled room had several patrons standing at the bar with large glasses of dark beer before them, even though it was only noon. The proprietor who had invited me inside grabbed an old telephone, cranked it several times, and when someone responded he gave a number. Then he said in a loud voice to whoever was on the other end of the line, "Get your bloody arse out here, matey. I've got a young chap here who needs to get to RAF Sculthorpe. Understand? Cheerio. Have a seat," he said to me. "Your transport will be here in an hour or so." And so it happened.

Within the hour an American air force pickup truck arrived driven by a British national. I threw my bags into the back of the truck and rode up front with the driver to my new home—Royal Air Force Station Sculthorpe, home of the 47th Bombardment Wing (Medium), which flew four-engined B-45 jet bombers. The 47th Bomb Wing was the most powerful American bomb wing stationed in Europe and armed with nuclear bombs, as I learned from my English driver. It wasn't long before the driver talked about the war, World War II of course, telling tales of German bombers coming across the Wash, flying so low he could see the faces of the air crew. He talked without letup until he dropped me off in front of the base billeting office. Other than saying hello and goodbye, I don't believe I added anything to the conversation. I was soon to discover that World War II was a topic that would come up continuously when I was with my English friends.

CHAPTER 21

RAF Station
Sculthorpe, England

B rigadier General Joseph R. Holzapple commanded the 47th Bomb Wing at RAF Sculthorpe in 1955. Fourteen years later, in 1969, after attaining four-star rank, General Holzapple served as Commander-in-Chief, United States Air Forces Europe, USAFE, with his headquarters in the lovely spa town of Wiesbaden, Germany. I met the general briefly upon my assignment to his headquarters on completion of a combat tour with the 355th Tactical Fighter Wing, at Takhli Royal Thai Air Base, north of Bangkok. From Takhli our fighter-bombers and electronic warfare aircraft flew combat missions against North Vietnam, a war very different from the one I experienced in Germany in the 1940s. The vice commander of the 47th Bomb Wing in 1955 was Colonel John Glover, holder of the Distinguished Service Cross, second only to the Medal of Honor. He and I were destined to meet again as well, in 1962, when Colonel Glover commanded the 55th Strategic Reconnaissance Wing at Forbes Air Force Base in Topeka, Kansas. My first operational assignment out of flying school was to the 55th wing, flying RB-47H six-jet reconnaissance aircraft into the teeth of the Cuban Missile Crisis of October 1962.

The 47th Bomb Wing had three bombardment squadrons, the 84th, the 85th, and the 86th, and one tactical reconnaissance squadron, the 19th. All four squadrons were equipped with B/RB-45 aircraft, the first American all-jet bomber. The 420th Air Refueling Squadron, equipped with KB-29 aerial refueling tankers, was there to support the B-45 bombers. It was a powerful armada of aircraft, positioned to deter the looming threat of the Soviet military colossus on the other side of the inner German border. As a lowly airman third class I was not aware when I arrived at RAF Sculthorpe that only five weeks earlier the 19th Tactical Reconnaissance Squadron had flown three of its RB-45Cs deep into the Soviet Union, far beyond Moscow, on a daring night reconnaissance mission. That foray was very, very secret then, and something my British driver didn't know anything about, or he surely would have told me.

RAF Sculthorpe had a temporary look about it, made up mostly of flimsy barracks-like structures with corrugated metal roofs and Quonset huts. Major Mengel's chapel was a Quonset hut, the large cross above the door the only identifying feature of its purpose and function. The shopping center, including the base exchange and numerous vendor shops carrying everything from Harris Tweed to fine English bone china and crystal, was a sorry-looking assemblage of concrete buildings with V-shaped, corrugated metal roofs. The wing headquarters building and officers' and noncommissioned officers' clubs were not much more than barracks, differentiated from each other only by the signs over their doors. If any money was spent on this barren air base, it was on the concrete of its runways and ramps and on the aircraft hangars, certainly not on the facilities which served the men and their families.

I arrived on a weekend. The base was quiet. No jets running up their engines, no trucks blasting down the concrete paved roads. Except for an occasional passing car, the electronic church chimes playing on Sunday morning, and the raspy blare of the Star Spangled Banner played over the base speaker system while the flag was being lowered at five o'clock in the afternoon, there was nothing to be heard. At the mess hall that evening I was one of only a few customers. Dinner, wouldn't you know it, was dried beef on toast. After dinner I walked around the base. It was a soft, gentle evening. The wind coming off the cold North Sea, only a few miles to the east, had died down. That night I awoke with my screams echoing in my ears, frantically clutching my mattress, half hanging out of my bunk. Another nightmare. I looked around to see if anyone heard. I was alone in the open bay barracks where I stayed for the night. I lay down again, trying to go back to sleep, hoping not to meet up with my past.

On Monday morning I quickly completed my in-processing at the personnel section and was assigned a very small room in the airmen's barracks, a room which I shared with another airman. He had homesteader rights and, of course, chose to occupy the bottom bunk. In the personnel section I learned that Detachment 28-2 of the 28th Weather Squadron was not located on RAF Station Sculthorpe, but in the nearby village of South Creek—in a building referred to as the "Shooting Box," a former hunting lodge. The little villages of South and North Creek were much more pleasant environments than the bland functional facilities at Sculthorpe. The Shooting Box served as a remote command post and communications center for the 47th Bomb Wing and the 49th Air Division, which was also located at Sculthorpe. Our small detachment provided weather support services to these two headquarters and their commanders. The Shooting Box was fully self-supporting, including its own messing facility. The air force cooks knew every one of us by name and cooked nearly every meal to order, something I had never expected to find in the military. Once, after I purchased a car, I accidently hit a pheasant on my way to work. I took the bird to our kitchen. The cooks then prepared the pheasant and ate it for lunch.

Our small weather detachment had a total of twenty-four men assigned, including eleven officers, ten of whom were weather forecasters. Of the thirteen airmen, all were weather observers except for me, the detachment clerk, and our supply sergeant. Colonel Hull was there to welcome me when I arrived and introduced me to his deputy, Major Coleman, who instructed me in my duties, which took all of ten minutes. I typed letters and reports, picked up and distributed mail, answered the phone, processed leave requests, and resolved pay problems. There were always pay problems for airmen; for some reason the officers never seemed to have any. I did anything and everything people asked me to do. Most of all, I made certain that Colonel Hull's desk was kept clean. My job was not terribly demanding, and I found plenty of time to learn from our weather observers the shorthand they used to plot atmospheric pressure, wind direction and velocity, and temperatures at different altitudes on the weather charts that the forecasters used to develop their actual forecasts.

Soon after my arrival I received orders announcing my date of rotation back to the United States. My DEROS, in military jargon, was April 29, 1958. I had just arrived, and someone was already worrying about my return home three years from now. The military paper mill churned out a seemingly endless stream of orders, directing every aspect of our lives—promotion orders, skill level orders, temporary duty orders, special orders, and personnel action memoranda. Orders meant paper, and there was lots of it every week for me to distribute. Weekends were usually quiet. By Saturday noon everything seemed to shut down. No flying after twelve o'clock noon. The locals didn't like airplane noise on Saturday afternoons or on Sundays, so flying or running up of engines during those "sacred" hours was prohibited. Most Americans lived off base in economy housing of often deplorable quality. Only low rankers like myself, without family, were required to live on-base, in barracks which provided little more than a bed, a small closet with one drawer at the bottom, a small table, and a lamp. Toilet and wash facilities were located in a common area down the hall. I thought back to basic training at Lackland and of the spacious facilities we had there. That was there; I was in England, a foreign country. It wasn't war, but that's why we were here, to prevent a war from happening.

On long weekends my thoughts turned to Harriet. I craved the smell of her perfume, the touch of her hand, the feel of her lips—to be honest, I needed her to satisfy my never-ending urge for the intimacy she had so freely provided. No matter what I was doing, a part of me always thought of her. So I decided to ask her to marry me. It crossed my mind that a girl brought up among wealth and privilege might not think that marrying an air force one-striper making all of one-hundred and some dollars a month was a good deal. I sat down and carefully composed what I felt to be the most important letter I had written in my life so far: proposing marriage. Two weeks passed. Finally the much anticipated letter from Harriet arrived, easily recognizable among the day's mail by its expensive, heavy, hand-rolled paper. I pulled the envelope from the heap and put it aside. I couldn't deal with possible rejection right away. I sorted the day's mail, put it into the individual boxes, and did all my other tasks. Only then did I feel ready to face whatever her letter may hold in store for me.

"Darling Wolfgang," she wrote. "What a surprise for you to ask me to marry you. Couldn't you have done that while you were still here? I always enjoyed being with you. But marriage? I never gave it a thought. I am only twenty years old. I like having fun. I am not ready for kids just yet, or being a housewife. Can you imagine me in a kitchen cooking a meal? It must be unspeakably boring. But then life around here without you isn't very exciting either. Parties, gossiping with my friends about their friends, dinners and dances, shopping at Neiman Marcus, it is all so boring. What I need is a night with you, darling. I don't want to go back to college. It isn't for me. I've been dating some of my old boyfriends. I hope you don't mind. After all, you are not here, and at times I just need the company of someone my age. Please understand."

The letter was progressing in a direction I had not anticipated. I put it down, wondering if I should go on. I had never considered that she would go out with anyone else once I left. It was both naive and selfish of me to think I would remain the only man in her life, but the thought of her lying in bed with another made my heart ache. Maybe I was reading things into her words. Maybe she was just going out to dinner, to the Wednesday church meetings, to a movie, or out for drinks and dancing. My thoughts, however, were less charitable. "Dad is still working on getting me presented to the Queen," her letter continued. "You have to understand that something like that is very important to people around here. It looks like it may happen soon. We could plan the wedding for late in the year. What do you think? If there is anything you think I need to do, please let me know. I need to run, darling. With love, Harriet." I didn't know if I should laugh or cry. She had accepted my proposal.

Over the next two weeks I learned that as a low-ranking airman I had to obtain my commanding officer's permission to marry. Colonel Hull gave me to understand with a nod of his head that it was fine with him. "I'll do all I can to assist you," he said, putting his feet on his desk and leaning back in his swivel chair, hands clasped behind his head. I thought the colonel was in his mid or late thirties, maybe eight years younger than my mother. "It was much easier for me when I got married," he said. I was standing near my desk. "Sit down," he interrupted himself, motioning for me to take my chair. "It's alright for you to relax around me. You are my assistant and doing a great job like I knew you would when I first laid eyes on you. You were the best of the lot. I interviewed everyone that morning, you last. I already decided to wait for the next batch of replacements to come in when I met you. Anyway, I'm just a light colonel," and he smiled, knowing he was far superior in rank and income to the airman he was speaking to in such familiar tones.

"Mary and I met while I was stationed in London in the war. We just went to a church and got married—that's all there was to it. Now I have a couple of kids, and she wants the boys to have a proper education, which, according to my wife, you can't get back home. So my boys are going to public school here. Eton. Public school in England means just the opposite of what it means in America—it's a private school and costs a bunch of money. Oh, yes, it puts a dent in my pocketbook all right, but my wife is happy." With that pronouncement he catapulted himself out of his swivel chair, grabbed his hat, and started to stomp out of the office. "Oh," he said, turning back to me, "it is only a small formality, but you have to put three hundred dollars into a Soldiers and Sailors Deposit at the finance office. The money is there to ensure that you can actually afford to get married. In your case, of course, that wouldn't be a problem, but rules are rules. It's a wicket you have to go through." Colonel Hull sauntered through the forecasters' room, looked at some charts the fore-casters were working on, and exchanged a few words. Soon I heard his car heading down the road for what I suspected was a recurring afternoon or two each week with a lady in nearby Fakenham. His wife lived in London, and to the best of my knowledge they only saw each other occasionally, not necessarily even every weekend. I liked working for Colonel Hull. His personal life was his own business.

The more I thought about getting married, the more I fantasized about Harriet. "We could marry as soon as August, before it gets cold and the winds start blowing," I wrote to her. "Let me know if that is alright with you. I would have to buy a car, arrange for an apartment or house, and we would need lots of household things to get started—towels, pots and pans, whatever else you might think we need."

Harriet wrote back, "I will be sending you things. Be prepared for a large number of boxes to arrive. I will have them sent directly from the store to you. August sounds fine. I've gone ahead and made reservations on the *Queen Elizabeth*, leaving New York on August 15 and arriving in Southampton on August 20. I'll take a private train to London where you can meet me. I will have the travel agent send you all the details once everything has been worked out. August is a busy travel month as you might suspect. It took a little doing to get a berth on the *Queen Elizabeth*. Dad has arranged for a letter of credit for you through the American

Express Company. When you identify yourself to them, they will provide you the funds you need for that strange account you tell me the army insists on before we can get married. Use the letter of credit for other expenses, don't be timid. I am planning on having an Announcement Party for family and friends. Will write Hedy and extend an invitation to her and your sister Ingrid. Love, Harriet."

I went to the American Express office on base, and after I showed the clerk my military identification, he provided me a check for three hundred dollars to deposit in the Soldiers and Sailors account at the finance office. His demeanor toward me, a one-striper, had been distant when I first entered the bank. He kept me waiting, while taking care of officers' wives who arrived after I had. Once he looked at the letter of credit, his attitude and demeanor changed. "So pleased to be of service to you, Mister Samuel. Call on me any time for any of your needs. Thank you so much, sir, for doing business with American Express." I then went to the Base Exchange where English dealers exhibited cars for purchase by Americans. The Morris Minor, a little runabout, was a popular car. Cheap for sure, but I knew Harriet wouldn't be seen dead in a Morris. Vauxhall, a General Motors car, looked clumsy and was much too big for us, at least I thought it was. I settled on a Triumph TR-2, a red two-seat sports car. I immediately sent Harriet a brochure and told her its cost—$1,335. Her next letter included a cashier's check in that amount. I opened an account at the American Express and went ahead and ordered the car. I was torn between the TR-2 and the Austin Healy. I settled on the Triumph after the salesman promised a delivery date not later than the first week in August. My friends assured me that the Brits never met their delivery dates.

Large packages began to arrive which would have quickly filled my little barracks room had I tried to store them there. I opened the first box from Saks Fifth Avenue, filled with luxurious bath towels. After that, I never opened another box, just stacked them in our supply room. Other boxes arrived from Neiman Marcus and other up-scale retailers. I suspected Harriet just picked up the phone and called in her orders. I couldn't imagine her going into a store and picking out pots and pans and towels and face cloths.

I talked to the vicar of an ancient church in North Creek who was pleased to host an American wedding, but insisted on reading the bans for three weekends in succession even though no one knew us. "It is tradition we must follow," he said. That done, there was one final task for me to resolve. I needed authorization from the 28th Weather Squadron to allow me to live off base and to ration separately. For a single airman the military provided housing and meals; once married and allowed to live off base, I would draw a housing allowance and payment in lieu of rations. Colonel Hull assured me that "Once you're married you can submit your request to live off base and ration separately." With his assurance I felt I could go ahead and start looking for a place to live. I also learned from him that I would be promoted to airman second class, A/2C, effective 1 August. With that second stripe, my pay, including allowances, would increase to around $240 a month. Additionally, once married, I would be eligible to receive $4.50 per day to defray housing costs, raising my total income to close to $400. I deluded myself into thinking that Harriet and I could probably live comfortably on that much money.

To be on the safe side, I called our squadron personnel section at Bushy Park. From them I learned that I had a little problem. Neither Harriet nor I were twenty-one, and the government required that we have our parents' permission to get married—in writing and notarized. Harriet's parents quickly gave their permission. Hedy wrote back, "You are too young to get married. . . . I suspect you are only marrying Harriet for her money. I am sorry, but I will not give my consent to something I don't believe is right for you." I had broached the subject of Harriet's and my relationship with my mother while on a short leave in Denver in January. She didn't want to accept the fact that there was a woman in my life and became quite angry. I dropped the subject. Now she came at me again, denying her support. What had I done for her to act this way? I was both shocked and furious. Although twenty years old and serving in the military, the law still considered me a child not fit to drink alcoholic beverages, vote in national elections, nor marry without parental consent. Didn't my mother give birth to me when she was twenty years old? I was born out of wedlock. Had she forgotten that? Certainly my father Willie came from a financial background superior to hers. She obviously didn't think of herself as marrying him for his money. As angry and frustrated as I was, I realized I wouldn't get anywhere with Hedy by pointing fingers at her own past. I wrote her what I thought was a reasonable letter, explaining Harriet's and my relationship, told her of our plans, and asked for her to relent and please send me her notarized consent. Two additional letters and an expensive transatlantic telephone call finally convinced her. It wasn't a good beginning.

CHAPTER 22

An Unlikely Wedding

R.M.S. "QUEEN MARY" Friday, August 12, 1955

PROGRAMME OF EVENTS
a.m.

7.00—7.00 p.m.—Swimming Pool and Gymnasium open for
      Exercise (weather and other circumstances permitting)

8.00—" A Storiette " Competition

8.15—Keep-Fit Class (Gentlemen)   Gymnasium

10.45—Meeting of Rotarians   Drawing Room

11.00—Keep-Fit Class (Ladies)   Gymnasium

11.15—Daily Run " Tote " (closes 11.50 a.m.)   Prom. Deck Square

11.30—Selections at the Hammond Organ   Main Lounge
        by Charles Saxby

p.m.

2.15—Recorded Music   Main Lounge
  Symphony No. 6 in F Major, Opus 68, " Pastoral " (Beethoven)
    The Vienna Philharmonic Orchestra. Conductor: Wilhelm Furtwangler

2.30—Table Tennis Tournament commences   Prom. Deck

2.30—Meeting of Lions International and Kiwanis   Drawing Room

3.45—AFTERNOON TEA DANCE   Main Lounge
  Queen Mary String Orchestra, directed by Edward Vigay

4.30—Movie :   Cinema
    " THE PRIVATE WAR OF MAJOR BENSON " (Tech.)
    Charles Heston and Julie Adams

6.15—News Broadcast (British)   Long Gallery

6.30—News Broadcast (American)   Long Gallery

7.30—Cocktail Dancing   Long Gallery
  Queen Mary Dance Orchestra, directed by Norman Hill

7.30—Cocktail Hour   Observation Lounge

8.45—Orchestral Selections   Main Lounge
  Queen Mary String Orchestra, directed by Edward Vigay

9.30—Movie :   Cinema
  " THE PRIVATE WAR OF MAJOR BENSON " (Tech.)
    Charles Heston and Julie Adams

9.45—KENO (Bingo-Lotto)   Main Lounge
    (Interludes at the Hammond Organ)
    followed by DANCING
  Queen Mary Dance Orchestra, directed by Norman Hill

DANCING will continue at approximately 1.00 a.m. in the Starlight
Roof Club (Verandah Grill) after completion in the Main Lounge
  Queen Mary Dance Orchestra, directed by Norman Hill
    (No Cover Charge)

B ob England, a weather observer who worked in the room next to me at the Shooting Box and who had recently married, invited me for dinner. He was a three-striper, an airman first class, who like myself was planning on going back to college once out of the air force. Bob and I hit it off immediately after my arrival. The apartment he and Celia lived in was thoroughly modernized and tastefully furnished, with large windows looking out on a bucolic tree-studded countryside. Their apartment was painted in yellow and brown pastels, hung with numerous hunting prints, and was light and airy, a comfortable place I thought. Their landlords occupied the first-floor apartment and, according to Celia, were "a thoroughly enjoyable English couple." Our dinner conversation focused on the local housing situation. "We were really lucky to find this place," Celia emphasized to me more than once. "Don't get up your hopes of finding anything like this anywhere near the base. Most of the places we looked at were small and cold, miserable-looking dungeons built hundreds of years ago and never modernized. County Norfolk is strictly agricultural, you may have noticed, Wolfgang, and one of the poorest counties in the United Kingdom." Celia addressed me by my first name, while Bob used my nickname, Sam, which I didn't like but couldn't do anything about. "As for housing costs? It's a classic case of supply and demand," Bob continued the conversation. "The rents are truly outlandish. I wish you luck in finding something that you and Harriet will find acceptable. You may have to consider Norwich, or even something near London."

First thing Monday morning I obtained a list of available off-base housing from the base housing office. Each listing gave a brief description of the unit and the monthly rent its owner was asking for. In most cases the descriptions were brief and of little value, forcing me to go and look at every place. The woman in the housing office wished me luck. Not a good sign. "There isn't much on the market right now, Airman Samuel," she said. "We had a large influx of people recently. And of course, there wasn't much there to begin with. Some people live as far away as Norwich. You may have to consider doing that."

Cabs sat outside the main gate in a disciplined queue—as the English referred to any line that was formed by accident or design by two or more people or vehicles. I rented one for the day. For the next five hours I covered much of the Norfolk countryside. Celia's cautionary comments proved all too accurate. Most places I looked at were dismal even when measured against the most rudimentary American standards. Old, built of stone, cold, damp, with small windows letting in little light. Some still had ancient coal or wood-fired kitchen stoves, as if electricity and central heating had yet to be discovered in this part of England, or inside plumbing for that matter. Celia told me to look for pipes running down the outside of a house, which often froze in winter and burst, leaving the occupants with a real mess on their hands. Four hours of looking left me dispirited. I had just about decided that my house-hunting was a bust. There was one last place for me to look at, a bit far from the base, along the coastal road to Wells-next-the-Sea, in the ancient village of Stiffkey. "Let's go and do the last one," I said to my driver, who turned out to be a modest, quiet man, making helpful but not intrusive suggestions, and never saying a word about the war, which I thought most unusual for an Englishman. We headed for Stiffkey, proceeding along Highway 149, a narrow, winding, road, lined by high hedgerows on both sides.

Stiffkey turned out to be a larger village than I anticipated, with some claim to fame as well. We passed an old church, its yard shaded by ancient trees. Pointing to a cemetery behind the church, my driver volunteered, "Sir Francis Bacon lies buried there. And then, there is that story about the mad vicar of Stiffkey. Maybe someone will tell you about him if you should move here," he chuckled. "That half-ruined castle there," and he pointed to it, "was Sir Francis Bacon's. An American major from RAF Sculthorpe lives there now. The place is haunted, you know. I wouldn't live there if you paid me. But you Americans don't believe in ghosts, do you?" He was right; I didn't believe in ghosts. The houses lining the cobblestone road looked very old—their steep tiled roofs moss-covered. I was looking for a three-bedroom apartment on a large estate. We had nearly given up when I noticed a narrow dirt lane leading up a hillside.

"That must be it," I said to my driver, who dutifully turned up the much traveled path leading into a cobblestoned courtyard fronted by a U-shaped, two-story brick building. It was the rear of the house, apparently now the principal entry. An iron gate barred access to a gravel path leading to the front. Although quite old, the building appeared well-maintained. I saw pipes running down the exterior walls. None of the previous places I looked at had indoor plumbing either. I decided I would just have to live with that aspect of English life. An air force captain and his family lived here until recently, according to a brief note on the small card given to me by the woman at the housing office. So I figured the place couldn't be too bad. I knocked on the massive oak door with a brass knocker of immense proportions. Bang, bang, bang—I could hear my knocks echoing through the house. I felt somewhat embarrassed at banging so loudly. I soon heard shuffling feet, a key turning in the ancient lock, and then the door opened slowly. A white-haired man stooped before me. He was probably in his seventies, about six feet tall, his left hand pressing into his side, as if he were in pain. He squinted at me over his reading glasses, a puzzled look on his face. Lieutenant Colonel Bailey, formerly of His Majesty's Indian Army, now living in retirement on his wife's estate, was clearly not pleased with what he saw before him: not an officer, just an American airman.

"Yes, what can I do for you?" Colonel Bailey inquired brusquely, lowering his head to better see over his glasses. His eyes were alert, penetrating—looking at me like he was examining an object of indeterminate origin which he didn't quite know how to dispose of. This is going to be fun, I thought, looking at the old man in his worn, baggy brown corduroy pants, his long-sleeved shirt carefully buttoned to the top, the way my grandfather Samuel always wore his shirts. A brown army leather belt held up his drooping pants, which seemed a size too large and surely couldn't remember a crease if they ever held one. He wore a Harris tweed jacket, which, like everything else, must have given him years of good service and was begging for retirement.

"I would like to look at the apartment you have for rent," I said firmly. "Is it still available?"

"Of course, of course," Colonel Bailey muttered, shuffling back into the house—the corridor was dark, exuding a smell of aging books, carpet, and upholstered furniture. Colonel Bailey shouted at someone unseen, then reappeared with a large, black, iron key, about nine inches long, like something out of Grimm's fairytales. He handed me the key, pointing to the wing across the courtyard, saying, "Do lock the door after you finish." And with that he closed the door in my face. I headed across the courtyard. My driver patiently waiting in his cab smiled and gave me a wink as I passed. The first room I entered seemed to be a pantry leading to the kitchen. The kitchen had an electric stove and was reasonably furnished. A window looked out onto the courtyard. Adjacent to the kitchen was a living room and a separate dining area. Stairs led to the second floor; creaky, but sound. At the top of the stairs was a bathroom with a large tub with ornate cast-iron feet. I flushed the toilet. It worked. The master bedroom was large and well appointed, as was a second, smaller bedroom. I looked for stoves and ovens, something to give off heat in winter, but all I saw were fireplaces. Celia told me that most places didn't have central heating so I wasn't totally taken by surprise. I knew I could check out kerosene space heaters at the base. Behind the house I saw a beech forest, and beyond the forest lay the open sea. I decided to take the place. This time when I knocked on the door I didn't slam the knocker quite as hard. Colonel Bailey reappeared promptly. "How much do you want for the place, sir?" I asked.

He looked at me curiously. Hesitated. I was in uniform, one stripe on my sleeves, no bars on my shoulders. Obviously, I was an airman, not an officer. He said, "The apartment is no longer available," and proceeded to close the door in my face.

I thought I knew what was going on. I put my foot in the door, preventing him from closing it, and said quite loudly, "The only reason you don't want to rent the apartment to me is because I am not an officer. I find your attitude disgusting. I am going to report you to my commander, and no American will ever again rent from you. I ask you again, how much do you want for the place?"

The colonel's face revealed his astonishment. He probably couldn't remember anyone of inferior status ever speaking to him in such a direct manner. Then he replied calmly, "Fifteen pounds, about seventy dollars in your money."

"I'll take it," I said.

"Please come inside." He acted as if nothing unusual had happened. The main house was cool, although it was nearly summer. I followed the colonel down the hall into a large living room where a couple of enormously large logs were valiantly attempting to give off some heat in an immense fireplace. He exited at the other side of the room through what must once have been the front door, to a patio, and asked me to join him at a small table. An open bottle of whiskey stood on the table. He poured himself a small glass. I declined. Colonel Bailey sipped his whiskey, explaining his conditions: A month's rent up front, a small deposit to be refunded once I left and no damages were discovered on the premises. In time, the old colonel and I became rather fond of one another.

Everything was ready, I thought, for us to marry—I arranged for our wedding at the church in North Creek, ordered a car, found a place to live, and went through all the red tape the air force required of me. Now all I could do is wait for Harriet to arrive.

Major Coleman, a pilot, the senior weather forecaster in our detachment and Colonel Hull's deputy, would rather fly airplanes than stand behind a light-table forecasting weather for other pilots. Whenever he had an opportunity to fly, he did. He flew with the base flight, which had an odd assortment of aircraft, including several old C-47 transports which had seen combat during the invasion of Europe, several newer C-119 twin-boom transports, a B-26 medium bomber painted black and used to tow targets for aerial target practice, and several newer two-seat T-33 jet trainers. One morning Major Coleman came to me and said, "Sam, this weekend I am flying to Munich. Have you been back to Germany since you came to the United States?"

"No, sir."

"This is a morale flight for airmen assigned to the bomb wing. The flights are very popular with the men. Would you like to come along?" Did I want to come along? You bet. I was elated to return to Germany, the country I had left only four years earlier, on a gray and windy January evening, thinking that I might never see it again. The 49th Air Division issued a set of orders authorizing me to visit Munich, Germany, for four days "for the purpose of rest and recreation. Travel by military aircraft authorized." I joined nine other airmen on a Friday morning at base operations. Major Coleman gave us a safety briefing, and we hopped into a truck which took us out to the aircraft. Everything was very informal. We strapped into web seats running down both sides of the fuselage of the C-47 aircraft. Major Coleman flew low, allowing us to view England from above, to see the white cliffs of Dover, the English Channel. We stayed in a military hotel in Munich and wore our uniforms when we went into town. It was 1955, ten years after the end of World War II, and Germany was still an occupied country. I thought it ironic that I, of German birth, a newly minted American citizen, should return in the uniform of the occupiers. I didn't feel like an occupier, nor did anyone else in our group, but that was in fact the situation. We were there to enjoy German hospitality, look at castles in Bavaria, eat Schnitzel, and drink some of that fabulous German beer.

One airman in our group asked me if he could accompany me that afternoon. "You speak German," he said, "and you know what to do."

"Sure, John. What would you like to do?"

He hesitated. Then said, "Do you really want to know?"

"Yes."

"I would like to eat in a really nice restaurant where they treat me just like anybody else." His request surprised me. I thought he might want to go to the Hofbräuhaus, Munich's famous beerhall. When I brought it up, he showed no interest. "A really nice restaurant would be fine," he repeated. That afternoon I found one of Munich's finest, a restaurant with lace curtains on the windows, waitresses who wore little white caps on their carefully combed hair, and white lacy aprons over black dresses. John hesitated when we entered—two Americans in uniform, one white, one black. Everyone in the restaurant stared. If my mother had taught me right, staring was impolite in Germany. I knew why they stared. There were no other Americans in the place, and quite possibly we weren't welcome. John thought they stared because he was black, but I knew that wasn't the case. The maitre d' approached with measured steps, head held high. I expected him to say he didn't have a table available, that every-thing was reserved—but he didn't. Instead, he seated us at one of the best tables.

"Let me do the ordering," I told John. He grinned nervously.

"I hoped you'd say that," he whispered. We enjoyed a typical German meal of *Ochsenschwanzsuppe* and *Wienerschnitzel*, accompanied by fried noodles, *Spätzle*, and a fine Bavarian salad. For dessert I selected *Schwarz-wälder Torte* and coffee. Our meal cost a little more than either of us had budgeted, but the service was impeccable. The other guests contin-ued to watch our every move—how we ate our soup, how we cut our meat, how we handled our silverware.

"Don't get nervous," I whispered to John. "Just imitate me as best you can." He did exceedingly well. We spent about two hours in the restaurant. After we were out on the street, John laughed loudly, slapped his thigh, danced a little jig, then put his arms around me. People looked at us, two Americans gone a little crazy.

"Sam," he said, "I never thought I'd eat in a place like that, with real silver and fine china. I always wanted to do that. Where I come from in Mississippi, they would have killed me if I'd gone into a place like that." I stared at John in disbelief. "My folks won't believe this when I write home." It was a big deal for John, and he never let me forget it. Whenever John and I saw each other at Sculthorpe, he'd wave at me and give me the V-sign.

The next day I visited Fürstenfeldbruck, the place where Hedy, Leo, and I started out in 1951 on our journey to our new world. The Fürstenfeldbruck railroad station looked just the way I remembered it; nothing had changed over the past four years. I walked the familiar path into town, across the market square, to the house of Herr and Frau Buck, Hedy and Leo's former landlords. I rang the doorbell and Frau Buck opened the door looking just the way I remembered her, with her slightly red-veined cheeks and a *Kopftuch* pulled tightly around her head. I thought she would recognize me even in uniform, but she didn't. I explained who I was, exchanged pleasantries, then returned to Munich. It was nice to visit Germany, but I was glad to return to England. The past was the past, and best left alone.

No letters from Harriet arrived, only more boxes to add to the growing pile in our supply room. I spent my weekends attending church in the small Quonset hut chapel on base and singing in the church choir. Anything to stay busy, to keep my mind off Harriet. I bicycled through the English countryside, visiting nearby castle ruins, or just rode along the narrow, winding hedgerow-lined country roads. When the sun shone, it was a pleasant experience, but there were all too many intervals of rain, not unlike the weather in the Lüneburg Heath. Harriet's letters became infrequent; one mentioned postponing our wedding. "It is so awkward getting married in a foreign country, darling," she wrote. "Don't you agree? None of my friends will be there." I tried calling her from a phone in the American Express office, but couldn't get through. My anxiety grew as did my need for her affection; it was like a fever devouring my body. I explained to Colonel Hull that something had come up, that I needed to go home on leave to straighten it out. Would he allow me to return to the States on military leave for thirty days? Colonel Hull was a generous and understanding man. "We'll manage, Sam," he said jovially. "Go home and get your love life straightened out."

I used some of the car money to buy a ticket on Pan American Airways via Shannon, Ireland, New York City, and Chicago to Dallas. The round-trip airfare was $660, nearly half the cost of the new Triumph TR-2. I thought of writing Harriet, but I knew the letter wouldn't arrive before I did. On July 24, I rode the train to London and boarded a Pan American DC-6 on the first leg of my long journey to Fort Worth. I had no idea what might await me once I arrived, how Harriet would take my sudden appearance, how her parents might react.

The flight across the Atlantic, while quicker than my recent crossing on the USNS *Buckner*, was long and boring. There was nothing to do but sit hour after hour and listen to the steady drone of the four engines. In New York I waited eight hours for a connecting flight to Chicago where I changed planes once more, and by late afternoon of the second day I was back in Texas. From Dallas I caught a commuter bus to Fort Worth, then took a cab. When my taxi pulled up in front of Harriet's house, I wasn't concerned about anything—I was tired, sweaty, and in need of a shower. I paid the cab and grabbed my bags. Suddenly it occurred to me that Harriet might not be home. I knocked on the door. Harriet opened it almost immediately and stood there in all her blonde, blue-eyed beauty, wearing shorts and a sleeveless blouse. She had cut her hair, I noticed. Then all I could think of was making love to her. "Darling, what a surprise," she gushed. "I was halfway expecting you. What took you so long? Mother is out." I heard all I wanted to hear.

I had no idea how Harriet's parents might take my appearance. Her father remained a shadow, passing through, yet nearly invisible to me. Her mother was her usual gracious self, acting as if my arrival was the most normal thing in the world. For the remainder of my stay she immersed herself in planning our wedding—not in England, but here in Fort Worth. Harriet and her mother settled on August 6 as the date. I couldn't believe a wedding could be planned that quickly and didn't really expect such a turn of events. Soon there were numerous parties and receptions to attend at the Petroleum Club, the Fort Worth Club, the Colonial Country Club, and various other clubs and private homes.

The *Queen Mary* was scheduled to sail from New York to Cherbourg, France, and Southampton, England, on Wednesday, August 10, 1955. The *Queen*'s sailing drove our wedding date. The wedding blossomed into a spectacle which fit right into Harriet's lifestyle—a never-ending string of parties with her at the center. Although I was the groom, I felt like an outsider looking in, like a spectator. I had nothing to do with anything and just went where I was told, dressed the way I was told, signed papers when told to do so, and generally kept myself available. As the days passed, I began to understand that Harriet had a decidedly distorted view of the England we were to live in. She and her friends gushed excitedly about London and its theaters, places to see, and places to dine, as if we were going on a long vacation, when in fact we were to settle down to the rather mundane life of a young couple making do on an old English country estate.

Harriet's father approached me one afternoon, shook my hand, and asked me to join him and another gentleman to "talk about a matter of some importance." The other man turned out to be an insurance salesman, and by the time "the matter of some importance" was settled, he had taken out a one-hundred-thousand-dollar life insurance policy on me with Harriet as the beneficiary. I thought it was an enormously large policy, but since I didn't have to pay for it, I didn't care. It was just another of the many things I was told to do and sign.

Harriet and I were married in St. John's Episcopal Church, with the well wishes of hundreds of Harriet's friends and business associates of her father's. The guests came from Dallas, Houston, Austin, Tulsa, Shreveport, Baton Rouge, and many other places where oil was king. My mother Hedy and sister Ingrid came for the wedding in spite of the short notice and in spite of Hedy's protestations that she didn't have anything to wear and didn't have the money to pay for the expense. Leo couldn't come, having only recently started his new job at Lowry AFB. Hedy and Ingrid's travel and hotel accommodations were arranged and paid for by Harriet's parents, giving Hedy no excuse not to be there. She and Ingrid were the only members of my family present. I could tell that Hedy felt utterly out of place. The flamboyant social setting was totally opposite from the struggling life she and Leo lived, working for modest wages. Suddenly Hedy was thrown into a world where money was never mentioned, yet everything spoke of wealth and opulence. The evening before the wedding Hedy refused to attend a dinner, claiming to be ill. With great difficulty I was able to persuade her to attend the wedding. In contrast, my sister Ingrid, a beautiful fifteen-year-old girl with a bubbly personality, went with the flow of things. By the time she and Hedy returned to Denver, Ingrid had acquired a following of eager young men, including one who made what appeared to be a serious offer of marriage. Ingrid took all of it in stride, offending no one and having a great time.

My best man was Tom Moran, my air force friend who married Harriet's friend Mary. Luckily he was still at Carswell. I was glad to have someone near me who came from my world. Harriet had five brides-maids, including my sister Ingrid. The "bridesmaids dressed in identical waltz length frocks of white Chantilly lace styled with bouffant skirts and strapless bodices worn with lace jackets" reported the *Fort Worth Star Telegram*. Flower girls wore "dresses of white tulle over taffeta with ruffled tulle berthas and full, carpet length skirts caught with blush rosebuds."

I was assigned a set of groomsmen, knowing none. It didn't matter. Harriet was given away by her father, who seemed to be caught up in the spirit of the occasion and actually looked as if he were having a good time. He remained as distant and aloof toward me as ever, yet proudly marched his daughter down the aisle. I thought Harriet looked beautiful, even regal, in her wedding dress. After the ceremony as we stepped out the church door, I noticed an enormous pile of presents on and around a large table in the vestibule, much too small for the largess provided by the invited guests. I never learned what was in any of the expensive-looking boxes tied with colorful ribbons. I believe Harriet's mother had them all unwrapped and inventoried, and sent out the obligatory thank-you notes after Harriet and I were well on our way to England. Many pictures were taken, mostly of Harriet walking up and down the aisle, cutting the cake, throwing her bouquet. There was one picture taken on the day of our departure for New York, which years later helped me understand our relationship—with me sitting on a chair looking up at Harriet, she standing looking down at me. The picture was to be all too indicative of our future relationship.

CHAPTER 23

RMS *Queen Mary*

Photographed on board
R.M.S. QUEEN MARY

A matched set of Neiman Marcus luggage, five rawhide-covered suitcases varying in size from a small cosmetics case to a huge travel trunk, was delivered to our hotel room. I had given up thinking about the cost of anything. I never even presented Harriet with an engagement ring, as I knew any ring I could afford on my airman's pay would have been an embarrassment to her. Instead, on her ring finger, she wore that enormous oval-shaped diamond, a multicarat ring she and her mother selected at Neiman Marcus before we met. Harriet flaunted that ring before her friends, but actually didn't need a ring to draw attention to herself. She had that pure-bred look about her, a casual yet studied walk which announced to everyone that she came from that world where people never thought about money, where having lots of it was a given, where everything you did was learned and studied from early childhood, especially how you walked, sat, and moved in public. Harriet learned all that and more, including how to spend money, an apparent art form in her world. How I became a part of Harriet's world remained a mystery I had yet to solve—a wealthy socialite marrying a poor immigrant boy. If I could figure out the answer, maybe I would know how to make her my wife in ways other than just name.

The five rawhide-covered suitcases, and more, went on the airplane that took us from Dallas to New York, where we stayed for the night in the Waldorf-Astoria before embarking on the *Queen Mary* the following morning. Everything was first class—the seats on the plane, the hotel room, our cabin on the ship. We flew from Dallas Love Field to New York's Idlewild airport the morning of the ninth of August. A red carpet was rolled from the first-class lounge to the stairs leading to the first class cabin. I had heard of the expression "red carpet treatment" but never expected it to be quite so literal. The *Fort Worth Star Telegram* reported that Harriet "wore away a chocolate brown silk suit with brown accessories. The couple will sail Wednesday from New York on the *Queen Mary* for England. They will make their home in Stiffkey, Norfolk, England." It all sounded so romantic, even could be, if Harriet was up to it. What was missing was the reality of life as the wife of an airman second class in the United States Air Force. On August first I was promoted, giving me an additional stripe and a little extra money, something I never mentioned to Harriet.

The *Queen Mary* was truly a beautiful ship, with her three enormous stacks towering over everything else at the dock. According to the *List of Passengers*, a small booklet distributed to every first-class cabin, the ship was 81,237 gross tons and driven by a quadruple-screw turbine, under the command of Captain R. G. Thelwell, O.B.E., R.D., and Staff Captain R. J. N. Nicholas, R.D., R.N.R., the junior captain, who did all the work and none of the socializing I presumed. The *Queen* carried a principal medical officer as well as a surgeon able to take care of most medical emergencies which might arise among its first-class passengers. A total of "2,828 souls" were onboard, including a crew of 1,272, and 257 first-class passengers. Segregation was absolute. No cabin or tourist-class passenger had an opportunity to penetrate the inner sanctum of the first-class world. The passenger list was rife with titles: Lady and Sir, Prince and Princess, Captain, His Excellency, Doctor, and The Honorable.

Harriet and I were escorted to our cabin by an attentive and solicitous member of the crew. B99 was a spacious and well-appointed cabin, looked after by two attendants who introduced themselves upon our arrival and put themselves at our service for the duration of the voyage. After getting settled, Harriet and I went up on deck for the departure ceremony. At twelve thirty sharp several tugs moved the huge ocean liner from its berth to the sounds of the ship's band. I couldn't help but reflect on my own arrival in the port of New York just four years earlier on a bare-bones navy vessel, a Liberty Ship painted ocean gray. Next to the *Queen Mary*, the USNS *George W. Goethals* would have appeared incredibly small.

Returning to our cabin we found a schedule of events for Wednesday, August 10, 1955, on our night stand. It noted that at 3:45 we were "invited" to a Passenger Lifeboat Station Muster and the Captain requested that we attend wearing our lifebelts. The mandatory drill was not going to be of any length nor interfere with anyone's personal life, because at 4:00 a ship's ensemble was scheduled to begin playing "Music for Tea Time." *The Naked Street* with Farley Granger, Anthony Quinn, and Anne Bancroft was scheduled for 4:30 that afternoon, and again later in the evening. Harriet and I never made it to a movie throughout the voyage.

The ship's August 10 "Programme" included announcements for upcoming meetings for onboard Rotary, Lions, and Kiwanis Club members—nothing was deemed too unimportant by the attentive hosts of the Cunard Steamship Line not to merit their considerate attention. A fancy headdress competition was scheduled for the ladies, and prizes of a humorous nature were to be awarded for the most original, artistic, and amusing entries. There was a "Game of Ants" competition scheduled. We never learned what the Game of Ants involved. An actually important announcement among all the trivia was that "Clocks would be ADVANCED 20 minutes at 5.00 p.m., 11:00 p.m., and 2:00 a.m." each day, so that by the time we arrived in Southampton we would be on English time. I thought that approach rather clever. Fitness classes were scheduled during the early morning hours, separate classes for ladies and gentlemen, of course; and British and American news broadcasts were provided late in the afternoons, just prior to the cocktail hour and dance. For our "pleasure and refreshment," we were informed that the Smoke Room was aft on the Promenade Deck, the Observation Cocktail Bar forward on the Promenade Deck, the Garden Lounge port side on the Promenade Deck, and the Restaurant Cocktail Bar was on the starboard side of the "R" Deck. The main events each day were, of course, breakfast, lunch, and dinner. While dress was casual earlier in the day, dinner was a decidedly dressy affair.

Harriet and I were by far the youngest couple in first class. From our perspective most passengers were well advanced in age. Fortunately the *Queen*'s dance orchestra began to play early in the evening in the Main Lounge, then moved to the Starlight Roof Club as the evening progressed. The orchestra played until one o'clock in the morning to a rather lively crowd, and that's where we spent most of our time. The sea was calm, the nights star studded. Our crossing turned out to be a picture perfect voyage.

The fun ended on the fifteenth of August when we docked fairly early in the morning in Cherbourg, France. Those traveling to the Continent disembarked. The rest of us packed and got ready for our own departure in

Southampton later in the day. We arrived in Southampton at ten o'clock in the evening and boarded the Cunard Steam-ship Company Limited R.M.S. Queen Mary London Special Train. In London we checked into the London Waldorf-Astoria. I had just over a week of leave remaining before I had to return to duty at the Shooting Box, plenty of time for us to take in a play or two before wrestling our pile of suitcases onto a train to Kings Lynn. After our opulent ocean voyage things finally took a turn toward normality, my kind of normality. There were no servants hovering around us anymore. We were finally on our own. I couldn't help wondering how Harriet would take to our new life, a life where she would be just another person.

One of our first stops in London was the American Express office, a well-known meeting place for American tourists. Harriet revealed to me for the first time that her father had sent a letter of credit through his bank to the London American Express office, allowing her to withdraw money at will. She promptly withdrew five hundred pounds in five-pound notes. The English note was a peculiar looking banknote, quite large when compared to the American dollar bill, and it was printed only on one side of a rather thin white paper. Like it or not, it was real money.

The train trip to Kings Lynn became a major chore because of our mountain of luggage. The cab I hired in Kings Lynn to take us to Stiffkey couldn't accommodate all of our stuff, so I engaged a second cab. The driver confided to me that he had carried many Yanks over the years, but never anyone who needed two cabs and owned so many suitcases. When we pulled into the Bailey's courtyard, Colonel and Mrs. Bailey welcomed us. While Harriet joined them for tea and crumpets, the cabbies and I carried our bags into our musty-smelling house. We didn't have a car yet, so I thought it best to take a cab to Sculthorpe to see if our new TR-2 had arrived, and stop by the commissary to pick up some food. The last thing I wanted was for Harriet to get disillusioned by her new environment and turn around and fly home. Our little English rental house was like nothing she had ever lived in. The cabby was pleased to have me once more as a customer, and we quickly agreed on the fare to take me to Sculthorpe, and if necessary back again to Stiffkey.

To my great surprise, our TR-2 was sitting in the new car lot, ready for pickup. Once I tracked down the salesman, I took the car papers across the street to the Base Exchange and paid the remaining amount due. The Triumph salesman started the car for me, gave me some driving hints, and off I went to the commissary. When I returned to Stiffkey, Harriet already looked despondent. My own anxiety level was correspondingly high. I suggested we try out our new car and drive to a nice restaurant near Wells-by-the-Sea. With the wind blowing her hair into her face, in a brand new sports car, driving down an English country lane, Harriet's spirits revived. By the time we found the thatch-roofed restaurant with a gorgeous view of the Wash, we were a happy couple once more.

Mrs. Bailey must have figured that newlyweds on their first morning in their first home were probably in dire need of help. The Baileys were early risers, and when Mrs. Bailey saw us running about in the kitchen, she came over and offered tea on the terrace. Oh, how wonderful you are, Mrs. Bailey, I thought. I had dreaded our first morning, and she saved it for me. Harriet and I decided to get the place fixed up. After tea we made several runs to the Shooting Box and picked up the remaining boxes. A Triumph TR-2 sports car didn't have much trunk space. After our first run, Harriet remained behind unpacking while I shuttled back and forth. Later in the day we went to the BX and purchased necessities—high on the list, a coffee pot. Things appeared to be coming together. It turned out that I had underestimated Harriet. She actually knew how to follow cookbook instructions, and at least for the moment thought of her new experience as fun.

August turned into September; the days remained soft and balmy. Little rain, lots of sunshine. Our car became the first object of contention. I proudly drove to work each morning, leaving Harriet stranded with no one to talk to but the Baileys. "It is utterly boring here being all alone," she protested. "I need to get out of here. Period. Find another way to go to work." So I walked over to the castle and introduced myself to the major who lived there with his family. He worked at the 49th Air Division headquarters at Sculthorpe and was quite amenable to giving me a ride each morning to the Shooting Box. Harriet picked me up after work. My friends Bob and Celia invited us for dinner. Harriet and Celia hit it off, and after that evening we saw each other frequently.

It turned out that Mrs. Bailey was related to the Windsors. She received frequent invitations to social events in London and to nearby Sandringham. One Saturday afternoon Colonel Bailey came over. We showed him around, and he feigned interest and approval, then he revealed the real reason for his visit. They had been invited to a reception at Sandringham on Sunday morning, and would Harriet and I, we insisted that they call us by our first names, be so kind as to accompany them? We gladly accepted. The next morning as Harriet and I stepped into the courtyard at the agreed to hour, Colonel Bailey came charging out of the house in tails, shotgun in hand. He marched into the forest behind our apartment and proceeded to shoot at the pigeons drawing circles above the tree tops. Apparently the birds annoyed him to no end. I don't know if he hit any, but he sure startled the daylights out of us. Harriet and I stood openmouthed, watching the comic spectacle unfolding before us. After firing five or six shots, the colonel returned, never saying a word as he passed. Several minutes later he and Mrs. Bailey emerged from their house and greeted us profusely. Mrs. Bailey wore a formal dress. I wore a dark suit and tie, expecting anything done by the English aristocracy to be on the formal side. Harriet wore a black cocktail dress and pearls. I thought she looked stunning. All four of us got into the Baileys' Landrover. Mrs. Bailey drove, something the colonel never had to do while he was on active duty in His Majesty's Indian Army and never expressed a desire to master in retirement.

It was a delightful gathering of the English gentry, and we had the immense pleasure of meeting the Queen Mum, as the adoring English public referred to the always smiling, ever gracious, unpretentious Queen Mother. She greeted Harriet and me with charm and personal attention. "Well, Harriet," I said to my new wife, "would you ever have expected it would be me who got you an introduction to the Queen Mother? Not the queen, but close enough." Harriet was in her element, meeting and greeting. What a tale she would have to tell her Texas friends. This was the time when the second cause of contention between Harriet and me revealed itself, the lack of a telephone. England wasn't Fort Worth where one called the phone company and within a day or two a phone was installed. Here it took considerable time and red tape. Colonel Bailey discouraged us from applying for a phone, but agreed to let us use his whenever we liked. Apparently Harriet worked things out to her satisfaction with Mrs. Bailey, because she never complained to me again about not having access to a telephone.

The Baileys were duly impressed with Harriet's social skills. Whenever they had a reception or hosted a dinner, we were invited. November was cold and clammy. I obtained several kerosene heaters from the base on loan for the winter to keep at least some of the rooms in our apartment at an acceptable temperature. To my surprise I discovered that there was a central heating system after all, and that our part of the house was connected to it. But the frugal Baileys turned the heat on only when it got really cold, and then set the thermostat somewhere in the lower-sixties. We were always cold and had our space heaters going nearly all the time. One day I heard the central heating crackling, and the heaters actually began to feel hot to the touch. Mrs. Bailey's mother had arrived for a stay of several days. It was obvious that the old lady would not have left her London West End home if her daughter had not assured her that she would make her comfortable. The Baileys gave a grand dinner for Mrs. Bailey's mother. The courtyard, usually populated only by our little red sports car and the Baileys' Landrover, was overflowing with Bentleys and Rolls Royces. In my dark suit and tie I was decidedly underdressed. Harriet, being the youngest female present, looked stunning in her revealing and figure-enhancing dress, eliciting many sideways glances from elderly gentlemen. At the dinner table, a huge U-shaped affair, Mrs. Bailey seated me next to her mother. Harriet sat further down the table near a couple of ladies who had traveled widely in the United States.

The dinner was a formal and scripted affair. I carefully watched Colonel Bailey and followed his example. There was of course the smoking room, a part of the library, which I had never been in before. There we men assembled before and after dinner, giving the ladies an opportunity to powder their noses. Cigars were lit, scotch and cognac was passed, and the conversation centered on very English things I knew nothing about. After a certain amount of time, the conversation ceased suddenly, the remaining whiskey was left standing, the cigars were abandoned, and the entire male contingent marched in unison out of the room to rejoin the ladies. Throughout the evening the water was left running in the ladies' lavatory to preclude anyone from hearing the flush of a toilet. Mrs. Bailey's mother turned out to be a delightful table partner. She spoke several languages—French, Russian, German—and told about the wonderful days before the Great War. She spoke of life in St. Petersburg, Russia, as the guest of Czar Nicholas and of visits to Berlin as the guest of Kaiser Bill, also a relative. Her German was flawless, accent free, and I presumed she was equally skilled in French and Russian. In the winter of 1955 to 1956 we attended several dinners at the Baileys and became very familiar with their routines and rituals. I often stood alone, nursing my drink by the huge fireplace in the main living room. Harriet was always surrounded by several gentlemen, who I presume liked being in the presence of a beautiful young American woman spinning her tales of Texas, oil, and money.

After four months in England it seemed to me that our married life had actually settled into a routine. On weekends we often went to London with Celia and Bob. We found a reasonable, well-located West-End hotel, the Strand Palace, across the street from the elite Savoy Hotel. The Strand Palace was less than half a mile from Buckingham Palace, within walking distance of excellent restaurants, and only a brief cab ride from most theaters. Bob and Celia didn't seem financially constrained; they had no children and were free to come and go as were we. In time we four saw nearly every performance worth seeing, from fabulous musicals such as *Kismet* and *The King and I*, to nearly every one of Shakespeare's plays at the Old Vic. We usually took off early on Friday afternoons and drove to London via Newmarket and Cambridge before hooking into the principal motorway into London. We parked our cars and wouldn't use them again until we left on Sunday afternoon—stopping on the way home for high tea in a favorite tea shop of Celia's in Cambridge.

We four decided to spend New Year's Eve 1955 at the Strand Palace Hotel in London. It was the usual New Year's Eve celebration with dinner, dancing, balloons, champagne, and lots of noise. Well after midnight, when I returned from the restroom, there, on a silver tray, sat a pot of strong black coffee. I rarely drank coffee at all, but Harriet insisted, "Have some, darling. We don't want to go to bed yet."

The coffee was very strong. Soon after I drank one cup, I began to feel ill. "Harriet, I think we better go to our room; I don't feel well." No sooner had we gotten to our room when I felt my heart pounding in my throat. I tried to take my pulse. After only ten seconds I counted fifty beats. I couldn't keep up. Feeling weak, I lay down on the bed, my chest heaving from my pounding heartbeat. Harriet looked down at me, smiling. "Run downstairs to the desk and ask them to send up a doctor," I urged her. "I fear I may die if I don't get help quickly. My heart is beating so fast, it may stop any second." There was no phone in the room. Harriet just stood there. A faint smile played around her lips. "What are you waiting for, Harriet?" I gasped. I had difficulty speaking. "Why are you smiling? Please, go and get a doctor!"

"You'll be alright, darling," she said. "Just relax."

"No, I won't be alright, Harriet," I gasped in panic. "My heart feels like it is going to explode. Please, get me a doctor. Please, run, don't walk. Hurry." She turned away, walked to the window, and looked out onto the dark street below. I was incapable of doing anything for myself. I put my hand over my heart and felt its racing beat. Then, as suddenly as it began, my heart rate dropped back to a normal eighty beats per minute. I remained in bed, weak, exhausted, too tired to move a muscle or say anything. Harriet remained at the window, looking out on the street. I lay there for about ten minutes. After I recovered sufficiently, I asked her, "Why didn't you get help for me? What were you thinking?" She didn't reply, didn't look at me. At that moment I knew with certainty that something very troubling had entered our relationship. I lay back down, not bothering to undress, and went to sleep. Never again in my life did I experience such a potentially catastrophic cardiac event.

The next day on the drive back she sat silently. I thought about what happened, thought about the hundred-thousand-dollar life insurance policy her father Thomas had taken out on me, and thought about the possibility that I was worth more to her dead than alive. Perhaps she envisioned returning home a widow with money of her own, a sought-after woman, the envy of her friends—terrible thoughts, but I couldn't get them out of my mind. I am convinced to this day that was the scenario she envisioned when she stood by the window looking out on the street, ignoring her husband's plea for help. I decided not to bring up the incident again. If I tried hard enough, I thought, we might make it. I wanted things to work out. I didn't want my mother to be right.

CHAPTER 24

Differences and Choices

Winter in Norfolk County was cold, wet, and miserable. Although there wasn't much snow, the high humidity made the place seem colder than it really was. Icy roads and frequent early morning fogs made driving in our little sports car a challenge. Harriet and I never really felt warm and comfortable that winter until we were in bed. Cold or not, I recall those winter months of 1955 to 1956 as the happiest days of our unlikely marriage, marred only by the bizarre New Year's Eve incident, which I rationalized away.

The American couple who rented Sir Francis Bacon's castle occasionally invited us over for tea. We continued to be part of the Baileys' social life and continued to share outings and evenings with Bob and Celia. Our social life, including frequent visits to London, was more than a young couple at age twenty, living in a foreign country, had a right to expect. Harriet did not complain, and I had hopes that she was actually accommodating to the realities of our world. She apparently managed to stay in touch with her parents and friends in Texas, although Mrs. Bailey, who handled the financial affairs in her household, never mentioned a telephone bill when I paid her our monthly rent in crisp five-pound notes.

In late March 1956 Harriet informed me that her parents would arrive in London in April on an extended visit. "You remember me telling you about being presented to the Queen? Well, it seems it's going to happen. Dad has it arranged. Texas politics. You know what I mean." She smiled. I didn't know what she meant. I had no insight into Texas politics. Then, as if in passing, or as an afterthought, she casually said, "I've missed my period, darling. I think I am pregnant."

"What? We were so careful."

"Well, it happened. And if I am going to be presented to the Queen, I can't go there with a big belly, can I? So you understand my presentation will have to happen sooner rather than later." I was totally unprepared for the news. Personally I didn't mind us having a baby. But I didn't think Harriet wanted children so soon. I had trouble imagining her as a mother, with her near total focus on herself. I wasn't sure about my role as a father either. It was all kind of scary. The subject of children had never come up between us. It was something remote, for older people, not kids like us barely out of our teens. So her casual acceptance of her pregnancy surprised me, as much as her continuing focus on being presented to a queen who meant nothing to us as Americans.

"Why do you, as an American, care about being presented to the Queen of England?" I asked her, unable to keep a little annoyance out of my voice. After all, she hadn't shared things with me until the last moment—her parents unexpected visit, her pregnancy, and what I thought to be a stupid presentation to a monarch of a foreign land. "It's not an American thing. Forget about it, and try to enjoy our stay here while it lasts. Why can't you do that? The Queen has no relevance in our world. Who the heck cares if you are presented to her or not? The Queen is an English thing, an anachronism left over from another time, good for the British tourist industry. Can't you see that? You've already met the Queen Mother, shook her hand, conversed with her one on one. That should be enough even for you."

Harriet gave me a cold stare. "It may not be important to you," she replied icily, "but it is to me." That was that. Queen, parents, and baby were things she meant to deal with in her own fashion. We drove to London the last Thursday in April, took a room in the Strand Palace, ate an early dinner, and attended a play. The next morning we took a cab to Heathrow Airport to meet her parents.

Their plane was three hours late, but eventually we saw it coming in for a landing, slow and low, a Pan American World Airways DC-6. A half-hour later, after having passed through British customs, Harriet's mink-stole-wrapped mother Harriet—both shared the same first name—and dark-business-suit-clad father, Thomas, emerged looking surprisingly rested. Our exchange of greetings was restrained and polite—no kisses, only polite hugs, inquiries about health, chitchat. I hurried off to find a porter to wrestle their luggage onto a cart. To my great astonishment, a Rolls Royce limousine was waiting to take them to the Savoy Hotel, London's finest—right across the street from where we stayed in the Strand Palace in much humbler circumstances. At the Savoy her parents had taken a suite of rooms, almost like an apartment, expensively furnished with French period furniture. They invited us to stay with them for the weekend, and we quickly moved from the Strand Palace into the luxury of the exclusive Savoy Hotel. I left London early Monday to return to work. Harriet stayed behind, giving me detailed instructions which of her many dresses and incidentals I was to bring back with me to London the following weekend.

In the coming weeks I saw little of my wife. I felt deprived, having gotten used to her presence, the warmth and comfort of her body. Weren't we supposed to be together? As my wife, she should be with me, I thought, not with her parents in London. I learned from Harriet that during the week her father attended to oil-related business matters, including visits with people at the American Embassy. She and her mother shopped and visited the sights of London. One weekend in May, Harriet and her parents drove up to Stiffkey, arriving in a chauffeur-driven Rolls Royce. They looked at our apartment, which they were paying for, and we introduced them to the Baileys. When they left, they drove down the coast road to Wells-by-the-Sea where they took a room in a pleasant country inn. Harriet's father for days afterward raved about the delicious sweetbreads they served for dinner. The next day, after a leisurely breakfast, they returned to London, taking Harriet with them. They moved from the Savoy to an equally luxurious suite in the St. James Court Hotel, owned and operated by the Savoy, just down the street from Buckingham Palace. When I visited on weekends, I rarely encountered Harriet's father. Then he flew back to Texas; her mother stayed. Harriet senior did go to the theater with us on occasion and to performances of the Royal Ballet which she much enjoyed. The presentation to the Queen was to take place sometime in May or early June, part of a larger planned social event I was neither informed of nor invited to when it occurred. Harriet showed no evidence of her pregnancy, looking as ravishing as ever. She acquired a new, expensive wardrobe at Harrods and Mark and Spencer's, stores equal in quality to Neiman Marcus in Dallas. I couldn't wait for her parents to return to Texas and for the whole thing to be over.

On September 1, 1956, I was promoted to airman first class, my third stripe. I was proud of my promotion, but didn't bother to mention it to Harriet. For her I was in the army, a life she put up with for the time being, but which was fundamentally incompatible with her own aspirations. I enjoyed every day of my air force experience, especially the ever-widening perspective it gave me on my new country and the world of military aviation. Although I wasn't a flyer, I sensed I was in the middle of a vast technological evolution transforming the air force. At Carswell Air Force Base my bomb wing flew huge B-36 bombers, technological hybrids using conventional powerplants augmented by jet engines. The B-45 bombers at RAF Sculthorpe were all-jet aircraft. Jets were the future, my future I hoped. In private moments I dreamed of one day flying one of those jets.

On occasion Harriet and I did talk about the future, but our views never were compatible. She decided for me that I would become a petroleum engineer, I would attend Rice University, and we would live forever in Texas. I had a totally different vision of what I was going to do, including returning to Colorado, to the mountains I loved so much. I knew if I had her choose between me and her parents, between her life of wealth and privilege and what I had to offer, I would be the loser. So I never pushed the issue, just let her talk.

In September my detachment was transferred from our bucolic location at the Shooting Box to Hillingdon Air Station, a World War II air defense bunker in the London suburbs. Colonel Hull remained behind at Sculthorpe. My new commander, Lieutenant Colonel Edward R. Dolezel, was in many ways a carbon copy of Colonel Hull—the same uniform, weight, and stature, equally generous, compassionate, and unmilitary in his disposition. Ed Dolezel was a scientist first, a graduate of the Massachusetts Institute of Technology, who much preferred immersing himself in the study of weather phenomena than getting involved in military routines. Especially boring to him were the administrative aspects of his position. So Colonel Dolezel, as Colonel Hull before him, relied on me to take care of the office. The only thing I couldn't do for him was attend the weekly staff meetings at the headquarters of the 28th Weather Squadron in Bushy Park—weekly meetings were the downside of being situated too closely to any headquarters. He would return from these meetings looking exhausted, hand me a list of things to do, and say, "Take care of this, Sam." Then he took off his blouse, loosened his tie, and disappeared among his weather forecasters to do what he liked doing best—analyzing meteorological phenomena. Our liking for one another was mutual. He treated me more like a son than the airman I was. I responded in kind.

Our desks faced each other in our small office, but we were seldom in the office at the same time. I made a daily mail run to South Ruislip Air Station, the location for the 7th Air Division headquarters of the Strategic Air Command. Ruislip served as our support base, provided housing for unmarried airmen, mess facilities, officers' and sergeants' clubs, a hospital, commissary, and base exchange. I looked forward to the mail run each day, the only opportunity I had to get out of our claustrophobic concrete bunker. In winter I would go to work in the dark and, except for the daily mail run, never again got outside during daylight hours.

Colonel Dolezel was a sensitive man and quickly deduced from our conversations that not all was right with his young clerk's marriage. He didn't probe, but I felt relieved when he occasionally encouraged me to talk, and he would quietly listen. Harriet was thrilled when she learned I had been transferred to London and immediately got busy finding a place for us to live. It seemed my transfer gave the two Harriets something to do other than dining out, shopping, sightseeing, and going to the theater. In my absence, with the help of a high-priced Mark & Spencer's realtor, she and her mother—who was still in England after five months—came up with a duplex in North Wembley. Harriet took me to the house and excitedly showed me around. A large foyer led to a bathroom, kitchen, breakfast room, living room, and dining room, the latter with an elaborate crystal chandelier suspended over the table. "Just think of the dinners we can give," Harriet swooned. The stairs leading to the upstair bedrooms were long, narrow, and steep. There were three bedrooms upstairs, a full bath, and a maid's room adjacent to a large walk-in linen closet. French doors led from the dining room out to a terrace Harriet thought charming. The house furnishings included bed linens, dishes, even an extensively stocked liquor cabinet in the living room. It was as if a wealthy family had walked out of the house and left everything behind. All we had to do was buy a washer, dryer, and refrigerator and the necessary transformers to be able to hook up to the English electric system which was double the voltage of our own—220 rather than 110 volts. Harriet was so enthusiastic about finding the place that I never even considered questioning her choice. She was happy, and that's what mattered to me. The greatest advantage of moving to London was that my wife came to live with me again, at least in the evenings. Her mother remained in her hotel suite at the St. James Court in London and either came out to visit her daughter during the day while I was at work, or more often, Harriet visited her in the city.

I suspected that Harriet became pregnant in March. By September she barely showed. One morning, dressed in a silk suit, getting ready to take the tube to town, she proudly announced, "Men are still looking at me."

"Why do you care about strangers looking at you, Harriet?" I asked, astonished that she would make a comment like that. "Isn't it enough that I desire you?"

"It's important to me how I look and how men look at me," she replied, clearly annoyed at my response. "I shouldn't have said anything to you." She grabbed her things and left for the city. We expected the baby in December. Harriet began to experience morning sickness. Her mother spent more and more time with us. On September 30, a Sunday, Harriet complained about feeling ill, went to bed early that afternoon, and declined to eat dinner. About seven o'clock that evening her mother quietly entered the living room and said, "Wolfgang, you need to go to the pharmacy and have this prescription filled." She handed me a piece of paper with scribbling I couldn't decipher. "The only pharmacy open this late on Sunday evening is Boots in downtown London, near the American Express office. Be a dear and run along. Harriet is really feeling badly and needs this right away." I put on my shoes, grabbed a jacket, jumped into the car, and drove off with only a vague idea where Boots was located. It was a long way from Wembley to downtown London. It took time for me to locate Boots, find a parking place, and then wait for the lone clerk to fill the prescription. I returned around eleven, about three hours later. When I walked into the house, I was greeted by silence. I ran upstairs and found the bedroom empty, the bed cold, Harriet and her mother gone. I looked for a note, there was none. I called the St. James Court: no answer. I thought of calling the police but figured that was too drastic an action. Don't panic, I told myself, there must be a logical reason for their absence. They will call soon. I had nodded off sitting in an easy chair in the living room when the phone rang.

"Wolfgang, dear," Harriet's mother said, "I am so sorry to wake you."

"Don't be sorry," I replied. "Where are you? What happened?"

"It is a long story, my dear. I will tell you everything later. We are at St. Marylebone Hospital, on Devonshire Place. Harriet delivered a baby boy. Both are well. Go back to sleep and come down in the morning." She gave me Harriet's room number and hung up. I was stunned. I thought Harriet wasn't due for another three months. I arrived at the hospital at ten o'clock Monday morning. Harriet looked fine; she even smiled at me. Her mother sat silently in a chair by her bedside.

"Have you seen the baby yet?" Harriet asked.

"No. He is in a special care unit and they wouldn't let me near him."

"Well, they will. Be patient."

"What happened? How did you end up in this hospital? Tell me."

"She needs her rest, Wolfgang," Harriet's mother interjected. "I will tell you everything." We went into an adjoining sitting room and sat down facing each other. "Let me tell you about the baby first," she said. "He is well, but in need of extended care. He only weighed four pounds, ten and one-half ounces when he was born."

"Isn't that very little?" I asked.

"Yes, it is. And that is why both have to stay here for two or three weeks." I knew nothing about giving birth and how much time a mother needed to recover, but I knew that after my sister Ingrid was born my mother was back on her feet in two days. I didn't understand why Harriet would have to stay in a hospital for three weeks.

"Harriet tripped at the top of your stairs and fell all the way to the bottom. I called an ambulance and had no time to leave you a note. I hope you can forgive me." Her eyes shifted downward when she said that; she didn't look me in the eye.

I saw the baby later that morning. He was incredibly tiny, wrapped tightly in a blanket, with black hair all the way down to his little ears. Driving home I thought about last night's events. It became clear to me that Harriet's fall probably wasn't accidental. Why was I sent to a down-town London pharmacy late on a Sunday evening for a routine prescription which could have been filled days earlier? Did her mother want me out of the house? Sending me off to Boots certainly insured my absence for two to three hours. What was Harriet doing at the top of the stairs anyway if she was so ill? I hated my conclusion: that neither Harriet nor her mother wanted the baby. They probably had talked about how Harriet could best avoid giving birth during their many meetings over the past months. Then jointly made the decision for Harriet to deliberately fall down the steep stairs on her stomach to lose the baby. That at last explained her mother's extended stay in London. My suspicions grew even more. How did Harriet happen to end up in one of London's very best hospitals? If it had been a true emergency, wouldn't an ambulance have taken her to the nearest hospital in Wembley? The longer I thought about what transpired, the more convinced I became that the supposed accident had been carefully planned and was no accident at all. The only accident was that the baby survived.

When I was about twelve, my grandmother Samuel was reminiscing one day about life on the family farm—how one of her brothers died suddenly from an infection, how her father was killed by a runaway team of horses, and how the maids always got pregnant but rarely gave birth, because they always seemed to lift things too heavy for their condition, fell down stairs, or took rare baths in water too hot. Maybe falling down stairs wasn't such an unusual way to deal with an unwanted pregnancy. Maybe it had been done for generations by desperate people. Our baby, however, survived in the excellent care of one of London's best hospitals, something the two Harriets probably didn't count on.

I no longer felt confident that I could save our marriage. Frankly, I was scared.

CHAPTER 25

A Shattered Marriage

Harriet remained with the baby in St. Marylebone Hospital for the next three weeks. I understood why the baby had to stay. At only four pounds and a few ounces he was very fragile and required nine feedings a day. The doctors and nurses were jubilant when the baby began to gain weight, an ounce at a time. On Tuesday, October 2, 1956, I went to the offices of the Metropolitan Borough of St. Marylebone and registered the birth of Wolfgang Thomas Samuel, son of Harriet Samuel and A/1C Wolfgang Samuel of Clarendon Gardens in Wembley. When I proposed Wolfgang as a first name and Thomas as a middle name, Harriet agreed. Whenever I visited, Harriet looked healthy and seemed to be in good spirits with no apparent complications from her fall. She seemed to thrive on the attention she received from the hospital staff and doctors.

"I can't tell you how cute he is," Harriet said to me one day. "I can't believe he is real. He looks like a little doll." But he wasn't a little doll. Wolfgang was a little baby with many needs his mother would have to tend to very soon. I wondered if Harriet was actually capable of doing that, but thought maybe such things came naturally to women. After all, Hedy had raised Ingrid and me under extremely difficult circumstances. Harriet's mother departed abruptly. I began to see the always polite, seemingly reticent and gentle woman in a different light. Concealed under her polished exterior was the toughness of a woman who expected to attain her goals no matter the cost. Precisely what goals she focused on in London was not clear to me at the time, but it seemed that things hadn't gone exactly her way. She completely avoided me at the hospital whenever I came to visit and left England without saying goodbye to me. I didn't even know of her departure until Harriet quite casually said, "Mother is flying home today." No explanation. I found it all very strange, even odd, that after spending months in London with her only daughter, she would choose to leave immediately after the premature birth of her one and only grandchild.

I tried to cope with the situation as best as I could. But coping for a twenty-one year old with no one to share the pressures and uncertainties of the past year was a tall order. Looking in the mirror I noted that I looked haggard and thin. I figured that whatever caused my weight loss would in time work itself out on its own. What did surprise me though was that I hadn't had any nightmares. Harriet began breast feeding baby Wolfgang, who continued to thrive. I loved holding my tiny son. I still wasn't sure if I was prepared to be a father yet, but then who is? My father Willie had been mostly absent and inattentive throughout my own childhood, so I had no fatherly example to follow. But I whispered a promise to be there for him when he needed me.

The third week of October both Harriet and baby Wolfgang returned home accompanied by a live-in nurse. The nurse was a tall, thin woman who had seen combat in North Africa and the Mediterranean. One evening she revealed to me the terror and helplessness she felt as a young nurse on a hospital ship off the coast of Italy under attack by German bombers. Her eyes took on that distant, faraway look I had seen all too often in combat veterans who tried to cope with memories too difficult to relate to others. "All those men drowned," she said. "They were so helpless. I can still hear their screams. What was worse, I couldn't help them. Helping them was my job. That's what nurses do. All I could do was save my own life and watch and listen as they drowned." She fell silent, tears rolling down her thin face. She wiped them away, embarrassed at having revealed herself to a stranger who might not understand. I felt compassion for the woman and wanted to put my arms around her, but of course I couldn't. She had no idea of my own background.

Our nurse, who was always in uniform, took charge of baby Wolfgang. All Harriet needed to do was be there for some of the feedings and occasionally change his diapers to practice for the day when she would be on her own. The nurse stayed in the third, smaller upstairs bedroom and turned the downstairs living room into the baby's room. Fortunately the house had central heating, unlike our drafty residence in Norfolk. I kept the temperature in the baby's room at 68 degrees Fahrenheit, considered a little high by our nurse, but she relented. Her word was law in matters baby. Harriet quickly returned to her old ways and kept herself busy shopping. She discovered a Wedgewood china pattern she just couldn't live without and had eight place settings delivered to the house. She rummaged through London's Silver Vaults and emerged with an intricately patterned silver service, including a huge tray which at one time must have belonged to British nobility who had come upon hard times. The silver service when fully assembled was so heavy I had difficulty holding it. Harriet didn't ask if I liked any of her acquisitions or explain how they fit into our lifestyle. Her independent and extravagant ways gave me an uncomfortable feeling of irrelevance. At one time we were close, I thought, but maybe it had all been a delusion on my part. Maybe nothing had really changed, only the way I experienced and understood our life. I wished her parents and their money would just go away and leave us alone. Maybe then we could find ourselves as a couple and have a chance at building a life together. But that wish was hardly in the cards.

Harriet had access to seemingly unlimited funds through her letter of credit at the American Express office in downtown London. She was not dependent on me in any way, certainly not financially. She never asked me for anything—other than compliance with her wishes. I tried to develop a savings plan based on my limited income, a plan that didn't include her parents and their money. But she didn't care to be involved in anything she considered so unrealistic. "I don't understand you at all," she said when I tried to discuss such notions with her. "Do you like being poor? I don't know what it is like, and I don't want to find out."

An important-looking envelope arrived in the mail from a legal firm in Fort Worth. The envelope, addressed to Harriet, contained signed, stamped, and certified papers providing for a hundred-thousand-dollar trust fund established by Harriet's father Thomas for his grandson. Baby Wolfgang was only days old and already a rich boy. The trust fund made me feel even more left out, pushed aside, irrelevant. The arrival of the documents led to a confrontation between Harriet and me about our son's name. "We should change his name from Wolfgang to Thomas," Harriet insisted.

"Why? I thought we settled the name issue."

"Don't you understand?" I noted the absence of the word *darling* when Harriet spoke to me. "My father was very hurt when we didn't name the baby after him."

"But Thomas is the baby's middle name," I said.

"It should be his first name. Just look at all my father has done for us. He pays the rent for this house, pays for our living expenses, bought our car, paid for our honeymoon, established a trust fund for the baby. Doesn't he deserve something in return? We need to change his name—now!" Her tone was demanding, and the level of her voice barely below shouting.

"It doesn't mean that much to me," I relented, wanting to end the confrontation. "I'll go tomorrow and change his name to Thomas Wolfgang. Does that suit you?"

"That's wonderful, darling," she replied mockingly. "I knew you would see it my way." I believe that was the last time she called me darling. I went to Marylebone city hall the next day and changed the baby's name.

The nurse stayed for ten days, then came by daily to check on young Thomas. Eventually she declared he was doing fine and didn't need her anymore. "Call me if you need me," the nurse told me at the door as she was leaving for the last time. She couldn't help but know that Harriet and I had marriage difficulties. "Call me any time, day or night," she insisted, "I'll always be there for the baby." I never called on her.

Upon my transfer to London in September 1956 I left my friends behind. Bob and Celia did not transfer to London, but stayed behind in Norfolk. I missed having them around. I missed the Baileys as well, their eccentric friends and the interesting dinner parties to which they always invited us. None of those pleasant diversions were available to us in London. There was the theater, but we attended less and less as time passed. The Wembley neighborhood we lived in was typical English upper middle class where neighbors minded their own business, remained invisible to each other, and seldom formed even casual acquaintanceships. Intimacy, the one thing that had bound Harriet and me together in the past, proved to be a brittle bond. After Harriet's return from the hospital, intimacy became increasingly less frequent between us and only at times of her choosing. When I showed a desire for her, she turned away, making herself unavailable. The departure of our nurse heightened our estrangement. Harriet no longer had the freedom to go into London to indulge herself. She became listless and unapproachable. Her temperamental side, always there before, now became dominant. Our conversations nearly always ended in arguments.

I thought we needed to talk about our future, but we could never reach common ground on any issue. My ideas about my future education quickly became a red flag, causing her to break into uncontrollable fits of profanity. I had never known that side of her, didn't even know she was capable of such vulgarity. I told her more than once that I didn't want her parents' money to finance my education and that I had no intention of studying engineering. "Engineering isn't me. I don't have the mentality to be a good engineer. What I want to do is fly airplanes. Become an officer in the United States Air Force. Serve my country. That's what I really want to do." She couldn't deal with that as an option and never gave up trying to interest me into attending Rice University to become a petroleum engineer—to make lots of money. "I don't care that much about making lots of money, Harriet, can't you understand that?" I once shouted at her in frustration. "I want to do something that is bigger, more meaningful than just making money."

She looked at me uncomprehending and, after she had thrown all the profanity she could think of at me, coldly said, "I told you this once before, and you better listen good this time, mister. You can't afford me on a stupid army salary. You need to think things through, and you are not thinking." Harriet drew a line in the sand, as we say in the military; so had I. I didn't quite realize that I was doing that at the time, nor did I comprehend the consequences of my actions. But I knew that I was not willing to compromise my lifelong aspirations, my dream. Not only did I not want to be a petroleum engineer and attend Rice University; I wanted to return to the University of Colorado where I failed the first time around. That's where I had to succeed. For Harriet there was only Texas. She had no interest in living in Colorado, even if it was only long enough for me to complete my education. We talked about what kind of house we wanted when we returned to the United States. The lavishness of her expectations left me speechless. It was no different when we discussed what kind of a car to buy now that we had a baby. Our little red Triumph was designed for two people to have fun in; we had to look at things differently now, get a bigger car. Again, there was no agreement. If I suggested a four-door, she wanted a two-door. If I named one color, she picked another. She wore me down until I said, "I don't care. You pick the car."

Then the telephone bill for the month of November arrived—over five-hundred dollars. Harriet had been on the phone with her mother each day. I was shocked by the size of the bill, regardless of whose money it was that paid for it. The telephone bill alone amounted to nearly my entire monthly air force salary. I knew we didn't have a chance to work things out between us if the financial umbilical tying us to her parents was not cut, or at least constrained. I confronted Harriet with the bill. Her response was violent. For the first time she berated my family, cursed my sister, my mother, anyone she could think of who was close to me, using words I last heard when I worked on the bull gang in the summer of 1952. In her anger she revealed that her parents had always opposed our marriage and only consented because she wanted it. "What a stupid decision I made!" she shouted, then locked herself into the bedroom. I didn't see her again until the next day. We made it through the Christmas holidays with difficulty.

Something new entered the picture that I had not been aware of before—alcohol. I came home one evening to find Harriet lying on the living room floor, passed out. Bottles of scotch, gin, rum, and other liquors lay about. She looked disheveled, unkempt, and had never dressed after getting out of bed—nothing like the young woman I fell in love with two years earlier. The baby had not been cared for and was crying loudly in his crib—hungry and dirty. I took care of the baby, changed his diaper, fed and burped him, and put him back to bed with a soft pat. Tommy was a good baby and didn't cry much, as long as his simple baby needs were met. When Harriet woke from her stupor, she turned into a screaming banshee. What was it she wanted? I asked myself. What could I do to change things? How did it all take such an awful turn? Alcohol was a development which scared me more than anything else I had discovered about Harriet. I knew what alcohol did to people, remembered the drunken Russian soldiers and what they had done to women. I wanted nothing to do with alcohol and feared its effects. I hardly ever touched alcoholic drinks and didn't even have a can of beer in the refrigerator. As far as I knew, the only liquor in the house were the bottles in the dining room which came with the house. I was certain Harriet couldn't have developed an alcohol problem from one day to the next. Drinking herself into a stupor had to be a deliberate choice, not an accident. I remembered her mother once cautioning me not to let Harriet drink so much Coca-Cola. "It isn't good for her," she said to me. "If you can, do something about it." Did she really mean Coca-Cola? Or did she think I knew something about Harriet's drinking and the word coke was just a euphemism for rum and coke, or something else. I realized I was still naive in many ways, tending to take things too literally. I guess I still had a lot of growing up to do, a lot to learn about human nature.

I tried coming home every noon to make sure the baby was taken care of, but Harriet viewed that as harassment. One day she acted perfectly normal, cooking dinner and taking care of the baby; the next she would make a scene, drinking herself into oblivion and caring for nothing. I didn't know what to expect when I got home. Life was turning into a living hell. Somewhere inside I still cared for Harriet and couldn't let go of the vision of the girl I once knew. I didn't know what was driving her, what it was she wanted, or if she even knew herself.

We took the baby for his final check-up in March 1957. The doctor who had delivered Tommy was pleased with his development, and when Harriet questioned him, he said that he saw no reason why Tommy couldn't travel. "He is quite alright," the doctor assured her. "A normal baby." Within days of the check-up Harriet booked a flight to Dallas. She didn't tell me about it until the evening before her departure. I had no idea when she was coming back. "I'll let you know," she said. "I'll call you." The thought crossed my mind that she might never return. Her being gone was actually a relief. For once I could sleep through the night, go to work rested, and come home that evening knowing what I would find—an empty house, yes, but not a drunken woman and a neglected baby. Spring passed and I never once heard from her. Then I received a cheerful call telling me that Tommy was doing just fine and that she was coming home. I was surprised and hopeful. Maybe being apart for a while had been good for both of us.

Tommy had grown quite a bit—that was the first thing I noticed upon their return. He smiled at me when I took him in my arms. One evening as we were lying in bed having a cigarette, she said out of the blue, "I dated some of my old friends while I was home."

"Your girlfriends, you mean?"

"No, boyfriends."

"Did you sleep with them?" I don't know why I asked that question, but once it was out I couldn't take it back.

"What do you think?" she replied, taking a long drag on her cigarette. "I was away for a long time. It didn't mean anything." I was in shock. I couldn't believe she would do that, then admit to it freely while making small talk with me. I turned out the light and tried to go to sleep. I knew there wasn't much, if anything, left of our marriage. Our life soon went back to the way it had been before she left. She drank to excess. At times I returned from work and found a strange sitter in the house. She had gone to London. One evening when I came home, the house was empty. There was no note. Harriet's suitcases and Tommy's things were gone. I went to our next-door neighbor, whom I had met casually, and he told me a man had come by in a Rolls Royce limousine, a bald man in a dark suit, an American, and driven away with Harriet and the baby. Her father. This time she wouldn't return.

It was the last week of July; the house rent was paid through September. We had planned to take a four-week vacation to Germany, France, Austria, and Switzerland. I had my leave orders in hand, the ferry reservations from Dover to Calais were made, and hotel rooms had been booked, so I decided to go. My father, who remarried soon after his divorce from my mother, had a little boy by the name of Gerhard, a half-brother whom I wanted to see. Maybe the trip would take my mind off my marital difficulties, allow me to gain perspective, even insight. Other than Colonel Dolezel, I had told no one at work about my marital difficulties, nor written Hedy and Leo. I was too embarrassed to admit failure after less than two years of marriage. It was a subject I just couldn't talk or write about easily.

On August 10 I locked the house and jumped into the little red Triumph TR-2 and drove down to Dover where I caught the ferry to France. It was just me and my little car, and as I drove into the sunrise through the French countryside, my cares and burdens began to drop away. I began to feel again like the young man I was.

Often, mine was the only car on the autobahn. In 1957 the German economic miracle was still in its infancy, and most people rode bicycles or motor scooters. It was an exhilarating feeling to speed down those beautiful four-lane highways with the top down, my hair blowing in the wind. On the autobahn from Munich to Berchtesgaden the fan belt broke. I pulled to the side of the road hoping some kind soul would stop to help me out of my predicament. I waited for a miracle, which came in the form of an American military jeep. The lone MP at the wheel was cruising the road as part of his assigned duties. I could have kissed him when he pulled over.

"Hey, fella," he shouted good-naturedly, "what seems to be your problem?" He got out of his jeep and ambled over toward me. He wore a helmet liner, 45-caliber pistol, pants bloused into paratrooper boots. "Nice car," he said before I could say anything. "You English?"

"No," I replied, "I'm American. Stationed in England. My damn fan belt broke. Do you have any idea where I can get a new belt on a Sunday morning?"

"Don't worry," he said. "Kilroy will provide." He laughed as he looked into the engine compartment, then walked around my car and nodded his head approvingly. "Nice," he muttered, "very nice." He motioned for me to get into the jeep. I looked at the name tag on his uniform shirt, and sure enough KILROY was his real name.

"I thought you were kidding," I said to him. "Your name really is Kilroy." Everyone knew there was no real Kilroy, only GIs leaving behind graffiti greetings wherever they went.

"You betcha," he said proudly, smiling broadly. "You've surely seen my signature before," he continued with his Kilroy charade. "I do say I get around." I learned he was from Minnesota, second generation German, and still spoke the language. How he acquired his name remained a mystery, since I thought it was English or Scottish. I didn't ask, he didn't say. "Don't worry about your car," Kilroy assured me, correctly interpreting my worried look. "No one will touch it. I know this area well. It's my turf. I patrol it every day." Kilroy's jeep was moving down the autobahn at maximum speed, and I was holding on for dear life. Jeeps at high speeds with their narrow wheelbase were not exactly the most stable of automobiles, and Kilroy's jeep was no exception. "Where you from?" he shouted over the road and wind noise.

"Colorado," I shouted back. "I'm stationed in London."

"Lucky you. They speak English there, don't they?" and he laughed at his joke. What a great guy to run into, I thought. "The Krauts," he shouted, "are learning fast, I have to give them that." He pulled off the autobahn into a small Bavarian village and headed for what looked like a garage, a gas pump out front. Kilroy jumped out of his jeep and knocked on a side door. A man in an open-necked white shirt opened the door and I heard the two talking and laughing. They obviously knew each other. The German disappeared into the house and soon emerged wearing a clean pair of blue mechanic's coveralls, entered his workshop, and reappeared carrying several drive belts in one hand. The mechanic got his tool kit and a crowbar, and all three of us jumped into Kilroy's jeep and drove back to my disabled automobile. In less than fifteen minutes my problem was resolved. I paid the German mechanic and added a carton of cigarettes in gratitude, remembering the power of cigarettes in the early postwar years.

"*Vielen Dank*," the mechanic said as I handed him the cigarettes, bowing slightly from the waist up. "I like Pall Mall. *Eine gute Marke*." We shook hands all around. As they drove off, Kilroy waved at me and hollered, "Kilroy was here."

I eventually ended up in Elmpt, near the Dutch border, where my father had found employment at Royal Air Force Station Brüggen. He worked in supply, a job he held until his retirement in his seventies. He had brought his parents, my grandparents, along with him to Elmpt, and Opa Samuel was busy planning to build a little house on a plot of land he had just purchased. The land was large enough to accommodate a second, larger house, which he intended to build after the first one was completed. The larger house was to be for my father and his family, the smaller house for himself and Oma. I had not seen them since 1950, seven long years. My grandmother could hardly contain herself when she saw me. She had resigned herself to never seeing me again in her lifetime. My father and his new wife seemed happy and making a go of their marriage after some early difficulties. Gerhard was a cute blond, blue-eyed boy of two. Willie's wife was pregnant again with their second child. I stayed a couple of days, then headed back to England.

Upon my return to London I had a letter waiting for me from Harriet's lawyers, informing me that she had filed for divorce. The letter advised that Harriet intended to keep the baby and deny me any visitation rights. In return, she would make no claims on me for financial support. I battled the issue within myself for a week, then decided to give Harriet what she wanted. I had nothing going for me to contest the divorce—I was stationed in a foreign country, had no financial resources to speak of, and the court which was to adjudicate the divorce was in her home town of Fort Worth where her family was well known and had a multiplicity of business and social connections. In time, surely Harriet would let me see Tommy again.

Divorce aside, I had practical things to tend to. For one, I lived in a house I couldn't afford. The monthly rent alone, not considering utilities, exceeded my net monthly salary. Fortunately the house lease contained a military clause which allowed me to terminate the lease with two weeks' notice. I gave notice and prepared to move out. I advertised the refrigerator, washer, dryer, and numerous transformers for sale at a reasonable price and sold them quickly. Whatever else remained behind of Harriet's things I packed and put in storage. Without my knowledge, prior to her departure, Harriet had shipped all the silver, china, and other valuables she acquired over the past year back to Texas. A most difficult decision was to sell my pretty little red Triumph TR-2. I had grown attached to the car and hated to let it go. But I had no choice. The car was just another expense. The proceeds from the appliances and the car, and a little extra money I had saved, I invested in IBM stock.

My boss, Colonel Dolezel, was an avid stock market fan. Much of his money was invested in yesterday's technology, as I saw things—Chrysler Corporation, General Motors, U.S. Steel, all industries with a huge infrastructure, massive overhead, a unionized labor force, but good dividends. Colonel Dolezel and I had some spirited discussions across our desks over where our future was leading us. I maintained that our future lay in electronics. "Can't you see that, Colonel," I remember telling him in late November 1957. "The Russians just shot up their second Sputnik. We are not going to be far behind. They scared the living daylights out of us, at least that's what I get from listening to you officers talk. So why don't you buy at least some IBM?" I never forgot that he was my boss, a lieutenant colonel; I, his administrative clerk and a three-striper enlisted man. But that didn't keep us from talking. I learned much from him about the market, economics, and how to think clearly and analyze things based on facts, not emotions. The facts as he saw them drove him to the industries of the past. I viewed the facts very differently, and they led me to the industries of what I believed to be America's future. So I bought IBM.

I continued to badger Colonel Dolezel to buy IBM and Texas Instruments. "If I had any more money," I told him, "I would put every dime into Texas Instruments." The Dolezels invited me for dinner more than once. They were old enough to be my parents and had no children of their own. I told Mary, "Talk to your husband and get him to buy some future-oriented stocks." She actually tried, but Ed remained superconservative. We stayed in touch over the years. Long after Ed died, Mary wrote, "I wished Ed had listened to you when you told him to buy Texas Instruments. I sure could use the money now that I am in a nursing home. God bless you, Wolfgang. Love, Mary." I never again showed such prescient farsightedness in picking stocks as I did that year as a twenty-two year old.

I finally wrote my mother about my marriage debacle, two long letters in quick succession unburdening myself of all the things that weighed me down. Hedy was the only one I felt who could relate to what I was going through. Not because she had gone through a divorce herself, but because of what we had experienced together in 1945 and in the early postwar years. Still, the letters were difficult to write since I wasn't convinced that I didn't contribute in some way to the failure of my marriage. I probably was too close to the situation to see what I could have done differently. I related some of the circumstances and events which led to Harriet's unannounced departure, addressed the role of her parents and how their money began to work against us, and conceded that the baby did not prove to be a unifying factor. "I beg you not to worry about me because everything is under control," I assured her after ten long pages. I knew she would know that nothing was under control for me.

It was more difficult than I expected to adjust to my new situation. It wasn't that I was looking for another woman. I was looking for myself. Trying to find out who I was and who I had become. I was lucky to find a charming room with a very nice English couple for only two pounds a week, about five dollars and sixty cents. My landlady woke me each morning with a cup of hot tea, made my bed, and tidied up my room. Four nights a week I attended University of Maryland classes at South Ruislip to prepare myself for my eventual return to the University of Colorado. "I do miss my little boy," I wrote Hedy, "but I feel he needs his mother more right now than he does me. I hope that when he is old enough to ask questions he will ask about his father, and we'll find each other again. I can't wait to see you and Leo. Can't wait to come home to Colorado. Love, Wolfgang."

Only days before my return to the United States for discharge from the air force, I received an official copy of the divorce decree. The District Court of Tarrant County, Texas, granted our divorce effective April 17, 1958. In the judgment it was "ordered, adjudged and decreed that the bonds of matrimony heretofore existing between the plaintiff, Harriet Samuel, and the defendant, Wolfgang Samuel, are hereby dissolved and that the plaintiff is granted a divorce from defendant." The court gave custody of the child to Harriet "with no rights of visitation insofar as the defendant is concerned," and ordered "that no obligation for child support shall be placed on the defendant." The court further ordered "that all costs of this proceeding having been paid, no execution shall ever issue for costs herein."

On April 29, 1958 I processed out of the 28th Weather Squadron at Bushy Park and took a train to Burtonwood in the north of England. There I boarded a civilian contract flight to McGuire Air Force Base, near Wrightstown, New Jersey. At McGuire, I was given new orders assigning me to Lowry Air Force Base, Denver, Colorado, for discharge from the air force, and a Greyhound bus ticket home—a ticket to Colorado and my future.

CHAPTER 26

Coming Home to Colorado

I saw Hedy and Leo waiting for me as the Greyhound bus pulled into the depot. My stepfather Leo wore a new blue suit and had tears streaming down his face when he saw me step off the bus. Leo always carried his emotions on his sleeve, and today was no exception. I was his son in every way but blood. Leo had always been there for me when I needed him. Nothing had changed. I hoped he knew how much I loved him. "Dear Wolfgang," he muttered in a tear-choked voice, hurrying toward me to give me a hug, "so good to have you home again."

Hedy, too, was dressed for the occasion, wearing an expensive new suit. She had excellent taste in clothing. Shoes, purse, gloves, hat, all complemented her suit; everything fit together as if designed that way. I knew it wasn't. Instead, she carefully collected each item until the whole ensemble gave the impression of a designer fantasy. Hedy was a fashion artist with a special knack for matching colors, fabrics, shapes, and textures into a coherent whole. She was a stickler for accessories. "Always buy the best accessories you can afford," she once lectured me, "even if the dress comes from Penneys." I didn't know where the little German farm girl, my mother, acquired her tastes. I loved her for who she was, for the many sacrifices she had made for Ingrid and me, for the stubborn woman she could be. Yet, she was a skilled compromiser when it counted, never losing sight of the greater goal she aimed to achieve. But there was no compromising when it came to her clothes. I hugged Hedy, gave her a smooch on the cheek, then grabbed my duffel bag off the station floor and slung it over my shoulder. I took the backseat in their new, white and blue, Chevrolet Impala. After seven years, my parents finally had the resources to buy a new car.

"How do you like it?" Leo asked.

"Looks great," I said. Leo was pleased with my response. He took the long way home, south toward Cherry Creek Reservoir. Near the reservoir he pulled over to the side of the road, a lonely stretch where all I could see was prairie grass and gopher holes. I had no idea why he was stopping. All three of us got out of the car. A slight breeze came off the mountains, behind us to the west. I turned around, and stretched out before me was the breathtaking array of Colorado's snow-capped Front Range, rising majestically into a clear blue Colorado sky. To the left I glimpsed Pikes Peak rising above Colorado Springs; on the far right, Longs Peak. In between lay a jagged array of snow-covered mountains. The sun reflected off the heavy snow pack, dazzling my eyes, the way I remembered the scene back in February 1951. Now I knew why Hedy and Leo had chosen to come this way. Turning toward Leo I saw this foolish grin on his face. "Welcome home, Wolfgang," he said softly. This time the tears came to my eyes.

"How did you know, Leo?"

"We knew," he answered, smiling broadly, unable to contain how pleased he was that he and Hedy had done just the right thing for my homecoming. Leo knew how much I loved the mountains, loved everything about Colorado, my home.

Not only had Hedy and Leo turned in their used 1951 Chevrolet for a new car; they also had moved from their simple frame house on Wheeling Street to a newer, all-brick house with a basement on Salem Street, just a few blocks south. In only seven years Hedy and Leo had attained a level of prosperity they would have found hard to believe had they taken the time to look back. Hedy never looked back. I admired both of them for all they'd achieved in such a short time—the once poor boy from Derby, the equally poor girl from Louisfelde.

"This is not my dream house, Wolfgang," Hedy said as she opened the front door, "but it's an improvement over Wheeling Street. It has much more space and a nice patio and garden out back. Come and look." She hustled me out the back door onto a lovely patio surrounded by a natural stone planter filled with flowers. "We just finished the planter two days ago for your homecoming. Isn't it lovely? I had to beg the stone mason to come and finish work on Saturday so I could plant the flowers on Sunday." I plunged into a comfortable patio chair, unbuttoned my uniform blouse, and took off my tie. Home at last. "Your bed is ready and waiting for you," she said, then she hurried inside, changed clothes, and started making lunch. When she came out again, I asked her where Ingrid was. Hedy frowned, busying herself with the flowers in the new planter. "She got married the other day."

"What?"

"She met a Marine last year. Home on leave. He is out of the Marine Corps now. They live in Greeley. He is going to school at Colorado State." She was tightlipped. I dropped the subject.

I freshened up, changed, and enjoyed the rest of the day just being with them. It was a Monday. Leo took the day off from work. Hedy went to work at Gertrude's dress shop later that afternoon. The orders I received at McGuire AFB gave me eight days' travel time to get to Lowry. My official reporting date was May 10. I signed in at Lowry that Friday morning and immediately began my out-processing. By afternoon I had orders in hand honorably discharging me from active duty effective the following Thursday, May 15, 1958. I still had two months to go on my enlistment, but for reasons known only to the air force, I was released early. I was paid for thirteen days accrued leave and received three hundred dollars mustering-out pay provided by a grateful, if not overly generous, 82nd United States Congress to those who served during the Korean War. By the end of the day, I was for all practical purposes, once more a civilian.

The next morning I grabbed my air force uniform and headed to a nearby photo studio to have my picture taken. I knew this moment in time would never be here again. I was truly excited about going back to college and promptly signed up for the summer session at the Denver extension of the University of Colorado. I took it as a good omen that its location was near the Emily Griffith Opportunity School where seven years earlier everything started for me, where I had struggled with the English language, struggled as a German boy to become an American boy. The next day I took a Trailways bus to Boulder and got off on the hill. It felt great to walk the campus again in the shade of its magnificent old trees, some planted when the university was established in the 1870s. I crossed Varsity Bridge, a carefully tended campus landmark, walked past Old Main with its peculiar Queen Anne tower, the oldest building on campus, and stopped before Macky Auditorium. Two towers flanked Macky, as if added as an afterthought, or put there as a senior prank. I registered for the fall semester at the admissions office in Macky, listing business management as my major. Of all the academic options I examined, management seemed to offer the best compromise and opportunities. Three years of course work lay ahead of me, about ninety credit hours, maybe a few more. I did some quick back-of-the-envelope figuring and determined I should be able to do it all in two years, including summer school.

I then walked over to the Air Force Reserve Officer Training Corps offices of AFROTC Detachment 105, located below the seats of the university's football stadium. I was received courteously and filled out various applications and questionnaires, then was scheduled to take the Air Force Officer Qualification Test, AFOQT, to determine my aptitude to be an officer and a flyer.

"I regret to inform you, Mr. Samuel," Major Vance L. Beebout, one of the professors of air science at Detachment 105, said to me, "but all of our advanced ROTC slots are filled. I will put you on a waiting list. But even if we should call you, it will not be in a flying slot. They were filled long ago." I sat there utterly stunned. I planned everything so carefully. Go to college. Take AFROTC. Get my degree. Get commissioned in the air force. Go to flight training. Was my dream ending? Major Beebout leaned back in his air force issue gray swivel chair, his eyes expressing no emotion. He was simply passing on a message, not knowing its impact on the young man sitting before him. "You have to understand," he said, sitting up, folding his hands before him, "that the Korean War ended not long ago. The air force is getting smaller. There is little need right now for new officers or flyers. Frankly, we have more than we need and are letting many go. Just look at me. I am a navigator and I am sitting here behind a desk. I would rather be in a cockpit, believe me."

As Major Beebout talked, obviously trying to make a bitter pill taste sweeter for me, I interrupted, "Sir, I don't know if this makes a difference, but I served nearly four years in the air force as an enlisted man. I was honorably discharged only a few days ago at Lowry Air Force Base. Does that make a difference?"

"Well, that puts a different light on things," the major replied. He left the office briefly and returned with the folder holding my application. He apparently overlooked my prior air force service when he scanned my application before the interview. "We have a special program for former enlisted men," he said in an upbeat tone of voice, smiling. "Relax, Mr. Samuel, we'll find a slot for you. Maybe even a flying slot if you qualify."

A few moments earlier I felt as if the bottom had dropped out from under me. Then it all turned around. I was thrilled when I walked out of the major's office. Two weeks later, I went back to Boulder to take the Air Force Officer Qualification Test. "Depending on how you did on the test," Major Beebout qualified his statement, "I will have a navigator slot for you. Unfortunately, the pilot slots have all been filled, but one may open up and you can switch if that happens."

I told him I didn't care what position I was offered, pilot or navigator. "All I want to do is fly."

"I like your attitude," the major told me as we parted. "I am looking forward to seeing you as a member of the cadet corps." In late summer Major Beebout called and told me my AFOQT test scores were satisfactory. "You've been admitted into the advanced Air Force ROTC program, and you'll like to hear this, I am sure. It is why I called you personally. We've been able to come up with a navigator slot for you." He interrupted my gushy response, "Let me be frank with you, Mr. Samuel. It was your attitude that convinced me to do everything in my power to help you get a flying slot. We like nothing better than giving enthusiastic young men like you a chance at their dreams. It's up to you what you make of it. See you in the fall. Goodbye."

Leo shared my joy when I told him the news that evening. Another small advantage came with my admission into advanced AFROTC—a small stipend of $1.85 a day. With my limited savings, and sole source of income the Korean War GI Bill benefits, any additional income was welcome. In the veterans' office, carefully hidden from the general student body on the third floor of Old Main, I located the all-important veteran's sign-in sheet. Once a month I had to show my face to verify that I was still on campus pursuing my academic goals, and this was where I picked up my monthly benefit check of $110. More importantly, the GI Bill paid my tuition and fees. The Korean War GI Bill of Rights, as did its World War II predecessor, gave many of us former servicemen the financial independence needed to obtain a college education.

The next stop on my agenda was to find a place to live. I needed a quiet place, no roommates, and a reasonable rent. I trudged over to the university's housing office. A kind woman greeted me as I walked in and listened attentively to my request for information. She gave me an application to fill out, and while I did she made a phone call. When I returned to the counter, she took my application, looked at it briefly, then asked, "Do you mind answering a few personal questions?"

"Of course not," I replied. "Go right ahead."

Smiling apologetically she said, "Have you served in the military? I mean, you look more mature than most students."

"Yes, I have," I replied. "Air Force."

"Oh," she said, "I served in the army air forces in World War II. I hate to have to ask you this question, but do you take women to your room, or have loud parties?"

I wasn't prepared for her question and must have shown it, for she seemed to cringe ever so slightly. "You sound like my mother," I said to her. "Do you really expect an answer from me? Those can't possibly be questions the university requires you to ask." She lowered her eyes. "Yes, I do like girls," I said, "but I don't have to take them to my room. And no, I don't intend to have loud drinking parties either. What I want is a quiet place where I can concentrate on my studies. I have three years of academics to complete in two. That doesn't leave me with a lot of extra time on my hands. Did I answer your question adequately?"

"Yes you did," she said softly. "I am so sorry to have asked you such a personal question, but I have a friend who is a librarian over in Norlin Library. She has a room available which might just be what you are looking for. And I believe, young man, you are what she is looking for," she said firmly, having recovered her poise. "I've taken the liberty of calling her, and if you have time, I'd be happy to take you over to the library and introduce you to Miss Virginia Holbert. She is a wonderful person. A better landlady you wouldn't find anywhere."

Virginia Holbert turned out to be everything her friend claimed she was. She lived in a small house on Fourteenth Street, a house she inherited from her invalid mother whom she had cared for until her death. As a result, Virginia never married. She was looking for someone to do a little grass cutting in summer, leaf raking in autumn, and snow shoveling in winter. I liked Virginia the second I laid eyes on her—she was the height of my mother Hedy, with a kind face, graying hair, gray-blue eyes, and dressed in a conservative blue dress with little red and white polka-dots. In her left hand she carried a tiny black purse, the perfect picture of a refined woman. Virginia didn't own a car, so her friend from the housing office drove the two of us through campus, up the hill past several ostentatious fraternity and sorority houses, to Virginia's little blue clapboard house that sat, as if wanting to be polite, farther back from the street than its larger neighbors. The charming little house within walking distance of campus was flanked by several huge Colorado blue spruce. I could see the Flat Irons looming through the trees, the distinctive slabs of sandstone rock rising from scree- and talus-strewn slopes, forming the backdrop for an incredibly beautiful university campus. A bed, a dresser, a small night stand, an old fashioned roll-top desk, two lamps, a bookcase, and a tiny table crowded a very small room. "We'll share the bath," Virginia said. "And feel free to use the kitchen anytime." Her bedroom was off the living room. The living room was furnished comfortably with her mother's heirlooms.

Virginia Holbert was born in Atchison, Kansas, at the genesis of the Atchison, Topeka, and Santa Fe Railroad for which her late father once worked. Her father died at a young age; soon after her mother was confined to a wheelchair, and young Virginia's future was sealed. She never complained, but through veiled comments I surmised that she missed marriage and children of her own. After her mother's death, Virginia made a home for several carefully chosen young college men, many of whom later reached important positions in their professional lives. Without exception, each shared his achievements with the woman who so generously housed and supported him during his student years at the University of Colorado. The twenty-five-dollar monthly rent I paid, she managed to give back for services rendered. Virginia became as close to me as my mother, at times more so, both as a friend and confidant. With her help I dealt with the trauma of my brief, disastrous marriage. In the two years we spent together, Virginia was the person who gently helped heal my invisible wounds, persuading me to take life as it came, not to blame myself for things I neither fully understood nor had control over. In days of long ago, in my days of war and horror, when I was saved so many times from death and calamity, my Oma Samuel ascribed my survival to a guardian angel. Obviously, that angel must have led me to Virginia Holbert as well.

I returned to Denver that day satisfied with all I had accomplished. One last thing remained to be done before leaving for Boulder in September. I needed to find a car. The cars I really liked were 1955 through 1957 Chevrolets. I checked out nearly every used car lot in Denver and quickly discovered that used cars were exactly that, someone else's rejects. Every '56 model Chevy I looked at turned out to be a clunker. The '57 models were a bit more expensive than what I wanted to pay; and '53s and '54s seemed to be nothing more than repackaged 1949 models. That left only the '55s. At the last dealership—tired, disappointed at what I had not found—I was ready to call it quits. Just then a salesman came up to me and said, "I have a car which just came in. It hasn't been cleaned yet. The couple who brought it in just drove off in a new model. Would you like to take a look?"

"What year is it?"

"A '55 hardtop." I couldn't believe what I saw sitting by the curb in front of the dealership. A green and white two-tone hardtop with white sidewall tires in near immaculate condition. I climbed in and drove the car around the block, looked under the hood, and decided to buy it then and there. I was certain I would never find a better used car. The salesman and I settled on a price, I wrote a check, he took the car into the shop to have it cleaned and to put on some new whitewalls, and I drove it home that afternoon. In late August, after summer school finals, I moved my things to Boulder in my new, used '55 Chevy hardtop.

In my two years at the University of Colorado I took at least six courses each semester, between eighteen and twenty-one credit hours. I was much better prepared for my academic challenges than in 1954. I not only had to pass every course I took to graduate in the summer of 1960, I also had to raise my terrible grade-point average. I was stuck with my sub-standard academic past, and it would take a lot of As to get me up to a B-plus or

A-minus overall grade-point average. I developed a study schedule each semester and stuck to it. Friday afternoons and evenings I left open to do as I pleased—nurse a pitcher of beer with a friend at the infamous Sink was one option, not often exercised. The Sink was still a smoke-filled bastion of adolescent iniquity, reeking of cigarettes and spilled beer. More often I took a date to Tulagi's with its more civil surroundings, dim lights, and dance floor. Three-point-two beer was served in all of the student-frequented establishments. The panty raids I remembered from 1953 were a thing of the past, gone with the members of the World War II generation who had graduated and moved on. The disappearance of panty raids did not detract from the university's reputation as one of the top party schools in the country, attended by many out of state students with deep pockets. Fraternities and sororities played a big role in fulfilling their members' wishes for a good time, continuous fun, and maybe finding a husband or wife in the bargain. I had absolutely no interest in the fraternity scene, much less in finding a wife.

I did precious little cooking in Virginia's kitchen and instead ate at McGinnis's, a boarding house down the street near the Tri-Delt sorority house, just a short walk from Tulagi's and the Sink. At McGinnis's I ate lunch and dinner five days a week, lunch only on Saturdays, and on Sundays I was on my own. Most of McGinnis's boarders were female students from Winnetka, Illinois. They drove MG sports cars and wore designer clothes and Dior perfumes—fun to be around, if frequently a little snobbish and naive. I dated some of the girls, but they reminded me all too much of Harriet and my recent past. Although many were quite attractive, I simply could not develop feelings for these young women. Neither was I ready for a close relationship with any woman—casual yes, close no. The food at McGinnis's was typical boarding house fare, filling but not particularly appetizing. I remember one occasion when fried trout was served for lunch. When I got my plate, I knew I was in trouble. The trout had swollen to immense proportions, which meant they hadn't cleaned the fish before frying. Oh, for some good ol' air force chow.

Saturday evenings I left open, having studied the rest of the day. My approach to studies paid dividends. Slowly my grade-point average began to rise, placing me on the dean's list every semester. In my senior year I was designated a Distinguished Air Force ROTC Cadet. As a distinguished graduate I would have the option of accepting a regular commission in the air force rather than a reserve commission. All military academy graduates received regular commissions in their respective services; ROTC, by definition, was a reserve officers' program. Therefore, regular commissions were the exception rather than the rule, a reward for exceptional performance and potential.

In ROTC I made many friends and one exceptionally good friend, Dean Stutz. A farm boy from Wiggins, Colorado, Dean was my height, my age, a little stockier than I, and like myself the first in his family to go to college. A football player in his high school days, Dean wore a crewcut and had a pilot slot. He pursued a degree in electrical engineering, which came easy to him. He had married his high school sweetheart, Shirley, and they lived in a small basement apartment—one bedroom and a kitchen with an expanded lounge area. I spent many hours with Dean and Shirley in their bare-bones place, watching *The Flintstones, Rifleman,* and other no-brainer shows like *Route 66* on their seventeen-inch black and white TV. We were sufficiently inundated with facts and theorems in our classes that when we relaxed we wanted to watch mindless programs that allowed us to laugh and act silly, our way to unwind. Dean was the one who introduced me to Giovanni Boccaccio's 1353 *Decameron. The Decameron* was not a no-brainer, yet it was light and hilarious reading. Dean and I would alternate reading its one hundred stories aloud to each other, with Shirley listening. All three of us laughed ourselves silly in the process. It took a whole year to get through *The Decameron.* Those were great days I've never forgotten.

Dean and I graduated in 1960, he in June, I in July, after summer school ended. He went on to pilot training at Reese AFB near Lubbock, Texas, and ended up flying the new 707-based C-135 jet transport. Dean got out of the air force after five years and went to fly for Pan American Airways, dying unexpectedly in his early thirties of a heart arrhythmia. A picture of Dean in his silver-tan air force uniform with the gold bars of a second lieutenant on his shoulders hangs in my study. I look at his picture almost every day. Dean was the best friend I ever had. His loss in the prime of his life was a tragedy for all who knew him. In our early air force years our paths crossed occasionally. I flew in RB-47H reconnaissance aircraft against the Soviet Union from diverse air bases around the world. Our aircraft were distinguishable from B-47 bombers by our black radome noses. I remember being shaken awake in my hootch one night at Clark Air Base in the Phillippines, in the early days of the Vietnam war. Opening my eyes, I saw Dean's grinning face looming over me. "Get up, you lazy bum, and let's go and have a drink at the club," he shouted. I threw on some slacks and a shirt, and we took a bus to the club. "I saw a B-47 sitting in a remote corner of the base," he said. "I figured it might be your spy plane and taxied as close to it as they let me. I saw it had a black nose, so I figured maybe you were here, ole buddy."

"What are you doing at Clark?" I asked him.

"Passing through," he said. "I'm in and out of here all too often."

"What do you carry?"

"You don't want to know what we take home with us." I knew what he carried home, the bodies of the fallen. He was terribly depressed about his cargo. Dean and I met once more before he left the service, that time at RAF Station Brize Norton, near Oxford, England. We were flying our RB-47H reconnaissance aircraft out of Brize Norton deep into the Baltic Sea, or high up north near the Kola Peninsula, to ferret out Soviet radar emissions, learn their technological secrets, aiming for them to reveal their wartime tactics. Dean landed his C-135 transport at Brize Norton. Again he saw a B-47 bomber with the telltale black nose, learned who the crew was, and immediately set out to find me. I was in London on a break, sightseeing and sampling London's nightlife. Dean tracked me down, and in the middle of the night I was awakened by a telephone call. "Hey, buddy. Guess who?" I caught a last train to Oxford where I had an air force staff car waiting at the station to rush me back to Brize where my dear friend Dean was waiting with a bottle of champagne. I miss my friend. I always will. Dean was the brother I never had.

In August 1959 I was ordered to participate in a four-week AFROTC summer camp at Hamilton Air Force Base, near San Francisco. Most cadets went to summer camp between their sophomore and junior years, a mandatory aspect of ROTC, the first chance for the military to look at their future officers in a stressful environment, as well as a chance to eliminate those who couldn't deal with the pressures. To me, summer camp was old hat, not much different from the eleven-week basic training course I went through as an airman at Lackland AFB in 1954. The emphasis was different, but the hours were much the same—up very early in the morning, to bed very late at night. We lived in old World War II barracks modified from open bay to rooms holding two bunk beds each. When we weren't attending lectures, exercising, touring, or observing firepower demonstrations, we scrubbed washrooms and toilets. Keeping young officers occupied was the mantra the military lived by. Young men had to be kept tired or they got into a heap of trouble, regardless of rank.

Hamilton was an Air Defense Command base which had recently transitioned to the newest air force fighter, the F-104. There I got to fly for the first time in the backseat of a T-33 trainer and had the opportunity to fly the jet on my own. It was a thrill cruising above the city of San Francisco, looking down at the Bay Bridge. At nearby Beale Air Force Base we went through a three-day survival course, a taste of things to come. In later years I took several survival courses in preparation for combat in Vietnam and multiple sessions of intense interrogation training as a member of a reconnaissance crew. At Hamilton, we qualified with .45-caliber pistols, instead of the M1 carbine I fired in basic training. Take a breath, hold it, aim, squeeze the trigger softly so you don't even know when the gun will fire. Boom! If you did it right, the bullet would hit the center of the bull's eye, or close to it. Just as in basic training, my target turned into one big mushy hole, my shots clustered so closely they were difficult to count. I fired the best score. Unlike basic training, here no one tried to deny my achievement.

For me, the most important event at AFROTC summer camp was the flight physical. Although I experienced numerous military physical examinations in the past, none had been as thorough and extensive as this one, nor as important. Failure of any part of the physical examination meant elimination from the flying program. Physicals remained personal nightmares for me. I remembered my first physical, that embarrassing experience in the American consulate in Munich in 1950. In the fall of 1951 I needed a simple high school physical. At Lowry Field a corpsman lined us up in four rows as if we were an infantry platoon—old men, middle-aged men, and a sixteen-year-old youngster, me. Age made no difference to the air force. Then the corpsman had us strip. All of us stood totally naked. I stood rigid, like an icicle, looking straight ahead. The doctor, accompanied by the corpsman came down the front of each row listening to heartbeats while examining genitals, telling us to turn our heads and cough. He then came down the back of our line and listened to lungs, commanding, "Take a deep breath. Hold it. Let out slowly. Bend over." Another physical from hell. After I went on active duty in 1954, I never again experienced physicals applied in such a rudimentary manner.

At Hamilton the vision test came last. Near and distance vision—pass; depth perception—pass; night vision, a test given in a totally blacked-out room with pupils dilated—pass. Then we were given a color test, which consisted of reading numbers off plates with colorized dots. I remembered taking the same test in basic training and failing. My flying career suddenly seemed to be on the line again. The corpsman flipped through the book of color plates, about twenty or so, with mingled colorized dots revealing hidden numbers; some easy to read, others hard. He flipped fairly rapidly through the plates one after another. I was hoping he would miss the plate I once failed to decipher at Lackland. He didn't. "Take your time," the corpsman said. "I have all day." My flying physical came down to this one color chart. If I failed, I was finished. I looked away, looked at the plate again, looked away once more, and finally thought I discerned the number 57—Heinz 57. Sounds right—57 it was. I passed.

After a raucous, end-of-camp party at the Hamilton Officers' Club, which included throwing our tactical officers, all captains, into the pool, I drove home from California to Colorado in my beloved '55 Chevy hard-top. It was the same road I traveled five years earlier in 1954 with my friend Al in search of a job in California. My prospects this time were all positive, compared to 1954 when I thought I had come to a deadend.

Passing through Winnemucca, Nevada, I saw the bulbous dome of a lone radar site visible on top of a nearby mountain peak. At Hamilton I learned about our air defense system and knew that the Winnemucca radar site was a backup to primary radar sites located at the coast, such as the one we visited on Mount Tamalpai. Several frame houses sat below the site, baking in the sun in the open desert. I presumed that they housed the families of the men who manned this lonely air defense outpost. I wondered if I would ever have to serve my country in a place like Winnemucca? I didn't care. I would go wherever they wanted to send me.

In my second year in Boulder I began to date a coed I first met at McGinnis's boarding house. Unlike most of the other girls, she wasn't from Winnetka, but from nearby Longmont, just up the road from Boulder. Her family operated a small chain of furniture stores in Colorado and Wyoming. Deanne Durning and her friend "Bunny" always sat apart from the other girls at the dining room table. One evening I took a chair across the table from them. The food came. I began to eat. Then the one named Deanne addressed me in German, "*Ich spreche Deutsch. Wo kommen sie her?*"

"How interesting," I replied. Actually I thought it was boring. I just wanted to finish dinner and get back to studying. What did I care if she spoke German? But I decided to be civil and respond.

"You speak very well," I complimented her. "Did you study German here at C.U.?"

"Oh, no. I'm a transfer student. I attended Principia, a two-year college in Illinois. When I graduated, I took the summer off and went to Europe. The usual stuff, you know. Down the Rhine River, Paris, Rome. I had so much fun, I didn't want to come home and cabled my parents. They came right back at me and wrote, 'Stay for as long as you like.' A girlfriend helped me get an interview at Mobil Oil Corporation in Hamburg. They hired me as a secretary. That's where I learned my German. I stayed for a year. Loved every minute of it. But I had to come home to finish my studies. So here I am." Suddenly my interest was aroused. I listened ever more attentively as she spoke. She was a pretty redhead with an open smile and a friendly, inviting manner. I knew it took courage and a high degree of self-confidence to do what she did, characteristics I respected. I began to see her in a different light.

"That's absolutely amazing," I responded. "I would like to hear more about your experiences in Germany." And actually I did want to. We finished eating, and I excused myself, promising to talk again. She studied in Norlin Library most evenings, as did I. We soon took our breaks together in the stairwell of the library. I smoked a cigarette, and we talked—talked about her experiences in Germany, about her growing up as the daughter of a furniture store manager in Cheyenne, Wyoming. In the stairwell of Norlin Library at the University of Colorado we became friends, and gradually I told Deanne about my failed marriage, and about the son I had and lost. She listened sympathetically. Deanne and I began to date, going to football games, Tulagi's, and various other functions around campus. Then she invited me to her home in Longmont for dinner, and I met her family. In the spring of 1960 we stopped seeing each other. An old boyfriend from her Germany days suddenly reappeared, and she decided to give that romance another try. I continued my own casual dating. I was young, twenty-five, and now and then needed to feel the warmth of a young woman in my arms, someone who, like me, was not looking for a long-term relationship but wanted to enjoy the moment. Many among the sorority crowd seemed to like it that way.

Graduation day, July 22, 1960, was the culmination of dreams that began to take shape nine years earlier, on a sunny December day in 1951, when on an impulse I, a sixteen-year-old, bought a set of shiny, gold second lieutenant bars at a pawn shop in downtown Denver. Nine years later I was awarded the coveted degree of Bachelor of Science in Business, graduated with distinction from the Air Force Reserve Officer Training Corps, and commissioned a second lieutenant in the United States Air Force. Most of my ROTC classmates were commissioned earlier in June at the time of the university's regular commencement exercises. Three of us—Horace Matthews, Carl Minkner, and I—still needed a summer course or two to finish. Matt and Carl were going into pilot training; I was the only one in my AFROTC class to enter navigator training. It was a great day for everyone, but most of all for Hedy. My mother couldn't stop smiling, couldn't believe her son was being commissioned an officer in the United States Air Force, couldn't believe I had earned a university degree. Leo couldn't believe that his stepson had not only finished high school, but college as well, and was being commissioned a second lieutenant in the very air force in which he once served as an enlisted man.

"Wolfgang," Leo said, emotion clouding his voice, "let me be the first to salute you." I saluted back, smartly. I loved the man so much, the Berlin airlift veteran who had become my stepfather on paper and my father in my heart.

"I can't give you that silver dollar, though," I said, referring to a military tradition of giving a silver dollar to the first enlisted man who saluted you. "It must go to our detachment sergeant." We both laughed and hugged one another. The sergeant soon came by to collect his due, clicking his heels and throwing me a smart salute. I gladly handed over that silver dollar. Deanne was there as well. Her romance had faltered once again, and we resumed our casual dating. During summer school she invited me several times for lunch and dinner at her parents' house, which looked out over the Longmont golf course. I found her mother, Patricia, and her father, Charles, to be nice and interesting people, hardworking and well educated. Chuck was an engineer with degrees from Colorado and MIT, a self-made man from Leadville, Colorado, a mining town high up in the Rockies, at the ten-thousand-foot level. Chuck's family immigrated from Nova Scotia and opened a coal business in Leadville; they later owned a ranch. As a boy Chuck delivered coal to Baby Doe Tabor, then living in a mining shack just outside the famed Matchless Mine, which had run out leaving her penniless. Fierce thunderstorms descended on the mountain valley in summer, and lightning struck his family's ranch house more than once. Chuck came down from the mountains as a boy and worked his way through the University of Colorado, later getting a master's degree in mechanical engineering from MIT, where he met his future wife, Patty, who was attending a Boston area college. He worked for years for United Fruit. Then Patty convinced him to go into business with her father. That's how Chuck the engineer became a furniture store manager. He and I had much in common. Both of us began our life journeys with only the will to succeed.

I invited Deanne to my commissioning ceremony at the last minute. She accepted. Together, Deanne and Hedy pinned the gold bars of a second lieutenant on my shoulders—the very same bars I had purchased on a whim in a Denver pawn shop. Years later I would pin those lieutenant bars on the shoulders of my son Charles, named after his grandfather Durning, when he graduated as an electrical engineer from Ohio State University in Columbus, Ohio.

At age twenty-five I had seen many of my dreams come to pass. There had been many obstacles, yet somehow, with the help of many mentors, supporters, and friends, I had overcome them all. I was proud of my achievement on that sunny July day in 1960, proud to once more wear the uniform of the United States Air Force, and grateful to the people who believed in me and helped make it all possible. Amongst all of those people—the kind and generous teachers at Opportunity School, my counselor at East High, my understanding commanders, Lieutenant Colonels Hull and Dolezel, Virginia Holbert—Hedy and Leo stood tallest. Where would I be if Leo had not insisted that I get a high school education? Where would I be if Leo had not come to my rescue when my first try at a university education failed? I owed him much. As I looked at him, I hoped he knew that I knew.

My debt to my courageous mother was unpayable. I was so glad she was there to share the moment. It was, after all, her moment as well. When she spoke of me to others, she'd always preface her comments by saying, "He did it all by himself. Put himself through college, became an officer in the United States Air Force. I had nothing to do with it." Hedy, of course, had everything to do with it.

CHAPTER 27

Harlingen Air Force Base, Texas

Military orders soon arrived terminating my enlisted status in the air force reserve. Then I received a letter from the Commandant of Air Force ROTC at Maxwell Air Force Base, Montgomery, Alabama, welcoming me to the officer corps of the United States Air Force. Last, but most important, a set of orders arrived directing me to report for active duty. "By direction of the President," the orders read, and Leo smiled approvingly when I read that sentence to him, "2nd Lt Wolfgang W. E. Samuel, AO 3123445, having volunteered for active military service is ordered to extended active duty to attend Navigator Class 61-11N. You will report to the Commander, 3610th Navigator Training Wing, Harlingen AFB, Texas, not later than 1200 hours, 30 Aug 1960. Effective date of duty 26 Aug 60. Retention of officer on extended active duty is subject to standard medical examination at first duty station. If officer fails to pass the medical examination he will be processed for separation." I read my orders several times. I pulled out a road map to find Harlingen, which turned out to be a little town in the very southern tip of Texas, squeezed between the Gulf of Mexico and the Mexican border, as remote a place as that radar site on top of the mountain near Winnemucca, Nevada.

Dreams are one thing, reality another. The stark reality for me was that the silver dollar I gave the sergeant at my commissioning ceremony in Boulder was just about the last dollar I had to my name. I had used every penny of income and savings on my education, sold my IBM stock, which I regretted doing, and ended up with nothing. I looked forward to going on active duty and receiving a paycheck, but until then I had to lay my hands on some money. Orders in hand, Leo and I went to the Bank of Aurora hoping to obtain a small personal loan of four hundred dollars to tide me over. It was the bank where Hedy and Leo banked since they moved to Aurora in 1952, eight years earlier. We didn't anticipate a problem getting such a small loan. The loan officer, however, saw things differently and curtly denied my application. I tried to persuade him that there was no risk as I was going on active duty as an officer in the United States Air Force and would repay the loan before the year was out. He wasn't persuaded by my plea, rose from behind his desk, and without saying another word indicated with his hand that our interview was over and we were to leave. In 1960 Aurora was a town where most residents in one way or another made their living from employment provided by the federal government, working either at Lowry AFB, at Fitzsimons Army Hospital, the Rocky Mountain Arsenal, or Buckley Naval Air Station. But apparently the bank's loan officer was not aware of the economic facts of his community, or perhaps he had another agenda. Whatever his motivation in denying my simple small loan request, I still needed money to support myself. I felt insulted; Leo was incensed by the loan officer's hostile manner. "Wolfgang, I know another place," Leo said. "The people at Household Finance always treated me fairly when I needed short-term financial help. Let's go there." The Household Finance office was across the street from the Bank of Aurora. Within thirty minutes I had a four-hundred-dollar check in hand. I paid off that loan before the year was out. Hedy and Leo promptly closed their account at the Bank of Aurora.

I enjoyed the few free days remaining before I had to report on active duty. The sun shone brightly every day, the sky paraded its pristine blue, and each morning arrived crisp and cool. I loved my Colorado and hated to leave. Two years passed all too quickly. I mapped out the route I intended to drive from Denver to Harlingen, over Raton Pass, New Mexico, through Amarillo to Lubbock, Texas. I thought I'd stay overnight with my friends Dean and Shirley Stutz. Dean was going through pilot training at Reese AFB in Lubbock, and they should have settled in by the time I arrived. But after taking a second look at the map, I changed my mind. Why not drive to Fort Worth? Maybe Harriet would allow me to see Tommy. I knew I had no parental rights according to the divorce decree, but hoped perhaps Harriet would allow me to see our son anyway.

Early on the morning of July 28, before the sun rose over the eastern plains, I said goodbye to Hedy and Leo. I arrived in Fort Worth late in the day and called Harriet's parents' home, the only number I had to get in touch with her. Harriet answered. Instead of hostility, I received a warm and friendly greeting. "I am delighted you called," she said. "I can't wait to see you again." That comment took me by surprise. "Why don't you come over? I am sure Tommy would love to meet his father."

"No, I can't do that Harriet." I didn't want to run into her mother and deal with her feigned hospitality and insincerity. "Isn't there some other place we can meet?"

"There is a playground just down the street, remember? I'll meet you there with Tommy." For the first time in three years I was to see my son. I was excited. Of course he would no longer be the tiny baby I remembered. Tommy was tentative when he exited the car. He politely came toward me and offered me his hand. His mother must have coached him, I thought. I picked him up and held him tight. He didn't resist, nor did he say anything when I gave him a kiss on the cheek. Then he turned toward his mother, pointed toward the playground, and said, "Mommy, I want to play." Tommy ran around the playground while Harriet and I talked. I kept my eyes on him, watched him. His hair was no longer raven black, but more like my own, light brown. He seemed quiet, maybe a little uncomfortable around the stranger who was his father. I was glad to see my son, sorry that I would have to leave him soon again. Harriet and I sat on the bench, she at one end, I at the other, quietly watching Tommy play.

I don't know what made me do it, but I turned toward her and asked, "Would you spend the night with me?"

She looked at me, smiled, and replied, "Let me take Tommy to my mother. It's time for him to go to bed anyway. I'll meet you at the Holiday Inn." We made love in familiar ways, ate breakfast together the next morning; then she went home and I continued on to Harlingen. I arrived early in the afternoon and signed in. The base looked dusty, tall palm trees lining the road from the main gate to the airfield's interior. I was assigned a room in bachelor officers' quarters, BOQ, a two-story barracks not unlike one I lived in in basic training at Lackland. The room was furnished with the usual functional furniture and a window air conditioner. I shared a bathroom with another officer. My windows looked out on an aircraft-filled flight line. One phone in the hallway served the entire floor. Whoever was nearest the phone answered, then loudly called out the name of whoever was wanted. We tried to keep our conversations brief as everything said on the phone echoed down the hallway for everyone else to hear. At four o'clock the next morning I learned the downside of being quartered next to the flight line. Crew chiefs began running up the engines on twin-engine Convair T-29 navigation trainers, parked practically under my window. Except on Saturdays and Sundays, it was impossible to sleep past four o'clock.

I called Harriet once I settled in at Harlingen and gave her my phone number. I also asked her to limit her calls because of the phone's location. She flew down to Harlingen the following weekend. We checked into a motel on Friday night, and she left again on Sunday. She seemed to harbor no residual animosity. It was all very puzzling to me. She acted as if we had just been separated for a while and now were picking up again where we had left off. She made the proposal during her visit, "Should we remarry?" she asked bluntly. "Tommy needs his father."

I had no ready answer to her question. Lying next to her in bed, I lit a cigarette, then replied, "We could give it a try. I don't know if it will work. I've thought lots about our son after seeing him in Fort Worth. I know he needs me as much as you. I want to be his father. But if we can make it work after all that happened between us, I don't know. I am just glad that you let me see him."

"It'll work," she said, "if we want it to. I'll keep my parents out of it this time."

"I'll have to think about it." I knew I couldn't deal with a repeat performance and make it through flight training. A rocky marriage and a demanding training program were incompatible.

"Well, think real hard," she said, "I would like things to work out for us, and Tommy." I knew we couldn't continue to meet like this. I had navigation dry runs to practice, plotting out routes from data provided by our instructors which was intended to get us student navigators used to our instruments, methodology, maps, and charts. There were tests to be taken, and on weekends like this one, I should really be practicing shooting the sun with a sextant, plotting out sun lines, and calculating positions. At night I had to do the same exercise on stars with my sextant. Soon we would start flying and do it for real—first, day missions over land and water using radio aids, LORAN, and shooting sun lines with our sextants; then more difficult night missions, using celestial navigation techniques and radar. I knew I didn't have time for weekend visits by Harriet.

At first Harriet called every other day. Then her calls became more frequent as well as annoying. She flew down a second time without my knowledge and called me from the airport. "Please, pick me up, darling." I was darling again. "I just had to come down and see you." After that surprise visit she called daily, starting in late afternoon until ten or eleven o'clock at night. Whenever the phone rang, I raced outside knowing that it was most likely for me. The T-29s would begin revving their engines at four in the morning. There was so little time to get any rest. "I've bought a beautiful dining room set, darling," Harriet announced on the phone. "You'll just love it when you see it. You must come and take a look at it. I bought a new TV as well. You can't believe how big it is."

I finally knew that things were heading right down the old garden path. "Harriet," I said to her firmly, "I am in the air force. I am the most junior officer there is. They will ship me to God knows where once I complete my training, and beautiful dining room sets and large TVs will only get in the way. That kind of life is not in the cards for me. You have to understand that. Quit buying things. I need to concentrate on my job, which is to learn to be a navigator. I don't have time to think about getting married, about dining room sets and large TVs." I paused. There was no response. "I have thought things through," I continued. "We are not getting remarried. It just won't work for us. Please, leave me alone. I have work to do." There was silence on the other end. Then a click. She hung up. It was finally over between us, I thought. But it wasn't to be. Harriet pursued me by phone for years to come, with an uncanny ability to track me down even at the remotest location, wherever I might have been stationed. I sent birthday and Christmas presents to Tommy, until one day a box was returned as undeliverable. Harriet died at the young age of forty-two from an alcohol-related illness.

Flight training became increasingly demanding, leaving me little time for personal matters. There were no opportunities to meet women my age. But I remembered that Colorado girl I dated while at the university, Deanne Durning. The girl with the red hair. I wrote her, and she wrote back. By November we progressed to a point where I considered asking her to marry me. She was a charming girl from an educated family and knew of my background. I thought we fit right into each other's worlds. I was sure she wouldn't mind traveling, something I was certain to do a lot of in the future. One afternoon I just picked up the phone and called Deanne at her sorority house.

"Hi, Deanne. It's me again."

"How are you," she replied.

"I have two weeks off over the holidays, Christmas and New Year's."

"Yes?" she replied. "Are you coming home? I'd like to see you."

I paused, then cranked up my courage, and asked bluntly, "Would you marry me?" A long silence followed.

"I don't know. It is so sudden, Wolfgang. It's the middle of the school year."

"After December I am up to my neck in work until I graduate next summer. Do we want to wait that long? Marry me, Deanne. Say, yes."

"I would have to leave the university. I need to talk to my parents. Can I call you back?"

"Yes, of course. Don't take too long!"

She returned my call the following day. "I talked it over with my parents. They advised me to follow my heart. Yes, I'll marry you. I can't wait to see you!"

Deanne and I were married on December 23, 1960, in the First Methodist Church of Longmont. Deanne was a Christian Scientist, I a Lutheran. My best man was Carl Minkner, who was home on leave from pilot training. Carl had been a member of my AFROTC class at the University of Colorado and had been commissioned alongside me in July. We wore semiformal air force mess dress. It was good to have a friend by my side. Our wedding was smaller than the elaborate affair Harriet staged five years earlier. This time both Hedy and Leo were there to share the occasion. Hedy did not feel out of place and freely gave her blessing to our marriage. Deanne and I spent several days honeymooning at the Broadmoor Hotel in Colorado Springs, a frequent destination for newlyweds. We then flew to Harlingen and set up our little household in a one-bedroom apartment

I rented before I left for Colorado. She knew all about my earlier marriage, about Tommy. There were no secrets between us.

In the weeks to follow there was little time for me to do anything other than concentrate on what I was there for—learning to navigate air force combat aircraft in all types of friendly and hostile environments. Our initial training flights focused on the basics of navigation—dead reckoning, map reading, sun lines, radio beacons, and tactical navigation aids. Our first real challenge was night celestial navigation, a technique widely used to navigate the bombers of the Strategic Air Command. For our final celestial navigation check-ride we took off at 0100 hours the morning of March 1, 1961, heading for a turn-around point at Natchez, Mississippi. The weather soon deteriorated. The air became bumpy, making it difficult to keep my sextant focused on a star. On the return-leg from Natchez the turbulence became severe. I wasn't going to let anything keep me from completing the assignment. While other students gave up and sat down at their positions and strapped in, I kept on shooting stars, holding on at times for dear life, calculating my position, keeping up with the aircraft. Our mission formally ended nearly six hours after take-off, at the let down point to Harlingen AFB. I sat back and relaxed. I did it; I was the only student to finish the assignment. Two days later I received my score: a near-perfect night celestial mission. After the instructor returned my charts and logs, he said to the class, "I commend Lieutenant Samuel for his perseverance and the quality of his work. However, the staff has decided not to count this mission because of the inclement weather on March 1. We will fly the mission over again." Everyone cheered. I was less than pleased with the outcome, since I had to fly the mission all over again, although I passed the earlier mission under severe weather conditions. After celestial navigation we practiced grid navigation, Loran, pressure patterns, and radar. Our last two missions on June 7 and 9, 1961, were day and night check-flights over land and water. We were allowed to use any navigation aid we chose except for radio beacons and tactical navigation aids—none of which would be available in a combat situation. I passed my flight checks with "flying colors," was designated a distinguished graduate, and awarded the wings of a navigator.

Being designated a distinguished graduate meant that I had the pick of assignments for our class. I wanted to fly transport aircraft. Both my fellow students and instructors thought I was crazy. "You want to go into fighters or bombers," I was told, not into "trash haulers." I resented the reference to transport flyers as trash haulers. It was those very trash haulers who, in 1948, saved the city of Berlin, a city of over two million people. They were the flyers who had made a lasting impression on this German boy, then living in a decrepit refugee camp near one of the airlift bases. I wanted to be just like those men, fly with them. But the rules changed for my class. The Strategic Air Command wanted the best navigator graduates as electronic warfare officers to man its growing fleet of eight-jet B-52 heavy bombers. Before I knew what was happening, I had orders sending me to Keesler AFB in Biloxi, Mississippi, for electronic warfare officer training. Another year of flying school lay ahead. I didn't like the assignment and protested to my squadron commander, trying to convince him to have my orders changed. He laughed in my face. "Samuel," he said, "this is the best thing that could happen to you. There is no career in flying trash haulers. Get out of my office, and thank your lucky star that you didn't get what you asked for."

Deanne and I packed our few things and headed for Mississippi via a long detour through Colorado. We spent most of our vacation in Longmont and Boulder, and in a mountain cabin near Longs Peak. I loved the Rocky Mountain mornings, the pungent smell of the towering pines, the crispness of the air, the rushing streams and waterfalls, the piercing cry of a hawk pulling lazy circles overhead. I loved Colorado, and I loved being alone with my Colorado girl.

When I reported to Keesler AFB, a surprise awaited me. Our training aircraft turned out to be converted C-54 transports, which during the Berlin airlift in 1948–49 had flown coal from Fassberg and Celle to Berlin. The aircraft still had traces of coal dust in their spars, attesting to their earlier use. To me it was like a reunion with old friends. On my first training flight I walked around the aircraft and patted its nose, as if it were a living thing. I said nothing to my classmates about how special these airplanes were to me, how they and I once were together in a place and time when I was still a German boy.

In Mississippi I learned not only how to collect electronic intelligence and jam enemy radars, but also about something many of my airmen friends had alluded to in years past but I never truly understood—racism. In the Mississippi of 1961, black was not a good skin color to have. Young black lieutenants were constantly harassed by the sheriff and his deputies. Riding with white classmates outside the base, they were frequently stopped and harassed by leather-jacketed police. Mississippi was still a place of white and colored water fountains, a place where segregation had been fine-tuned to its ugliest. The situation reminded me all too much of Strasburg under the Nazis, and later, the Communists. After graduating from electronic warfare training, I was glad to leave Mississippi behind. I had several assignments to choose from—electronic warfare liaison officer at air defense centers in Kansas and California didn't involve flying. I wasn't interested. Air Defense Command C-121 four-engined patrol planes cruising the east and west coasts of the United States seemed boring. Electronic warfare officer on a B-52H bomber at Grand Forks AFB, North Dakota, was more like it, a real combat aircraft. What I finally chose was an assignment to a secretive reconnaissance unit based in Topeka, Kansas. The unit flew its RB-47H jets along the periphery of the Soviet Union. People called them spy planes. There was only one assignment to the 55th Strategic Reconnaissance Wing. I thought others might take it before I had my turn. No one did. The reason was simple. On July 1, 1960, less than two years earlier, an RB-47H had been shot down by Russian fighters over the Barents Sea. The two survivors of the six-man crew spent months in Lubyanka prison before being released in 1961 by Premier Nikita Khrushchev as an "inauguration gift" to President John F. Kennedy. None of my classmates seemed to want to have anything to do with an outfit that flew such risky missions. America was at peace in 1962, or so we thought. But it was just the kind of assignment I was looking for, and I grabbed it. Nothing would give me a greater thrill than flying against the Communists. I had talked my options over with Deanne, and she supported me fully in my choice of assignment. Topeka was only a day's drive from Colorado.

CHAPTER 28

A Dream Come True

On a hot Mississippi day in early July 1962, Deanne and I loaded up our new 1962 Chevrolet Impala hardtop and headed north for Topeka, Kansas. The car had no air conditioning—we couldn't afford that—and it soon became miserably hot when the sun got up high in the milky white sky. Deanne, seven months pregnant with our first child, incessantly dabbed perspiration off her nose with a small linen handkerchief. Sweat rings formed under her arms, attesting to her discomfort with that big baby inside of her. She made the tan top and the matching skirt herself, to save us money. She was proud to have made her own maternity clothes, never before in her life having used a sewing machine. There were moments when she wanted to just throw her arms up in the air and give up, but she didn't, and she was wearing what she had sewn with such determination.

We arrived in Topeka two days later. I reported to my squadron and immediately was entered into a training program more hectic than anything I had ever experienced. There was little time to settle in. We found a small two-bedroom apartment in a fourplex apartment house, which, we were happy to discover, included most of the appliances we couldn't yet afford to buy. Our next stop was the base hospital, a big red brick building that Deanne was to visit frequently over the next eight weeks.

The officers' wives of the 343rd Strategic Reconnaissance Squadron, my new unit of assignment within the 55th Strategic Reconnaissance Wing, extended a warm welcome to Deanne and quickly made her feel as one of them. The women cautioned her not to ask too many questions of the men—where they went and what they did. Deanne also learned about men who died flying for their country, and she met the widows they left behind. If I, a motivated and enthusiastic young lieutenant, felt privileged to serve my country, so did Deanne in her role as an air force wife.

I was one of a dozen newly assigned electronic warfare officers, EWOs, to arrive at Forbes. On August 20, 1962, soon after our arrival, I flew my first training mission in an RB-47H north toward the Canadian border, over the empty and barren northern states. Lumbering F-89 Scorpion air defense fighters vainly tried to practice intercepts on us as we sliced through the cold, blue northern skies. It was a daytime mission of eight hours' duration in a downward firing ejection seat which, someone whispered to me in confidence, was a seat designed not to work. Apparently the knowledge we EWOs possessed was too sensitive to allow us to be exploited by Soviet interrogators should we be shot down and captured. Three EWOs sat in a sealed capsule in the aircraft's former bomb bay. Our sole mission was to glean the secrets from enemy electronic emissions; our only window to the outside world, the electronic equipment we had been taught to operate—direction finders, search receivers, pulse analyzers, recorders.

"These are short training flights," my Standardization Board evaluator informed me after administering a no-notice Emergency Procedure Test, "especially designed to give you new guys the most training in the shortest possible time. Once you're checked out and certified you'll rarely fly during the day, and your missions will frequently be up to fourteen hours long," he paused, "and take you to places where the bad guys will be waiting for you, waiting to shoot you down. Enjoy your short eight-hour missions while you can." He laughed at me as if he had just let me in on a private joke.

Our training program was hectic—fly, critique, plan the next mission. Fly August 20, fly August 23, fly August 24, fly August 27. Fly, critique, plan, fly, critique, plan—day after day. I had no idea why the pace was so hectic. I would have liked to have had a little more time with Deanne, who was growing bigger by the day and had to cope with her new life as a flying officer's wife all on her own. She never complained, instead busying herself settling into our new home, buying what she needed for the baby's arrival.

On Wednesday, September 12, 1962, I sat at the end of the Forbes runway in my RB-47H reconnaissance aircraft on yet another training flight. Over the intercom I heard the navigator count down the seconds before brake release, exactly on the minute—ten, nine, eight—while the pilot increased power to the six General Electric J47 engines. The aircraft rocked under the strain of the thrusting jets. When the navigator's count reached zero, the pilot released the brakes, activated the water-alcohol injection sequence to increase our take-off power, and our sleek jet slowly started its long roll down the ten-thousand foot runway. Black plumes of jet exhaust followed the aircraft, hanging in the Kansas sky long after the roar of the departing plane had dissipated over the parched prairie. Seven hours later we landed, debriefed with maintenance and intelligence, then left for home after first checking the next day's flying schedule at the squadron.

When I arrived home at nine o'clock that evening, Deanne was not feeling well. As the hours passed her pains became more regular, and I drove her to the base hospital. The doctor on emergency room duty seemed unconcerned and assigned her to a bed. The duty nurse sent me home to get some sleep. "We'll call you if we need you," she promised, with a smile that said, we don't need you. You'll just get in the way. The phone rang early the next morning, Thursday, the thirteenth of September 1962.

"Hello?"

"Airman Samuel?" said the voice at the other end of the line.

"Yes."

"Your wife had a baby boy. They are fine." The phone went dead. I stood there stunned, still in my green flight suit from the night before. I had been too exhausted to take it off before falling asleep. I changed into 505s, the summer uniform. Flight suits were not allowed on base except on our way to or from the flight line. At the hospital I briefly spoke to Deanne, who was happily holding our little baby boy in her arms.

"He is mine," she said, smiling broadly. "When the nurse handed him to me this morning, he had two little sweat beads on his nose. Only he and I have that characteristic. No one else that I know of. The minute I saw that, I knew he was my baby." I was afraid to touch the little person, his head lying near her breast, for fear I might hurt him. "Can we name him Charles, after my father?" Deanne asked.

"Charles is a fine name, and it will make your father proud." I hurried off. I was late for a formation. No excuses allowed. Two weeks later, on September 26, 1962, I passed my flight check which certified me as a fully qualified crew member of an RB-47H reconnaissance crew. I received my permanent assignment to crew S-67, a select standardization crew, commanded by Major Howard Rust. My flight check had been a night mission. Upon our return to base, as the aircraft initiated its final approach, we all glimpsed a beautiful sunrise. On take-off and landing we three EWOs, called Ravens in the 55th Reconnaissance Wing, sat in the aisle below the pilots to give us a better chance at escape in case of a crash landing. The wheels touched down with a jolt, and after eating up much of the runway, we blew the approach- and brake-chutes off to the side of the runway with our jet exhaust, then turned onto a taxiway to find our parking place among nearly 150 B-47 bomber and KC-97 tanker aircraft. Exhausted we slid down the aluminum access ladder to the oil-stained concrete of the ramp below, glad to be able to stretch aching muscles.

In the distance I could see one of our RB-47K photo reconnaissance aircraft from the 338th Reconnaissance Squadron rolling down the runway for an early morning training mission. We watched its take-off roll out of habit, as airmen are apt to do. The aircraft gained speed, then suddenly veered to the right and disappeared from view. The next thing we saw was a black mushroom-shaped cloud rising into the clear, blue Kansas sky; tongues of flame shot through the smoke as if it were a vicious thunderstorm. Shocked by the suddenness of the tragedy, we stood rigid and transfixed, witnessing the death of four of our own—two pilots, a navigator, and a crew chief. That morning before I got home the phone rang in our home. Concerned wives called Deanne, knowing that I had a check flight and should have landed about the time of the crash, an accident visible far beyond the base. The phone calls of potential death were a heart-wrenching experience for Deanne, the young air force wife.

There was some good news for Deanne and me. I was promoted to captain on October 1, 1962. The pay increase was sufficiently large for us to buy an air conditioner for our 1962 Chevy and a new gas stove for the kitchen.

I soon learned why our training pace had been so hectic. The Soviets were moving SS-4 medium-range ballistic missiles and IL-28 Beagle light bombers into Cuba, a threat that was a closely held military secret. For the protection of the missiles and bombers, the island of Cuba was being ringed with SA-2 surface to air missiles and anti-aircraft guns. There were no more training flights for us. The Wing's aircraft were entirely committed to flying operational missions in support of the emerging national emergency. Twenty-four hours a day, day after day, one of our RB-47H aircraft circled the island of Cuba, searching for surface to air missile radars and their locations. It was not a good time for a new father to try to get to know his newborn son, or to comfort and support a wife in her new role as mother. Deanne had to manage on her own, and she rose to the task. When I got home, I fell exhausted into bed. There was little time to relax and talk. One day blended into the next; one flight into another. On the way to and from Cuba there was a little time for me to think of my new baby boy, who was always asleep when I returned home. I would look at him, bend down to kiss his cheek, try not to wake him. I loved our boy, my boy.

On Monday, October 22, 1962, President John F. Kennedy, in a televised speech to the nation, announced that the Soviet Union was in the process of installing nuclear-tipped missiles ninety miles off our shore. A naval quarantine was to be imposed on the island of Cuba until all missiles were removed. Missile-carrying ships would be intercepted and not allowed to proceed. The quarantine would take effect on Wednesday, October 24, 1962. By presidential directive, the Strategic Air Command went from Defense Condition 5 to Defense Condition 3—from a routine alert posture for the nuclear-armed bomber strike forces to a readiness posture where all aircraft were loaded with nuclear weapons and ready for launch. There were no more leaves granted, no more training flights. The United States got ready to go to war. On the day the quarantine went into effect, General Power, the Commander-in-Chief of the Strategic Air Command, unilaterally ordered SAC forces from Defense Condition 3 to Defcon 2. Over one thousand bombers sat on their dispersal bases crewed and loaded with nuclear weapons ready to strike at the Soviet Union. Over one hundred Polaris nuclear-powered submarines went into their final launch positions, ready to execute the order for which they had been built. The nation was on the brink of a nuclear holocaust. It seemed to many of us aircrews that General LeMay's carefully crafted strategy of nuclear deterrence had failed. I survived World War II and thousand-bomber raids, and I knew neither I, nor my young family, would survive a nuclear exchange with the Soviet Union, should it occur.

It was an apparently routine surveillance mission on October 26. We had taken off from Forbes AFB. Three hours later, at 32,000 feet altitude, we coasted out over Key West toward the island of Cuba. We three Ravens searched for radar emissions from hostile MiG fighters and surface to air missile sites. The aircraft interior was bathed in a soft, red glow as we went about our tasks, hour after monotonous hour. The deafening roar of six jets slicing through the frosty night air strained my ears. I adjusted my helmet to relieve the pressure of an earpiece. Major Harry Tull, the senior Raven on board, searched the I-band for hostile fighter radars. I, as Raven II, searched Echo, Fox, and Golf bands for surface to air missile tracking radars. Captain Chuck Myers, the Raven III, searched in the lower bands for SAM acquisition radars. The monotony was broken when our copilot's threat-warning receiver went off with a shrill sound. Simultaneously Harry Tull picked up a powerful airborne tracking radar off our tail. The unknown fighter flew a tail-cone approach, making him easy prey for our 20 mm tail guns. Our copilot, Captain Joe Racine, swung his seat around, locked his radar onto the unknown fighter and reported to Major Rust, our aircraft commander, that he was ready to open fire.

"It's an unknown," the Raven 1 announced over the intercom. "We can't identify him."

Rust ordered Racine to "stand-down your guns." Joe Racine put his radar in standby, ceasing its emissions which could be misinterpreted as hostile intent by a trigger-happy friendly fighter. We Ravens knew Soviet radar characteristics, not those of friendly fighters, so by definition, the approaching fighter should be one of our own. The unknown fighter continued his approach, his exhaust shaking our RB-47 from tail to nose as he passed over us at close quarters. Several days later we learned from our intelligence people that the unknown fighter making that dry firing pass on us was a US Navy aircraft whose pilot thought he had a Soviet Badger bomber in his gunsight. How easy it was to make a mistake in judgment: a navy pilot, an air force crew of six, or all seven aircrew could easily have died that night off the coast of Cuba. It was all part of doing business.

Our flights around Cuba, labeled Common Cause, continued around the clock, day after day, to locate surface to air missile sites, to provide support to high-flying U-2 photo reconnaissance aircraft, and to locate one last ship on its way from the Soviet Union with a cargo of SS-4 intermediate-range ballistic missiles. We Ravens found the surface to air missile sites. One of our RB-47Hs, ranging across the open spaces of the North Atlantic, found the elusive Russian ship carrying the offensive ballistic missiles. All members of the 55th Strategic Reconnaissance Wing were proud to find "the needle in the haystack." Once located, navy P-3 anti-submarine aircraft took over shadowing the Soviet ship. American destroyers approached—and the ship turned back toward the Soviet Union. The Cuban Missile Crisis ended on Sunday, October 28, 1962. There was no nuclear war. Premier Khrushchev agreed to remove all offensive missiles and aircraft from Cuba, never again to reintroduce them. In return, the United States, in time, would remove Jupiter missiles aimed at the Soviet Union from the soil of our NATO ally Turkey.

Although no shots were fired in anger, there were losses. One of our RB-47H aircraft searching for the Russian ship crashed on take-off from Kindley Air Base, Bermuda—four of our friends and fellow flyers lost their lives. Another aircraft crashed on take-off from MacDill Air Force Base in Florida. Its crew of six perished as well. In six short weeks, fourteen men from the 55th Strategic Reconnaissance Wing died flying for their country. Three funeral services were held in the base chapel at Forbes AFB. We young officers who had reported to our new duty station only four months earlier were sent on the sad task of escorting our dead brothers-in-blue to their graves in places like Kansas, Iowa, and Nebraska. Freedom wasn't free, never had been. We learned that lesson very early in our careers.

Three months later, on January 3, 1963, a cold, blustery, and snowy Kansas morning, Deanne drove me to Base Operations. I was leaving for RAF Brize Norton in England, to fly the periphery of the Soviet Union to glean secrets the nation desperately needed to counter the Soviet threat. The Kola Peninsula, Novaya Zemlya, Kaliningrad, Klaipeda, and other strange sounding place names few Americans ever heard of, were on our target list. Deanne bade me farewell with a hurried kiss. I swallowed hard. I couldn't let her see my pain. She held our tiny son Charles close in the blustery Kansas cold. Our baby boy was ill. We didn't know what he was suffering from, but his temperature was inordinately high. She touched my face with her hand, put the baby into his carry-cot next to her in the car, and drove off toward the base hospital. I wanted desperately to be with her and Charles, but I could not.

Crew S-67—Rusty, Howie, Joe, Harry, Chuck, and Wolf—flew out of England for three long months. Our aircraft would lift off from dimly lit runways at night with no radio calls to alert a vigilant foe that we were coming. On one mission north to the far off Kola Peninsula, a KC-135 aerial refueling tanker flying in trail behind us, gave us one last drink of precious fuel near Bear Island, then turned back for Brize Norton. His mission was over, ours was just beginning. High over the Barents Sea, in the dark of night, we flew nearly wing tip to wing tip with the bombers of Russia's strategic forces as they tested their newest air to surface missile. We had surprised them. Russian fighters frantically searched for us, the uninvited intruder. As we flew amongst our foes, we took their secrets with us.

We returned to Forbes Air Force Base on the second of April 1963, after flying eighteen lone reconnaissance missions. Each of us was awarded the Distinguished Flying Cross. On the Forbes Air Force Base flight line we were met by our wing commander, Colonel Marion C. Mixson, who congratulated us for a job well done and for coming home safely. Then it was time for us to meet our anxious and smiling families. Deanne looked more beautiful than ever, with her soft features, red hair, and shining brown eyes. She held Charles up high for me to see him as I approached. At seven months he had grown so much, I thought, added inches and pounds. Deanne gently pushed our baby boy into my open arms. I held him up high to get a good look at the son I didn't really know yet. I kissed his fat little cheeks over and over again. I loved being home, being a husband to my wife, a father to my son.

A fleeting thought rushed through my mind as I held Deanne and Charles close—I had a family of my own to love and be loved by; was serving and flying for my country as I always wanted to; and I was just another American boy.